The Adjunct Professor's Guide to Success

Related Titles of Interest

Successful College Teaching: Problem-Solving Strategies of Distinguished Professors
Sharon A. Biaocco and Jamie N. DeWaters
ISBN: 0-205-26654-1

Faculty Work and Public Trust: Restoring the Value of Teaching and Public Service in American Academic Life
James S. Fairweather
ISBN: 0-205-17948-7

Emblems of Quality in Higher Education: Developing and Sustaining High-Quality Programs
Jennifer Grant Haworth and Clinton F. Conrad
ISBN: 0-205-19546-6

Writing for Professional Publication: Keys to Academic and Business Success
Kenneth T. Henson
ISBN: 0-205-28313-6

Revitalizing General Education in a Time of Scarcity: A Navigational Chart for Administrators and Faculty
Sandra L. Kanter, Zelda F. Gamson, and Howard B. London
ISBN: 0-205-26257-0

Multicultural Course Transformation in Higher Education: A Broader Truth
Ann Intili Morey and Margie K. Kitano (Editors)
ISBN: 0-205-16068-9

Sexual Harassment on Campus: A Guide for Administrators, Faculty, and Students
Bernice R. Sandler and Robert J. Shoop
ISBN: 0-205-16712-8

Leadership in Continuing and Distance Education in Higher Education
Cynthia C. Jones Shoemaker
ISBN: 0-205-26823-4

Shaping the College Curriculum: Academic Plans in Action
Joan S. Stark and Lisa R. Lattuca
ISBN: 0-205-16706-3

For more information or to purchase a book, please call 1-800-278-3525.

THE ADJUNCT PROFESSOR'S GUIDE TO SUCCESS

Surviving and Thriving in the College Classroom

Richard E. Lyons
Indian River Community College

Marcella L. Kysilka
University of Central Florida

George E. Pawlas
University of Central Florida

Allyn and Bacon
Boston • London • Toronto • Sydney • Tokyo • Singapore

Executive Editor: Stephen D. Dragin
Series Editorial Assistant: Elizabeth McGuire
Marketing Manager: Ellen Dohlberg/Brad Parkins
Editorial-Production Service: Omegatype Typography, Inc.
Electronic Composition: Omegatype Typography, Inc.

Copyright © 1999 by Allyn & Bacon
A Viacom Company
Needham Heights, MA 02494

Internet: www.abacon.com

Library of Congress Cataloging-in-Publication Data
Lyons, Richard E.,
     The adjunct professor's guide to success : surviving and thriving
in the college classroom / Richard E. Lyons, Marcella L. Kysilka,
George E. Pawlas.
       p.   cm.
     Includes bibliographical references and index.
     ISBN 0-205-28774-3
     1. College teaching–Vocational guidance—United States.
     2. College teachers, Part-time–Training of—United States.
     3. Education, Higher—United States.   I. Kysilka, Marcella L.
     II. Pawlas, George.   III. Title.
     LB1778.2.L96 1999
     378.1'2–dc21   98-29466
                                                              CIP

Printed in the United States of America

10   9   8   7   6

To the thousands of committed adjunct professors who bring to our classrooms the wisdom of their years in the "real world" and the passion for their life's work that enrich the education of us all.

CONTENTS

PREFACE

In recent years, institutions at all levels of higher education—universities, liberal arts colleges, and community colleges—have turned to respected resources within their communities to staff increasing numbers of their courses. Over a quarter of a million adjunct professors are employed annually by U.S. institutions—a number that is expected to increase in the next five years. Although these adjunct professors commonly possess a significant knowledge base in their area of expertise, they often lack formal training in teaching skills. Most colleges and universities have so far done little to develop formalized programs for preparing their adjunct faculty members to enter the classroom. This highly practical handbook is designed to provide an essential conceptual foundation for college teaching, along with a toolkit of teaching and classroom management ideas that are critical if you are to effectively meet the needs of students. As a result of applying the techniques presented here, you will accelerate the achievement of classroom competence and personal confidence.

The Adjunct Professor's Guide to Success begins "where the inexperienced adjunct professor is" intellectually and emotionally, and addresses sequentially the major issues impacting classroom success. It employs nontechnical language and makes frequent connections to the nonacademic world. Most of each chapter is dedicated to "classroom survival skills," and each chapter concludes with tips for achieving a distinctive teaching style. The book concludes by addressing the state of mind of an adjunct professor thinking about whether to continue part-time teaching.

This book is written for nonteaching professionals—businesspeople, attorneys, medical professionals, and others—who are increasingly staffing the largely evening and weekend courses offered by nearly all institutions of higher education. *The Adjunct Professor's Guide to Success* is not specific to a particular teaching discipline, nor, in fact, to academic *vis-à-vis* occupationally focused courses. It is designed as a toolkit to be read and used as its sequentially arranged chapters are required by the developing adjunct professor. Active reflection and perhaps a little re-reading before tackling each succeeding chapter will solidify your understanding of the most critical concepts of college teaching.

We have among us served as adjunct and full-time college professors, teacher–educators, department chairpersons, and instructional deans at the community college and university levels. In the process, we have come to know scores of adjunct professors well, understanding the motivation that prompts them to teach and applauding the passion they bring to the classroom. Each of us has become concerned about the underpreparation of adjunct professors, and we thus offer this book as a partial remedy. Much of the book is based on extensive, recent research conducted and thoroughly reviewed by the authors.

ORGANIZATION

Each chapter of the book is introduced by a series of questions designed to clearly focus your attention on the key issues addressed within it. One or two paragraphs are designed to get you on common ground with each chapter's theme. The text of each chapter addresses the key survival skills of your first college teaching assignment.

Chapters 1 and 2 are designed to provide the aspiring adjunct professor with an understanding of the culture of contemporary higher education in the United States and suggestions for strategies for obtaining a part-time teaching position.

Once you have interviewed and achieved a tentative teaching assignment or arranged a developmental relationship with a veteran professor, Chapter 3 will guide you through a comprehensive orientation to the specific institution. Appendix 3.1 provides the first of several highly useful tools—a checklist to focus your self-directed orientation efforts.

Among the most critical chapters in the book for most readers, Chapter 4 will help you more effectively understand the changing nature of college and university students. Increasingly, institutions of higher education are becoming "customer-driven." Surviving and thriving in this culture requires a factual understanding of higher education's client—one who is far different from those with whom you probably interfaced while a college student yourself.

Many readers of this book will have a business orientation, and therefore clearly understand the important role of Chapter 5—effective planning of your course. The time invested in developing a grounded, comprehensive plan will maximize learning for your students and minimize the problems you encounter as the manager of the classroom.

It is difficult to achieve long-term success in any endeavor when its beginning is ineffective. Chapter 6 provides the key components of getting your course off to the type of start that will have students looking forward to succeeding class meetings.

Chapter 7 provides you with practical and proven communications tools and course management techniques designed to help you retain the overwhelming majority of students throughout the course. "Retention" of students is one of the key concerns instructional leaders face today as declining budgets make funding of their programs increasingly challenging.

Chapters 8 and 9 focus on what might be called the two major categories of instructional methods—instructor-directed and student-directed. These two chapters are a "must read" before you get very deep into your course.

Poorly designed and administered examinations are one of the major contributing factors affecting the professor's success in retaining students. Chapter 10 is designed to provide the essential tools for developing more effective objective and essay tests.

In recent years, there has been growing interest in more authentic assessment of student learning. Few students take paper-and-pencil tests at work or in their everyday lives, but are instead challenged to apply the concepts they have learned in the classroom to solve real problems. Chapter 11 will sensitize you to the appropriate uses and techniques of "authentic" forms of assessing student learning.

Students tend to react disproportionately to the first and last meeting of each course they take in college. Chapter 12 specifically focuses on conducting an effective final class meeting, as well as determining final course grades and the other tasks associated with bringing a course to a successful end.

Chapter 13 focuses on assessment of the course and your performance as the instructor. Increasingly, colleges and universities are relying on student evaluations, and to a lesser extent, other forms of assessment, to improve the quality of their courses. This chapter provides highly useful suggestions for ensuring that your course is evaluated positively.

The final chapter is designed to help you objectively evaluate the personal dividends provided by your teaching experience. It provides tactics for continuous improvement of your teaching skills and leveraging your teaching experience in other aspects of your life.

At the close of each chapter are four recurring components designed to help you further digest the material. The first is entitled "Through the Adjunct's Eyes," a compilation of perspectives we have experienced with adjunct professors over the years. The "Tips for Thriving" component is designed to provide ideas that will enable you to more quickly develop your own distinctive teaching style—increasing the psychological rewards of your new part-time position. The "Review of Key Points" sections provide a reminder of the key ideas addressed in the chapter, and the "Suggested Readings" provide some resources for expanding your knowledge base on the theme of the chapter.

The Adjunct Professor's Guide to Success is the type of book you will want to refer to often as you teach, and one you will want to share with other adjunct professors with whom you forge lasting relationships in this most rewarding of part-time occupations.

ACKNOWLEDGMENTS

This book would not have been possible without the contributions of several special people. We thank Edwin Massey, Raymond Isenburg, Jack Maxwell, and Dottie Vandegrift of Indian River Community College for their whole-hearted support of the research that led to the book's development. We also thank Norma Thompson, Donald Lucy, Jack Burns, and Gary Sullivan of the same institution for their meticulous review of the manuscript, as well as Patricia Profeta for her help in researching key components. We appreciate as well the perspectives on the project extended by Jeff Cornett and Tom Kubala of the University of Central Florida and Silvia Zapico of Valencia Community College. Thanks also to our colleagues who reviewed the manuscript: Imogene Ramsey, Eastern Kentucky University; and John Travis, Texas A&M University. Finally, we thank the over one hundred adjunct faculty members who have read and provided valuable feedback on the book's content. Their embracing of the material speaks forcefully to its potential for helping you achieve success in your classroom.

R. E. L.
M. L. K.
G. E. P.

The Adjunct Professor's Guide to Success

1

SO YOU'VE DECIDED TO PURSUE PART-TIME COLLEGE TEACHING

Focus Questions

- Why do deans and department chairs want and need effective adjunct professors teaching their students?
- What are the intrinsic and extrinsic rewards of part-time college teaching?
- What specific qualities do instructional leaders value in the adjunct professors they hire?

Periodically, we each are driven to pursue a dream whose seeds were planted many years before. In the few quiet moments of our busy and perhaps undersatisfied lives, we find ourselves revisiting and in a small way nurturing that "Someday I'll..." dream. Then, for reasons we can't fully explain even to ourselves, we are launched by a triggering event or internal realization to profoundly and openly embrace our dream. Confronting our self-doubts, we extend our deeply entrenched comfort zones and mentally project ourselves into the arena of our dream fulfilled—vividly reliving memories of unique experiences long ago. Our senses are dramatically activated to distinct sights, sounds, and emotions no longer so far away and we begin to more fully contemplate the differences which the achievement of that special dream could make in our lives.

In recent years, thousands of professionals like you—both working and retired—have been drawn to teaching part-time at their local colleges or universities. While a few have had previous teaching experience of some kind, most have been primarily observers of others' teaching. New adjunct professors are attracted to teaching for a variety of reasons, both material and psychological. Conditioned by their own undergraduate experiences, many perceive academia as a stimulating, yet somewhat mysterious and daunting environment in which to work—even part-time.

Achieving success in this challenging environment must begin with a grounded understanding of the expertise you are capable of sharing with students. While neither this chapter nor the remainder of this book will address directly your specific discipline area, one of the major rewards you undoubtedly will derive from teaching is a deeper understanding of that chosen field. Ultimately, your success will hinge on your ability to assimilate into the culture of your institution and understand the perspective of students who are far different from those of only a few years ago. The authors believe that more than teaching your subject, you teach *students*—individuals who hold diverse motivations for learning your course material, but who each need all the expertise, passion, and professionalism you can impart. Thus, this and subsequent chapters seek to provide you an enlightened understanding of the nature of today's students and methods of fostering their true learning. Only through that emphasis in your teaching style will you achieve the quality of success which the reading of this book indicates you seek. In the end, intentionally or not, you will not so much teach a course but your perspective of life and your vision of the future. So let's get started in bringing your dream to life!

THE CHANGING ENVIRONMENT OF HIGHER EDUCATION

Not so long ago, the culture of the typical American college or university was perceived, from both inside and outside, as quite removed from the rest of society. Nearly all professors taught full time and invested many hours pursuing somewhat abstract ideas in what many conceived as "ivory towers." Then, war veterans attending college on the G. I. Bill and, subsequently, throngs of middle- and lower economic-class students who were the first from their families to attend college challenged all institutions of higher education to reconsider their fundamental missions. While the cultures of many institutions cling to elements of bygone days—as exemplified in the traditions revisited during each graduation ceremony—the overwhelming majority have made dramatic, albeit sometimes reluctant, changes in the way they interface with the rest of society.

In very recent years, the widely perceived distance between academia and the rest of society has largely evaporated. Professors write books which the multitudes read, consult regularly with a wide range of businesses to transfer theory into practice, and appear on television talk shows to discuss matters of widespread concern. A college education has become the ticket to upward mobility in an increasingly more materialistically conscious society. Colleges have reacted by more actively marketing themselves, first to the mass market through their sports teams, then to niche markets, through cultural programs, elderhostels, executive M.B.A. programs, and the like.

The environment of higher education has evolved increasingly to blur the lines that have separated it historically from the corporate world. Competition has flourished, not only with other traditional colleges and universities, but with upstart institutions with accelerated programs provided in locations more convenient to "customers." As in the business world, pressure on colleges and universities has intensified to cut costs and to provide more value for the tuition dollar. This pressure largely has fueled the more widespread employment of adjunct professors.

Along with these changes has come a reconceptualization of individual career development. Today, more individuals than ever before work for reasons beyond the financial consideration. Increasingly, professionals have adopted an independent, "self-employed" mindset to create careers with multiple income streams. Many plan for a more balanced lifestyle, derived from a collection of richly satisfying components—both occupational and recreational. Many seek ways to increase growth within their overall career by carefully leveraging equity in each component, much the same way as astute individuals utilize a variety of investments to achieve their diverse financial goals. Just as the traditional business culture has embraced these collective changes, the environment of higher education has adapted to ensure the retention of its brightest and most productive contributors.

BACKGROUND AND MOTIVATION OF ADJUNCT PROFESSORS

Our contemporary society/marketplace has stimulated a rich variety of individuals to pursue a part-time career in higher education. Their reasons for seeking this path were first illuminated in a study by Howard Tuckman published in 1978. Through surveys of over 3,700 respondents from all levels of higher education, Tuckman delineated seven categories of adjunct instructors and, in the process, established a foundation for further research on adjunct faculty by others.

In the landmark work *The Invisible Faculty*, Judith Gappa and David Leslie (1993) built on Tuckman's findings to more thoroughly and contemporarily explain the factors that differentiate adjunct professors. Through interviews with deans, department chairs, full-time faculty, and 240 adjunct instructors at eighteen U.S. and Canadian colleges and universities—both public and private—they developed a typology of four loose categories, predicated on the work experience and motivation of those they studied.

Their "career enders" include those who are fully retired, as well as those who are in transition from well-established careers to a lifestyle in which part-time teaching plays a significant role. As the nature of the international economy changes, increasing numbers of highly successful people, including former full-time professors, are expected to pursue part-time teaching during their later years.

Over half of all adjunct faculty members are employed full time and are categorized by Gappa and Leslie as "specialist, expert, or professionals." Their percentages are lowest among the faculties at liberal arts colleges and highest at private, doctorate-granting institutions. They are often pursuing new contacts, either social or professional, and the opportunity to fulfill themselves through sharing their expertise. These individuals often have advanced training and rich experiences in fields critical to the mission of the college or university.

"Aspiring academics" are building their credentials and teaching skills while making professional contacts that might improve their chances for obtaining a full-time teaching position. Others seek recognition that would enable them to achieve success in a nonteaching capacity within the academic arena. Some are long-term part-timers who, while continuing to pursue a full-time appointment, work at another job in a closely related environment. Some teach concurrently at several institutions.

"Freelancers" are teaching for an increasing number of varied reasons other than those identified by members of the other categories. Some freelancers own their own business and view their part-time teaching as an opportunity to develop their business contacts. Others are homemakers or have primary care responsibility for family members. Some, including many artists and musicians, choose to build their careers around a series of part-time jobs that are interrelated. Because they tend to be resourceful and possess professional contacts who could enrich their teaching, freelancers have much to offer the institutions at which they are employed.

It's not uncommon for members of these categories to move, at least temporarily, into another category, perhaps to later return or shift to a third when life circumstances dictate. Hopefully, you have found your motivation and lifestyle position amplified within this discussion and can begin to see a broader perspective of the role of adjunct faculty members in the culture of higher education. A key characteristic of effective college instructors is the ability to continually move between the individual and generalized perspectives and understand the short- and long-term implications within each.

The publication of *The Invisible Faculty* fueled a greater appreciation for the role of adjunct instructors and increased interest in their more effective use by colleges and universities. Subsequently, a number of additional books and articles have been published that could enhance your understanding of a range of issues affecting adjunct professors.

In summary, the factors that motivate individuals to pursue part-time college teaching positions include:

- Opportunity to share wisdom gathered over years of professional experience and to engage in intellectual stimulation
- A strategy for developing credibility in the marketplace and/or a client base for a full-time job, sometimes called *rain-making* or *networking*
- Opportunity, especially for newcomers to a community, to meet and interact with a rich cross-section of bright citizens—both students and college employees—establishing primarily personal relationships
- The chance to psychologically repay the time and emotional energy invested by a cherished former teacher or family member
- Opportunity to actively explore a potential new career
- The chance to perform before a potentially grateful audience, and to be recognized for special skills or knowledge
- Opportunity to supplement a personal income

Recently generated data indicate that literally thousands of individuals are having a rich variety of their needs satisfied through adjunct college teaching. Many have come to define themselves largely in terms of their part-time teaching role. They would no more pass up a regular teaching assignment than they would the opportunity to take an annual vacation or participate in some other valuable self-development activity.

In reality, you and others drawn to adjunct teaching would probably cite several of the above or related reasons as significant motivating factors. As you pursue your interest in teaching, be sure to reflect regularly upon and clarify your goals and expectations within the specific institutional environment in which you teach. Keeping a journal can be an especially rewarding and useful activity at this time. Many adjunct instructors have overestimated the extrinsic rewards of part-time teaching, as well as the chances for obtaining a full-time teaching position, only to have their hopes dashed. Veteran adjuncts report deriving their principal satisfaction from the intrinsic rewards of teaching—the intellectual challenge, the social interaction, and the opportunity to play a role in the development of others. Over time, you will find your self-efficacy and confidence levels improve markedly as you immerse yourself in the rich dynamics of the academic culture and regularly evaluate the impact of your teaching experiences.

THE DISCIPLINE LEADER'S PERSPECTIVE

Increasingly in recent years, the discipline leaders in higher education, i.e. department chairs, deans, "lead teachers," and persons with related titles who are responsible for making teaching assignments, have come to greatly value your potential contributions to their individual students and their program-building efforts. You enrich their curricula by providing up-to-date expertise, especially in highly specialized courses, which their full-time faculty members frequently lack. You provide contemporary "real-world" applications of the theories and practices described in textbooks, making courses "come alive." You provide students a sense of current professional trends and a connection with the working environment that many students aspire to enter. You introduce students to resources they might not otherwise encounter, through your guest speakers, field trips, and related activities. You build a stronger connection between the institution and the varied elements of its surrounding community. You provide scheduling flexibility, cost savings, and other efficiencies, enabling instructional leaders to offer more courses, at times and places convenient to their increasingly busy and knowledge-thirsty students. In short, you help create "win–win" situations, enriching the education of students within the increasingly more market-driven environment of higher education.

Sometimes, however, a few rushed, flawed decisions have made some department chairs and deans extremely cautious about employing adjunct professors. More often than many would like to admit, new adjunct professors have been assigned to teach courses—often on very short notice—for which they were not an appropriate fit or were not effectively prepared. Anxious to get their foot in the door, many new adjunct instructors have accepted teaching assignments without fully and accurately assessing the match between their backgrounds and the requirements of the assigned course, and with insufficient knowledge of the classroom challenges they might face. Regrettably, many also lacked the appropriate support resources to overcome either. To prevent repeating these common mistakes, aspiring adjunct professors must be very careful to familiarize themselves thoroughly with the full range of issues that impact their success, and to identify and fully utilize the resources available to support their teaching.

Increasingly affected by today's realities, instructional leaders feel pressure from their stakeholder groups—students and their families, employers, full-time faculty members, legislators, benefactors and others—to hire adjunct professors with the following characteristics.

- Clearly like most students they meet, regardless of age, gender, socio-economic status, ethnicity, motivational level, or personality type
- Are poised to "think on their feet" in challenging situations
- Have a genuine sense of humor and consistently display a positive attitude
- Present a professional image and demeanor, without being stuffy
- Invest out-of-class time to talk with and ensure the success of students
- Display consistent enthusiasm for the subject matter and institution

- Regularly recruit a few students from their full-time workplace or other arenas of influence
- Submit final grades and other reports in a timely fashion and adhere to other college policies conservatively and consistently

Most discipline leaders have experienced at least one negative situation involving an ineffective adjunct professor and vividly remember the valuable time and emotionally draining energy invested in attempting to fix those problems after-the-fact. Such leaders therefore have come to fear hiring adjunct professors who have the following characteristics.

- Spend inordinate amounts of class time telling "war stories" or overly promoting themselves or their full-time careers
- Read extensively to students from the textbook or their notes
- Arrive late to class, leave early, or otherwise misuse scheduled class time
- Fail to meet, or arrange to have a suitable substitute meet, their class for every scheduled meeting
- Make insensitive statements of a racial, gender, political, or other nature
- Demonstrate lack of respect for the ideas of stakeholder groups
- Administer examinations that include material not appropriately covered in class, ambiguous questions, or other problems
- Miscommunicate or criticize institutional policies or the motives and competency of those who created them
- Assign too many high or too many low grades to students

In addition, each discipline leader typically has a number of individual foibles, developed through years of teaching and supervising others who teach. Invest the time to discover and more fully understand these personal nuances by carefully observing your instructional leaders' actions, listening intently to their comments and asking appropriate questions that can enrich your perspective. One of your greatest potential rewards from adjunct teaching can be the relationships you develop with your instructional leaders. While often appearing aloof, the typically shy instructional leaders, you will probably find, are immensely interesting individuals, who, given a quiet moment, will openly share perspectives that will facilitate your development as a professor.

THROUGH THE ADJUNCTS' EYES

Appearing at the conclusion of each chapter, this section relays the experiences and perspectives of three new adjunct professors—each composites of individuals the authors have each experienced. At this point, the three will introduce themselves and share how they came to pursue part-time under-graduate teaching.

Karen:

My name is Karen and I'm a practicing attorney. Upon graduation from law school and admission to the bar six years ago, I took a position with a large metropolitan firm. I "paid my dues" clerking and working 70- and 80-hour weeks, but I found building a career in that firm would require me to sacrifice my personal life for a good long while. Several months ago, I relocated to a smaller city to work for a highly respected, traditional law firm. Soon thereafter I learned that among the responsibilities of all aspiring partners in the firm was the cultivation of new clients—what is called "rainmaking" in our profession. I read an interesting article on rainmaking strategies in a legal profession periodical to which the firm subscribes. One especially appealing strategy featured was teaching part-time at a local college. One of my longtime role models has been a terrific high school English teacher, Mrs. Miller, who encouraged me to consider all sorts of possibilities for my life—including teaching! Vivid memories of my many discussions with her no doubt partly explain why I was drawn to pursue college teaching now.

Juan:

My name is Juan. Upon completing my bachelor's degree, I went to work for a large multinational corporation and traveled overseas a great deal for several years. At first, it was very exciting, but living out of my suitcase (and countless superficial relationships with clients, hotel staff members, and the like) began taking a toll on me emotionally. I didn't seem to have a home or any truly grounded relationships. One Sunday afternoon, while sitting in a Barcelona park, I finished reading an especially meaningful book and developed a pronounced feeling of emptiness. Over the next few weeks, I pondered my situation and decided to examine more psychologically rewarding career options.

Shortly thereafter, I applied for and was accepted into a Master's program at a renowned state university. After starting classes, I became totally immersed in the academic environment, and in my second semester I obtained a teaching assistantship. I developed especially rewarding relationships with two prominent professors, completed my Master's, and entered their doctoral program. Now about halfway through my coursework, I have decided to more effectively explore a teaching career in higher education. While continuing as a teaching assistant, I have come to meet several "post-doc" Ph.D.'s who are very frustrated about being unable to obtain a tenure-track position. They each say this is a growing situation nationwide. I have also heard that some universities are modifying their promotion and tenure systems to reward not only research, but teaching success as well. Several of the ABD's (all but dissertation) are exploring alternative ways of building their careers, emphasizing teaching over the pursuit of their research interests. One in particular has become very excited about working at a community college, enabling her to dedicate herself totally to her first love—teaching. I find myself more drawn than ever to interfacing with students in the classroom and helping them pursue interests that will improve the quality of their lives.

Margaret:

I am Margaret, recently retired from a Fortune 500 corporation and relocated to a medium-sized Sun Belt city. I earned an Executive M.B.A. while still employed and in the process developed an appreciation for the give-and-take of classes populated by career-building working professionals. I guess that's when the thought of teaching first entered my mind. In the past few years of my work life, I noticed that newly hired management trainees were increasingly ill-prepared to deal with the complexities of corporate life. I got special enjoyment from mentoring several of them who have gone on to firmly establish their corporate careers. Like many of the other retired executives in my area, I find that the recreational and social activities within my community fail to provide the type of challenges and rewards people like us need. Fortunately for me, our area is home to an independent college, a state university, and a multi-campus community college. I am actively exploring part-time teaching at all three institutions.

TIPS FOR THRIVING

As you contemplate this rewarding part-time profession, actively solicit the feedback of every supportive member within your sphere—including those from the college, your other employment arena(s), and personal friends. In Chapter 5, you will be asked to assess your strengths and weaknesses as they relate to preparing and delivering a course. That activity will be far more beneficial when you have processed a rich variety of inputs to achieve a more grounded understanding. Use the occasion of your preparation for this journey to access perhaps the richest single source of information on your potential to teach—your own former teachers from high school and college. You will probably be pleasantly surprised at the value their insights can foretell.

More than ever, nurture a relationship with someone who can view education through the eyes of a contemporary student—who is willing not only to listen to you unconditionally, but to regularly provide frank and constructive insights. There will likely be times when you return from class extremely puzzled over something that occurred there. Your self-efficacy will sometimes be threatened, making it difficult to objectively process these experiences when they first occur. Having an easily accessible and trusted "sounding board" may relieve a great deal of frustration and provide the perspective necessary to bring your challenges back into realistic focus. As early in your teaching experience as possible, start to identify potential teaching mentors who might provide a professionally grounded perspective, but continue to nurture the relationship with that non teacher, whose opinions will prove especially valuable in your efforts to more fully understand your students and to achieve the type of success that you desire.

REVIEW OF KEY POINTS

- The historical boundaries between higher education and the corporate world have become increasingly blurred in today's environment.
- Adjunct professors are attracted to teaching by a wide range of psychological, social and financial factors.
- College discipline-leaders value adjunct professors for their discipline expertise and their potential to make "real world" applications, as well as the operating efficiencies they offer.
- Discipline-leaders have a fairly universal set of criteria that drives their decision-making on hiring new adjunct faculty members.
- Begin developing mentoring relationships early with several key individuals who might later play a role in your development as an adjunct professor.

SUGGESTED READINGS

Gappa, J., & Leslie, D. (1993). *The invisible faculty: Improving the status of part-timers in higher education.* San Francisco: Jossey-Bass.

Hakim, C. (1994). *We are all self-employed.* San Francisco: Berrett-Koehler.

Roueche, J., Roueche, S., & Milliron, M. (1995). *Strangers in their own land: Part-time faculty in American community colleges.* Washington, D.C.: Community College Press.

Sinetar, M. (1987). *Do what you love, the money will follow.* New York: Dell Publishing.

2

OBTAINING AN ADJUNCT TEACHING POSITION

Focus Questions

- How do you get your "foot in the door" of the local college or university?
- What are the unique elements of job interviewing in a higher education environment?
- What are some prudent follow-up activities to an interview with an instructional decision maker?

The degree of effort required to obtain an adjunct teaching assignment varies a great deal between institutions, and even between departments within the same institution. Through your full-time employment or community affiliations, you may already have established a relationship with an instructional leader that might rather easily be leveraged into obtaining an adjunct teaching assignment. If so, and especially if your assigned class begins in the very near future, you might want to skip this chapter for the time being, returning when you must put forth a more extensive effort to obtain a subsequent position. If you are beginning the pursuit of a part-time teaching position "from scratch," the insights this chapter presents will prove invaluable to the success of your effort. Obtaining a rewarding adjunct teaching position requires a thorough understanding of the perspective of the instructional leader making the hiring decision, grounded knowledge of what you "bring to the table," and the use of employment-seeking tactics highly regarded in this environment.

THE DISCIPLINE LEADER'S
DECISION-MAKING STRATEGY

Perceptions of the role of adjunct professors among discipline leaders vary markedly. Some traditionalists view full-time faculty in an exalted status and part-time faculty as little more than a source of cost savings and course-scheduling convenience. An increasing number of enlightened leaders, however, have come to value adjunct faculty for the wider range of potential benefits they provide, as discussed in the previous chapter. Such leaders understand the long-term value of fully integrating adjunct professors into their institutional culture, and dedicate resources to that goal. Obviously, you would be wise to access the opinion of the key decision makers in your situation prior to beginning efforts to obtain a position.

Higher education, probably more than nearly any other institution within our society, has a highly paradoxical culture. Although the over-whelming majority of its population is young (or at least "young at heart"), many of its customs and procedures are very traditional—if not arcane. Its employees are, on the one hand, among the most loyal you will find in any environment, but, on the other, among the most independent. The traditions of "academic freedom" and collegiality provide much more latitude for the performance of college teaching duties than employees in most other work settings enjoy. Gaining employment, including a part-time teaching position, is fraught with all sorts of unique challenges that must be proactively addressed by those seeking entry.

First, you must, as much as possible, manage the timing and circumstances of obtaining your initial teaching assignment. While a few enthusiastic adjunct professors have secured their first teaching assignment by contacting the college or university the week before the beginning of a new semester, such tight time horizons have often contributed to rushed and inadequate planning of their course and later to very unfortunate experiences in their classroom. Often, adjunct professors unsuccessful in their initial teaching assignment with a college or university are not invited to teach again. In approaching the institution, your chances of long-term success are enhanced by making contact at least six weeks before the beginning of the semester. Before seeking an appointment with the instructional decision-maker, obtain a copy of the college catalog (usually readily available at the bookstore or registrar's office) and review its explanation of the college mission, structure, and curricula. Unlike those in many private sector organizations, the human resource or personnel departments of colleges and universities, while perhaps a valuable resource for information, typically play little role in actively recruiting qualified part-time instructors. In some cases, they even serve as a barrier to your entry into teaching, so plan accordingly.

The department chair typically should be your initial official contact at the college. Build your knowledge base about him or her early by accessing biographical information likely to be published in the college catalog or other institutional publications. Note the highest degree and university from which it was earned—colleges and universities are especially credential-conscious organizations. Continue your information-gathering process later through careful observation and attentive listening. A telephone call to the instructional leader's office on a midweek afternoon would probably have the best chance of a positive reception. Avoid calling in the morning and beginning games of "phone tag" that might contribute to an unfavorable impression. Leaving well-developed e mail messages is typically especially effective with time-challenged discipline leaders, who are often involved with multiple tasks and unable to talk effectively on the telephone for even a few minutes. Regardless of your communication medium, identify yourself succinctly, relay the general types of courses which you feel equipped to teach, and ask for an introductory meeting only.

Expect to be asked to mail or fax a resume or curriculum vitae (CV) before being granted an interview, so have one prepared before you call. Modern word processors enable you to turn your traditional resume into a CV within an hour or so. While most of the resumes you have developed throughout your career were probably designed to clearly communicate your potential to increase profits, reduce costs, or achieve some other common organizational goal, the CV should be developed to convey succinctly your depth of experience and training in the discipline area. Communicate your potential to teach by prioritizing and highlighting training sessions and other types of presentations you have delivered, in industry, civic, or religious settings. Emphasize your commitment to the community by identifying the offices you have held in civic organizations and roles you have played in community activities, especially those related to young people. In addition, provide details of your academic background, such as key courses completed, title of your thesis or other major projects, awards, and related school achievements. Depending on the discipline in which you hope to teach, it might be useful to add a section on your travel experiences, technology skills, or other personal interests. While one-page resumes seem to have become especially valued in the private sector, academics looking out for the best interests of their students tend to value somewhat more detailed and formalized documents. Therefore, include specific and focused information on your CV—softening the puffery common on resumes used in the business world. Be mindful of time constraints on the reviewer of your CV by listing your most critical information toward the beginning. Two pages are typically about right for most community college situations, while a university setting might call for three or (on rare occasions) more pages. There are frequent exceptional situations however, so confirm that approach with each instructional leader's administrative assistant and adapt. Submit your CV in a timely fashion, including with it a cover letter that effectively accentuates your major teaching attributes.

Strongly consider submitting your CV in person, thus not only ensuring that it gets to the correct destination, but giving yourself a chance to meet someone who might later serve as a friendly face when you arrive for an interview. A personal visit also provides you a chance to become a bit more familiar with the culture and values of the organization, and perhaps enables you to spontaneously meet and "break the ice" with the decision-maker. Your strategy should emphasize being proactive and persistent, without being pushy, until you are granted an interview. At the time an interview is scheduled, be sure to note the names and roles of all of those who will attend, so that you might more effectively manage follow-up conversations, such as sending thank you notes or letters to appropriate parties or for other reasons that might emerge.

PREPARING FOR THE INTERVIEW

If you have not already done so, visit the campus—its classroom buildings, student union and library, and talk with professors, staff, students, and anyone else who looks like they might have a minute for you. Note the degree of formality, the demographic composition of its student body, and its values—expressed both overtly and in a multitude of subtle ways. Since there will be a great deal of information to process, take written notes or use a pocket tape recorder to retain significant perceptions from your visit. Visit the campus bookstore and note the textbooks for the courses you would most logically be assigned to teach. Assess their level of difficulty and cost—these are clues to the approach the instructional decision-makers embrace. Get a soft drink or cup of coffee in the cafeteria and sit down to observe the dynamics of the institutional environment.

Walk the campus to absorb the ambiance. Locate the offices of the dean and department chair with whom you might later interview. If the opportunity presents itself and the environment is not overly hectic, you might introduce yourself to the discipline leader's administrative assistant. Listen carefully to information shared about the department or personality nuances of key players. Avoid asking probing questions that might create the perception that you are being anything other than friendly, open, and professional.

Read as much of the college catalog, schedule of classes, and related institution publications as you can acquire before going for the interview, with your primary focus on the department, courses, and persons of greatest impact on you. If the college has an Internet website, review it carefully for the most current additional information. To gain additional background information and, possibly, material for an effective opening to the interview, talk with those from the community (employers, public school teachers, and administrators) who might logically interface with the discipline leader with whom you will later talk.

In preparing for your interview, determine first who the probable participants will be. In interviewing potential adjunct professors, some instructional leaders rely totally on their own opinion to make hiring decisions. Others employ a single interview by a group of two, three, or more discipline leaders and faculty, each with a "territorial" stake in the success of each professor the department employs. Still others may employ a series of screening interviews, prior to a final interview that includes a top administrator. Project yourself into each decision maker's perspective and—using the list provided in Chapter 1—identify the information each is likely to seek from you during the interview. Be prepared to showcase your abilities effectively without engaging in what might be perceived as egotistical self-promotion.

DURING THE INTERVIEW

As with any job interview, there are a few basic rules. Bring several additional copies of your CV and your copy of the college catalog, complete with margin notes and dog-eared pages. Arrive early, in case traffic, weather, parking or some other environmental factor, is a challenge. Make a positive impression on the receptionist and others you meet in the office—they may later have input into decisions impacting your hiring. Regardless of distractions— colleges and universities are typically hectic places—remain focused on the preparation you have made. Expect a delay, and more formality than is common in the business world. Therefore use "doctor," "dean," or other appropriate title unless you are explicitly asked not to do so. Make effective eye contact, shake hands firmly, share your name, and thank each participant for taking the time to meet with you.

When you finally sit down with the interviewer(s), take a moment to focus your thoughts and visualize the positive facial response you would like to see. In the moment during which the interviewers give your credentials a final review, note clues that communicate their values system. Commit yourself to active listening rather than speaking. Stay focused on your primary goal—establishing your credibility to deliver effective instruction. Having the key decision-maker express that you have potential for contributing to the program, rather than assigning you a specific class to teach, is probably the best news you can hope to hear at the end of the initial interview. So avoid pushing hard for a more definitive outcome.

Expect first to be asked an open-ended question such as, "Why are you interested in part-time teaching?" while the interviewers continue to review your credentials. As in the business world, the department chair and dean need to discover rather quickly "What you can do for them," so be prepared to state your case positively and succinctly. Your potential is being compared not only to that of other new adjunct professors, but to veteran teaching professionals as well. Be prepared to effectively evaluate your ability to deliver specific courses in their curriculum. Avoid indicating you can teach "anything"—and in the process discount the integrity of their program. Listen very carefully and observe attentively when they share their history in education, their expectations of an effective adjunct professor, and their vision of the department's future. As the dialogue evolves, seek to increase your understanding of the decision-making process, the time frame related to teaching assignments, and which two or three courses you are perceived to have the best potential in delivering. Ask if copies of course syllabi are available. Ask what you can do to better prepare yourself for an assignment, such as observe a veteran's teaching, serve as a guest speaker or teaching assistant for a class, establish a mentoring relationship with a full-time or veteran adjunct professor, or read particular materials. Give the decision maker multiple reasons to perceive that you will be an effective fit with his or her mission.

Conclude the interview by formulating a clear understanding of the follow-up steps that need to be addressed. Since colleges will need to complete a detailed data file prior to assigning an adjunct professor a class to teach, it is typical to provide the standard employment package immediately following the initial interview. Begin and maintain a file of photocopies of all the critical paperwork you submit to the college. Formulate a list of key answers and other comments made to you, as well as your personal perceptions of significant occurrences. The major bottleneck in the approval to teach process is often securing official transcripts from the colleges and universities you have attended. Unofficial photocopies, or transcripts marked "issued to student" will not satisfy the final hiring requirements of the accrediting associations that set many standards of institutions. Many colleges have developed handbooks for adjunct faculty that you might obtain from the interviewer, or perhaps the human resources department. Close your interview by expressing your understanding of their concern about the critical nature of the hiring decision and by assuring them that you are well worth the risk they might take on you.

FOLLOWING UP THE INTERVIEW

Within a few days, send each instructional leader who interviewed you a formal, correctly written business letter warmly expressing your gratitude for their time investment and demonstrating your reflection on some of the key issues that emerged during the interview. Once again, reassure the decision-maker of your understanding of the process and your willingness to complete the extra acts of preparation, and compliment something which you saw or heard that reflected their commitment to excellence. Close by stating the two or three most significant contributions you could make immediately to the increased success of their program. Expedite the paperwork process as much as possible to ensure that you meet institutional requirements if called on soon to teach.

If all goes well, the discipline leader will call soon with a tentative teaching assignment or with a plan for activities that move you closer to attaining that goal. In this day of tight budgets, your assignment often will depend on sufficient enrollment being generated—not only for that class, but also for classes taught by full-time faculty who must carry a minimum teaching load. It is common at many institutions for a number of tentative assignments to be modified at the last moment, with adjunct professors shifted to a different section (time or place) of the same course or to another course—or to have an assignment cancelled. No dean or department chair enjoys making those telephone calls, for reasons including the negative perception it might create of their management capability. While such cancellation calls may be frustrating to receive especially if you had prepared a great deal for the course, it is critical that you demonstrate understanding and support to the discipline leader in these situations. If you receive such a call, you might express again your willingness to serve as a guest speaker, substitute instructor for emergency situations, or volunteer teaching assistant in a course you seem especially suited to later teach. You could also offer to "team teach" the course with a veteran instructor. Your goal should be to get your foot in the door, so consistently demonstrate a cooperative and unselfish nature. Your initial assignment will come soon enough, and the more exposure you have to the factors that impact success, the better off you will be in the long run.

THROUGH THE ADJUNCTS' EYES

Margaret:

So far, I have been able to schedule and complete interviews with two of the three department chairs at local institutions who hire part-time instructors in my field. The first interview felt really odd. After having interviewed hundreds of applicants over the last thirty years, it was the first time I had been "on the other side of the desk." It really sensitized me to what it means to be an "older person" in a "young person's world." I was actually nervous and talked way too much, bragging about my achievements and dropping names of executives I had worked with over the years. The chair surely concluded that her students didn't want to listen to somebody spout on like that for a whole semester!

The second interview went much better. I was relaxed and just tried to be myself. The department chair was nearly twenty years younger than I and clearly a little nervous himself. I got him to talk about himself and the accomplishments of his department—he has a very positive vision for the future. It was exciting—like old times at work! At the end of the half-hour we seemed to have "hit it off." He was especially interested in my real-world approach and ideas about making my classroom team-oriented and interactive. He has agreed to let me try a section of a management class during the upcoming semester, but he wants me to make an appointment to review my syllabus before the course actually starts. He also suggested that I observe a section of the same course now being taught by a veteran professor, to get a feel for the students and the level at which the material is delivered.

Karen:

Soon after being attracted to part-time teaching, I had a conversation about my career-building strategy with a senior partner in my law firm, Mr. Jackson. I brought up possibly teaching at our local liberal arts college and he was ecstatic. He said that he had been teaching one class per term there for a number of years and had met many interesting and enthusiastic students—some of whom later became clients or made referrals of their families and friends to him. He had been wanting to stop teaching to spend more time with his family. But the department chair, who had grown to be a close personal friend, said, somewhat jokingly, that he couldn't do so until he found a suitable replacement. Mr. Jackson said if I was really interested, he would mentor me, provide me all of the exams and other materials he had developed over the years and introduce me to the department chair. I jumped at the chance!

The following Monday, we went to talk with the department chair together and closed the deal on my teaching the same course as Mr. Jackson, beginning next term.

Juan:

In pursuing a part-time position outside the university, I asked one of my professors for referrals. He gave me the name and telephone number of the department chair at a nearby community college, with whom he apparently has a professional relationship. Later, I sensed he had made a telephone call to support my effort. I knew other graduates students have successfully taught at the community college part-time, so I felt I had a little edge in the interview. The department chair was primarily interested in my perceptions of how students differed between universities and community colleges. Luckily, my major professor had told me that community colleges tend to have "nontraditional" (older) and more diverse students. Most also work full-time and have other obligations on their time. We seemed to "click" in the interview, and she assigned me one course to teach next term. I think the community college environment, with its emphasis on teaching rather than research, will be well worth my time to explore.

TIPS FOR THRIVING

Every effective department chair and dean has a few key adjunct professors whom they count on using every single term. Your success in gaining an assignment would be enhanced if you could clearly visualize being included in this top echelon. Besides positive evaluations of your teaching, the most critical factor in your long-term success is to communicate regularly your personal loyalty and understanding of key issues to your discipline leaders and other institutional decision-makers. Continually seek to better understand their personalities, motivations, and challenges, then support their progress toward success by providing them regular evidence of your support. Initially, forwarding copies of journal and magazine articles, especially those which are specific to your full-time job and therefore perhaps not as familiar to academics, is an inexpensive and genuine way to demonstrate your commitment. After beginning your teaching, you should plan to share copies of outstanding work produced by students in your classes. Later, more personal feedback—oral and written—would effectively convey your interest and loyalty.

Also, remember the administrative assistant who supports each decision maker. She is probably deeply grounded in everything of any consequence that impacts the operation, and if properly treated, has the potential to help eliminate barriers to your success. Thank you cards and other modest expressions of gratitude may well pay large dividends in the future.

You have begun your journey to achieve one of the most rewarding part-time occupations in our society. Strive to fit into this rich culture before taking any action to stand out. Seek to understand rather than critically question practices that might seem unusual by comparison to your experiences in the nonacademic world.

REVIEW OF KEY POINTS

- Entry into the academic environment requires a fundamental paradigm shift for most adjunct professors.

- Many of the basic rules of enlightened job interviewing apply in obtaining an adjunct teaching position, while a few are significantly different.
- Discipline leaders have a fairly universal set of criteria that drives their decision making on hiring new adjunct faculty members.
- Begin developing relationships early with all those who might later play a role in your success as an adjunct professor.
- Be persistent, positive, and professional in your follow-up efforts.

SUGGESTED READINGS

Bolles, R. (1997). *What color is your parachute?* Berkeley, CA: Ten Speed Press.
McCormack, M. (1984). *What they don't teach you at Harvard Business School.* New York: Bantam Books.

3

A SELF-DIRECTED
ORIENTATION PROGRAM

Focus Questions

- What aspects of the institution must you understand before entering the classroom?
- Which resources of the discipline leader will help most in your preparations to teach?
- How can you build your teaching skills in the brief time before starting your course?

We begin this chapter with the assumption that you have been given a tentative teaching assignment, or that discussions with the dean, department chair, or other discipline leader have identified one or more courses that might be assigned to you at some future date. At best, most colleges or universities schedule a meeting or two annually and perhaps provide a handbook to their adjunct professors with critical information about their institutions. In most cases, these practices are woefully insufficient to address the wide range of challenges that might come your way. It is critical that in the limited time you have prior to the beginning of your course you more thoroughly orient yourself to the institution's policies, procedures, and culture and clarify expectations of your role as an adjunct professor. An orientation checklist (Appendix 3.1) will effectively facilitate this process.

GETTING FOCUSED

Upon their initial tentative assignment, most new adjunct instructors delay further preparation until a commitment or clarification call comes from their discipline leader. Such delays guarantee that they find themselves woefully under-prepared to begin teaching their assigned class. Discipline leaders cannot predict precisely how many sections of a given course are needed until students complete their registration. Thus, you may be contacted to guarantee a particular teaching assignment with only a few hours' notice. Factor in the simple fact that it is difficult to recover from a poor first class meeting, and that an invitation to teach a second course is predicated wholly on your success in your initial effort, and you have two strong reasons for self-directed preliminary preparations as soon as the tentative assignment is made. The time and energy you invest in these preparations will invariably be rewarded, albeit sometimes later than you might prefer, by the decision-maker who has become adept at identifying the committed new adjunct professor. Your planning should focus on developing your knowledge base in four arenas: human resource issues, general college-wide and department logistical procedures, services to support your teaching, and resources for developing your teaching skills.

While your department chair or other discipline leader is your most valuable resource, you should be continually cognizant of the many demands on their time, especially immediately before the beginning of a term. It would be a major mistake to depend solely upon them for answers to the many questions you will develop before you enter the classroom. As stated before, the college catalog, course schedule, and other institutional publications can provide answers to many of your questions. In addition, many colleges and universities have developed handbooks exclusively for adjunct faculty members, designed to provide answers to the specific types of questions new instructors are likely to have. Many institutions also have developed web pages that communicate valuable information to their instructors via the Internet. Learning to utilize these resources early in your adjunct career, before taking your questions to support staff (much less the discipline leader!), will build your knowledge base and confidence level, earn you goodwill, and contribute to establishing positive relationships with the instructional leaders and others on campus with whom you will later interface.

HUMAN RESOURCE ISSUES

When compared with most other employment arenas, institutions of higher education, which depend more heavily on highly specialized workers to deliver their missions and collaborative practices to make decisions, typically exhibit a very complex human resources function. Decisions are especially complicated in the case of faculty, whose credentials require careful review to satisfy the requirements not only of the institution but also the standards of accrediting associations and perhaps various governmental entities as well. A high level of functional support for the needs of full-time faculty is typical, but that provided for adjunct faculty is often less than desirable, even though certification and related standards nonetheless apply. Therefore, it is incumbent upon the adjunct professor to proactively manage his or her employment and, where required, certification applications. The institution's receipt of appropriate official transcripts from colleges and universities you have attended and related documentation from other sources tends to be an especially challenging process requiring your persistence. Many potential adjunct professors have been stymied in their efforts to teach by incorrectly assuming that their employment file was complete, when it in fact lacked one or more key documents.

While it is accepted professional practice to be on good terms with all of the institution's staff, we recommend that you develop an especially positive relationship with one particular competent and reliable clerical employee in the human resource department. Ask for that person any time you have questions about your file and other human resource issues, and regularly demonstrate your appreciation through "thank you" notes or other small gestures. Her or his competence and willingness to serve as your advocate can save you many headaches, not only in the application process, but far into the future. Rely on this person especially to help you confirm your emerging understanding of the college's human resources processes, while being extremely careful about creating potentially compromising situations.

Upon receipt of your teaching certificate or other document clearing you to teach, promptly communicate that fact to your immediate instructional decision-maker. Since it might not otherwise be brought to his or her attention, it would be appropriate to send a photocopy of the certificate or other approval document, attaching a note that serves as a "memory jogger" and reinforces your commitment.

Other human resource matters that should be clearly understood prior to your initial teaching assignment are employment contracts and the amount, frequency, and method of remuneration. The pay for adjunct professors, most frequently based upon the level of education and typically not negotiable, may well be outlined in an adjunct faculty handbook or similar document readily available from the human resources department. Accessing the information this way might save an uncomfortable interchange with the discipline leader. Salary is typically very modest, as are "fringe benefits" (if available). Although some colleges offer a few limited benefits, such as tuition or bookstore discounts, or perhaps total reimbursement for courses you take to remain current in your teaching field, most will not supply insurance, an office, travel reimbursement, or related benefits.

Take a moment to calculate the pay on an hourly basis and the nonmonetary benefits you believe you will receive from teaching. Factor in the hours of preparation you will need to invest outside of class (especially for the initial teaching assignment) and any additional costs, such as travel, that you will incur. If the financial and potential psychological rewards do not outweigh the costs, terminate your pursuit of adjunct teaching, or at least delay it until the inherent limitations become acceptable. Becoming disgruntled over such factors after the term has begun has a negative impact not only on your morale, but also on students who depend on you to make their one chance at this course come alive.

GENERAL LOGISTICAL INFORMATION

While you are admittedly limited in the amount of information you can gather and process prior to teaching your first class, there is certainly a fundamental knowledge base you should start immediately to build. This information is a foundation for the more specific and detailed course planning that will be addressed in Chapter 5. First, develop a clear understanding of the missions of the institution and the program within which you will be teaching, by gaining answers to the following questions.

- Does the instructional program seek to provide students with a theoretical foundation on which they might build advanced study at this or another institution, or does it equip students for immediate entry into the workforce?
- What is the overall demographic makeup of the institution and the student population of your specific program?
- Are the students in the program typically full-time or part-time? If students are usually employed, are there particular industries or organizations in which their employment tends to cluster?
- Do the students in the program tend to have an especially dominant academic strength or weakness?
- Are the courses the discipline leader identified as being your potential assignments required courses or electives? Are they introductory level or advanced courses? Are there prerequisites? What degree programs do each support?

You should also develop a clear understanding of the methods employed to evaluate the performance of adjunct faculty. Specifically determine answers to the following questions.

- Will the discipline leader or designee visit one of your class meetings? If so, will the session to be visited be announced in advance? Will an evaluation form be used, and if so, is it available for you to look over in advance? How and when will the observation be "debriefed"?
- Will students evaluate your performance at the end of the term? If so, is a copy of the form available in advance? What are the procedures and timing of the evaluation? When can the completed forms be reviewed?
- Is an evaluation conference conducted with the discipline leader? When? If so, what are its procedures and ramifications?
- Have targets of success been defined, against which your performance will be compared? These might include goals related to the retention of enrolled students, defined percentage limits of "A" or "F" final grades, etc.
- Who makes the final decision on whether you will be asked to teach again?

Early in your adjunct career, develop an understanding of how the institution shares information with you. Specifically, determine answers to the following questions.

- When and where are faculty meetings held? Are they for all faculty, or solely adjunct faculty? If they are mandatory, how do you document attendance? Are minutes from previous meetings available?
- Are mailboxes provided? Where are they located? What times are they available?
- Is a newsletter or other form of periodic information update available? Where, when, and how are such resources made available?
- Does the college/university have an adjunct faculty committee or other vehicle for dealing with issues peculiar to adjunct instructors? How does it function? Where and when does it meet?
- Which, if any, social events or ceremonies are open to adjunct faculty members?

Before meeting your class for the first time, you will also want to determine the following information:

- What are the parking arrangements for faculty and students? Is a decal required? If so, where, how and when is it obtained?
- What other transportation considerations affect students in the course, e.g., location of bus or subway stops?
- What is the general state of safety on campus? What are the security provisions? Do you need a specific form of identification? How do you reach a security guard in a hurry? Where are telephones located in relation to

your classroom? What is the procedure for locking and unlocking your classroom?

- Where are refreshments available? Is their consumption permissible in the classroom?
- Where do students purchase textbooks and required supplies, if any? What are the hours?
- Where and how do you obtain class rolls and grade sheets? Are midterm grades reported? When are final course grades due?
- If you teach at a satellite campus, what provisions are available for transporting materials to the discipline leader?

Dozens of questions will no doubt emerge as the time to begin your course approaches. Keep careful track of the answers that affect the specific plan you will develop and implement for your course.

SERVICES TO SUPPORT YOUR TEACHING

Next, develop an understanding of the support resources available to you as an adjunct professor, including the procedures that affect their availability and convenience. The effective use of these resources can not only save you time and money, but also markedly enhance the overall quality of your instruction.

Although most colleges and universities make photocopying and even word processing services available to their adjunct faculty for developing handouts and examinations, these services often have several days' turn-around time and require effective long-term planning. Audiovisual equipment, including overhead projectors and videotape players, is commonly available also, when reserved sufficiently in advance.

The college library typically provides an array of services for all its faculty, including a "reserve section" where you can provide students with supplementary reading materials. If your course lends itself to assignments that require library research, be sure to know its resources and limitations prior to making such assignments. Most college librarians would be pleased, if asked, to give you a personal tour of their facilities. Should the library lack resources that you perceive as critical to the effective completion of your tentatively planned assignments, you may want to re-think your strategy. Asking students to complete assignments that require research at less convenient libraries might be logistically impossible and opens you up to criticism.

Lastly, your students, many of whom arrive at college with less than an ideal preparation, may require access to computer equipment or specialized tutoring to master the skills and concepts in your course. If the college provides computer laboratories, it is critical that you become familiar with their operating hours and somewhat with their procedures. Therefore, you may well want to take a brief tour to learn first-hand about the resources available. In addition, with the hectic lifestyles of today's students, which will be highlighted in Chapter 4, you will no doubt want to inquire about the facilities your college provides for administering "make-up examinations" to students who were unable to take them during regular class hours. Effective use of each of these resources can make your job a great deal more manageable.

RESOURCES FOR DEVELOPING YOUR TEACHING SKILLS

An increasing number of colleges are providing professors—both full-time and adjunct—with resources for improving their teaching. These include courses, workshops, videotapes, books, and others. Sometimes these are housed and coordinated through a centralized "teaching and learning center," "faculty development center" (or similar-sounding title), or they might be available through a less structured delivery system. Institutions especially dependent on adjunct professors sometimes provide additional developmental activities, such as informal lunches and weekend workshops, that focus on a key aspect of teaching effectiveness. Each of these offer great benefit and will be known to your discipline leader if you remember to ask.

While there are few books devoted specifically to the issue of adjunct teaching, there are many broader focused books you are likely to find helpful in developing your knowledge base. In this book, those perceived as especially pertinent for the new adjunct professor are cited as "suggested readings" at the end of each chapter. Others are cited in the bibliography. Many of these books are readily available in college libraries, or through interlibrary loan arrangements your library may have with other libraries in your region. There is also a growing body of articles that would be helpful in building your knowledge base. The following periodicals and journals, available in the library of many colleges or universities, are especially useful resources:

- *College Teaching*
- *The Teaching Professor*
- *Innovation Abstracts*
- *The Chronicle of Higher Education*
- *Journal on Excellence in College Teaching*
- *Change*
- *The National Teaching and Learning Forum*

Probably your single most valuable developmental resource, however, would be the establishment of a mentoring relationship with a full-time faculty member or a veteran adjunct professor—ideally from the department in which you would subsequently teach. Before you teach your first course, you would be wise to observe your mentor delivering a similar course. In later discussions with your mentor, you should focus on building your knowledge of teaching strategies and materials, developing a better understanding of the types of students you observe in their classroom, and other related activities. After you begin teaching, it is invaluable to have a mentor with whom you can discuss challenging situations that arise so your solutions are more likely to be effective. Research strongly validates the importance of promptly discussing student ratings and observation results with an experienced practitioner. You might ask your discipline leader about potential mentors, or you could attempt to build a spontaneous relationship yourself with those you might meet in departmental or adjunct faculty meetings.

An especially key point to remember is that you must offer the potential mentor a benefit for the time you are asking him or her to invest in you. Offer to serve as a guest speaker on a key concept in one of their courses, volunteer to serve as a substitute if they need to miss a class meeting, or periodically invite them to lunch and pick up the tab. Mentoring has proven most effective when it builds on a base of knowledge in teaching methods you have developed for yourself. Therefore, it is critical to take full advantage of books such as this one, courses and workshops your institution might offer, and other resources, rather than rely on the mentor to answer all of your questions.

Recall that, from the discipline leader's viewpoint, one of your major strengths in the college or university classroom is your ability to bridge the academic and "real world." Therefore, in addition to methods of development internal to the institution, you should learn to effectively leverage the resources available to you within your full-time position and related professional association. You will also benefit from becoming a keener observer of your acquaintances who possess the types of skills typically associated with successful teachers—corporate trainers and other human resource professionals, presenters at conferences and meetings you must attend to stay current in your field, and professional salespeople. Each of these, no doubt, exhibits some behavior which you might model and incorporate into your emerging "teaching style."

You probably have additional resources that could enrich the learning opportunities for your students. These might include a work environment that, through a field trip, could provide students with insights difficult to grasp in a classroom setting, colleagues who might be excellent guest speakers, and videos unavailable in the academic department or library that might be used to clarify an especially critical point. Using those resources may present a range of interpersonal and perhaps ethical issues, but nonetheless, considering them expands the perspectives you might bring to your classroom.

THROUGH THE ADJUNCTS' EYES

Juan:

Following up on the point my community college department chair made during our interview, I have tried to further understand the differences between the cultures of the university and the community college. Much of the difference can be attributed to the formation of the institutions. Whereas universities are likely to be a century or more old, nearly all community colleges have come into existence since the later 1950s—the time of Sputnik and the Civil Rights movement.

There seems to be a stereotypical perception by people at the university that community college students are not as prepared as those who come to the university right out of high school. I talked with two instructors from the department at the community college and, while not totally dismissing the stereotype, each said I needed to better understand the complexities affecting community college students rather than accept the stereotype at face value.

Karen:

Mr. Jackson set time aside for me several afternoons to thoroughly review the college catalog, with particular focus on the "political" aspects of the culture, as well as the materials he had developed for the course. At the end of our meeting at the college, the department chair had provided me a copy of the textbook and some materials the publisher provides to support the teaching of the course. He also gave me the syllabus of a section of the same course being taught by one of the department's full-time faculty members and encouraged me to arrange a meeting with her before finalizing my course plan and syllabus.

Mr. Jackson was clearly invested in my success in the classroom— he wants me to make the firm and him look good. He has assumed the role of mentor, making himself available so freely that I noticed some other young attorneys in the firm seem to get a bit jealous. In one of our sessions, he mentioned a conversation with the college president about his potentially being named to their board of trustees, so I felt even more compelled to follow his suggestions and course plan closely.

Margaret:

Since free time is available to me, I invested a great deal in reviewing the college catalog and their adjunct faculty handbook. While there were not many surprises, it did strike me that there had been perhaps more change within higher education since my days as a graduate student than I anticipated. These materials seem more "reader-friendly" and marketing-oriented than I remembered colleges being when I was a student. There was, however, still a sizeable section on policies and procedures that was a bit difficult to digest in one setting. It's comforting to know that so many answers are readily available when situations in my classroom might call for clarification. I sure don't want to be calling my department chair every time I have some little problem—he expects more of a veteran than that!

TIPS FOR THRIVING

While you have been selected to teach based on the strengths you bring to the course, you must manage to become fully aware of the context within which you teach. It is important that your course and methods are perceived by other faculty members, full-time or adjunct, as consistent with the departmental mission. Stated another way, it is critical that you are perceived as a "member of the team." In your first teaching assignment, you should plan to not only structure your course in a manner similar to those of veteran instructors, but to give similar types of assignments and examinations. Your method of dress and the degree of formality you project should meet the expectations of the department chair. For your own peace of mind and broadest acceptance of others, clarify those as explicitly as possible before entering the classroom for the first time.

Besides accessing the printed and human resources mentioned, ask the discipline leader for copies of syllabi or course outlines of others who have instructed the courses likely to be assigned to you. Ask for whatever textbooks and "ancillary materials," such as instructor's manuals, might be available. If the assignment becomes imminent, a bank of test questions developed by the textbook publisher to correlate with the content and structure of the text, transparencies for use with an overhead projector, and coordinated videotapes would be especially valuable. These materials are typically furnished by the textbook publisher to the discipline leader at the time the textbook is adopted. In some cases, such materials are made available through the college library. Since these materials are not always perfect for your needs, be sure to evaluate each objectively before incorporating them into the plan for your course.

REVIEW OF KEY POINTS:

- Your planning process should begin as soon as a tentative assignment is made by the discipline leader.

- From the beginning, turn to college publications and staff employees for answers to most questions; only consult the discipline leader for especially difficult and ambiguous questions.
- Proactively manage your employment and certification applications through the college's stated process.
- Nurture a working relationship with a member of the human resources department staff.
- Evaluate the full range of potential benefits from teaching before you commit to an assignment.
- Develop a clear understanding of the institution's and program's missions, evaluation procedures, information sources, and logistical matters that impact teaching before you begin your actual course planning.
- Investigate any support services and develop an understanding of their purposes and procedures.
- Begin a self-directed plan for building your teaching skills that includes formal instruction provided by the institution, observations of veteran teachers, reading, and initiating a mentoring relationship.
- Assess your full-time employment arena for teaching role models and potential resources for the courses you might teach.

SUGGESTED READINGS

Bianco-Mathis, V., & Chalofsky, N. (Eds.) (1996). *The adjunct faculty handbook.* Thousand Oaks, CA: Sage.

Dunham, S. M. (1996). What college teachers need to know. In Robert J. Menges & Maryellen Weimer (Ed.) *Teaching on solid ground: Using scholarship to improve practice* (pp. 297–313). San Francisco: Jossey-Bass.

McGuire, J. (1993, June). Part-time faculty: Partners in excellence. *Leadership Abstracts,* 6(6).

O'Banion, T. (1995, December/January). "A learning college for the 21st century." *Community College Journal.*

Phillips-Jones, L. (1982). *Mentors and proteges.* New York: Arbor House.

Senge, P. (1990). *The fifth discipline.* New York: Currency-Doubleday.

APPENDIX 3.1 ADJUNCT PROFESSOR ORIENTATION CHECKLIST

Use this form to guide your orientation to teaching at the institution. You might want to refer to the college catalog, the adjunct faculty handbook, and the department chair (or his or her designee) as resources.

I. *Human-Resource Related*

- ☐ Employment Application Package Complete
- ☐ Teaching Approval/Certification Process Complete (if applicable)
- ☐ Faculty ID card
- ☐ Other

II. *General Instructional*

- ☐ Understanding of Institutional/Program Mission
- ☐ Demographics, Needs of Student Population, Probable Class Size
- ☐ Class Rolls, Student Attendance Procedures
- ☐ Classroom Procedures: Schedule, Breaks, Housekeeping
- ☐ Grade Rolls, Submission Procedures
- ☐ Faculty Evaluation Procedures
- ☐ Release of Student Information
- ☐ Books/Bookstore Logistics/Sources of Required Materials and Supplies
- ☐ Student Retention and Counseling Procedures
- ☐ Security/Reporting Incidents/Parking Procedures
- ☐ Library Logistics/Learning Resource Labs/Computer Labs
- ☐ Auxiliary Resources: Printing, Wordprocessing, Audio Visual, etc.
- ☐ Regular Sources of Information: Meetings, Newsletters, etc.
- ☐ Other

III. *Department/Division/Program Specific*

- ☐ Room Keys/Security Codes
- ☐ Required Forms/Reports
- ☐ Mailbox/Materials Distribution System
- ☐ Office Space/Procedures for Availability
- ☐ Specialized Facilities and Equipment
- ☐ Introduction to Key People
- ☐ Faculty Development Resources: Mentors, Workshops, etc.
- ☐ Other
- ☐ Other

Comments:

4

TODAY'S UNDERGRADUATE STUDENTS

Focus Questions

- What are the significant demographic changes occurring among college students?
- How have perceptions toward attending college changed in the last generation?
- How should instructors structure their teaching to maximize results?

New adjunct professors, most of whom attended college full-time directly after completing high school with cohorts largely similar to themselves, are often surprised when they enter the classroom of their first assignment. Over the past twenty-five years or so, the undergraduate student populations of most colleges and universities have become increasingly diverse—in age, gender, ethnicity, working status, and other significant factors. Before a new faculty member can become successful, this new student population must be significantly understood, not only in the unique characteristics engendered by its demographic makeup, but in terms of the societal conditioning to which it has been exposed. This chapter will help you understand the dimensions of the increased diversity of undergraduate students, but more than that, build your understanding of ways in which students vary in attitudes toward school and learning styles.

THE BIG PICTURE

According to data provided by the National Center for Educational Statistics, total enrollment in all forms of higher education increased 66% between

1970 and 1994. Much of this increase was among part-time students, who now comprise over 70% of total college enrollment. In most teaching assignments, adjunct professors will deal overwhelmingly, if not exclusively, with part-time students. Between 1984 and 1994, the number of men enrolled increased 9%, while female enrollment increased 24%. Today, female undergraduate students outnumber males, and among part-time students, women students exceed men by 50%.

The number of "nontraditional" students, typically defined as 25 years of age or older, has been growing more rapidly than the number of younger students. Between 1980 and 1990, enrollment among younger (or "traditional-age") students increased 3%, while enrollment among nontraditional age students grew 34%. Enrollment increases, especially among older students, have been fueled by the growth of community colleges and extension programs by four-year institutions, as well as by changes in the economy that demand higher levels of academic skills from workers at all levels. Though there is a great deal of common ground between students of any age, it is very useful for the new adjunct professor to understand some of the key differences between younger and older students.

TRADITIONAL STUDENTS

Students under 25 years of age comprise about 75% of the full-time undergraduate students in American college and universities, but considerably less than 50% of part-time students. Increasing numbers of traditional-age students are staying close to home to attend college while working full-time or in several part-time positions. Many have been at least partially supporting themselves for several years, often while accumulating significant debt through tuition costs, which have risen faster than the inflation rate, and/or the purchase of what were once considered luxury possessions for students.

Much more than in previous generations, these students are the product of dysfunctional families. Many younger students have parents who have divorced one or more times, sometimes remarrying other divorcees with children to form "blended families." Other students' parents have never been married. Such situations have contributed to the stifling of psychological and academic development during some students' most formative years, residually affecting their college-age performance. These students have often "discovered" that commitment to others hurts as much as it heals.

The parents of today's younger college students were more likely to have been employed under the unsettling circumstances of "downsizing" and corporate mergers and to have changed jobs and residences. As a result, their now college-age children have changed elementary and secondary schools far more often than was the custom only a few decades ago. Such students often exhibit socialization problems throughout their college years, isolating themselves, becoming medically depressed, and sometimes turning to unhealthy lifestyles. Many traditional-age students have been "latch-key kids," entertained too much by television programs and videos with violent and otherwise negative themes. Parents, exhausted when they arrived home after working long hours and sometimes an extended commute, have failed to read to them or to provide coaching for homework assignments during students' early years.

More likely to have worked part-time while in high school—often well past what most adults would consider reasonable hours—today's traditional-age college students have not been as focused on school success as those of two decades ago. Because of their employment, younger students are less likely to have played organized sports or to have been involved in other constructive school activities; consequently they may not have had the opportunity to learn the skills of cooperation and compromise. Barely old enough to drive an automobile, many have maintained their own households, frequently cohabitating with equally challenged peers. They have engaged in all sorts of other "adult" activities for which they were insufficiently prepared and have developed extensive coping mechanisms for dealing with the obstacles in their lives. Without structure and consistently communicated standards, many have not developed the self-discipline (some might call it "responsibility") that we typically associate with success in higher education.

From another perspective, traditional-age students have grown up in a society largely influenced by consumerism, materialism, increased demands for individual rights, and decreased time horizons for nearly everything. One fast-food chain has promised to deliver their products "your way"—a theme replicated in thousands of other advertising messages that have inundated young college students' minds. Traditional-age students have been conditioned by the aftermath of Watergate, Three Mile Island, "insider-trading," and other high-profile ethical scandals, contributing to a mindset of cynicism and lack of respect for all authority figures—including college professors. Speaking spontaneously and angrily of alleged misdeeds by others and lodging complaints—even lawsuits—have become common behaviors. Students of this generation are quick to proclaim their "rights." Many of today's students perceive professors as service providers, class attendance as a matter of individual choice, and grades as "pay" to which they are entitled for meeting standards they perceive as reasonable.

A litany of reasons, including (but certainly not limited to) depersonalized schools, public school teacher turnover, and overemphasis on standardized tests, have contributed to a less than effective primary and/or secondary education for many students. A large number begin college requiring remediation in reading, writing, and mathematics skills. Conditioned by their "surfing" through MTV and dozens of other cable channels, violent computer games, instantaneous access to the entire world through the Internet, and other widespread technology, traditional-age students often exhibit extremely short attention spans and an affinity for color and rapid movement—qualities difficult to recreate in many traditional classrooms. These students have heard themselves identified as members of "Generation X" ("Generation Y" or the "Baby Boomlet" is just over the horizon) and perceive an outside world that dislikes and—perhaps even worse—is unwilling to invest the time to understand them. This self-image often drives a self-fulfilling prophecy of boredom, negativity, and lowered academic expectations that exhibits itself in the classroom.

Many college professors who remember a time when students were perceived as more "responsible" and "appreciative" seem to expect today's students to miraculously act the same way, and become frustrated when it doesn't happen. Investing quality effort only with students who display more conservative, traditional values is not a prescription for achieving the degree of learning success that instructional leaders expect. All educators have a responsibility to all students and to the profession to accept all students "where they are," and to guide them toward an outcome that our highest standards indicate are appropriate. In his blockbuster book *The Seven Habits of Highly Effective People,* Steven Covey, himself a professor, encourages us to "Seek first to understand, then to be understood"—a requirement for achieving success with today's students, especially the traditional-age.

NONTRADITIONAL STUDENTS

"Nontraditional" students have seen their ranks grow dramatically in recent years, especially in the evening and weekend classes that adjunct professors are most likely to teach. Many of these students have lost their jobs to "the new economy," been displaced by technology, and/or been unable to sustain an income that would enable them to provide adequately for their families. Although a disproportionate number of evening students are single women, many are single men, often also with children. They often lack the support from family and long-time friends, who now live far away. Even though their employers may support their education financially, nontraditional students feel resented by their co-workers when leaving work early, or arriving late, to pursue their college education.

Many older students are attending college after a long layoff, frequently doubting their ability to succeed. The other time-consuming challenges in their lives—children and other family responsibilities, caring for aging parents, work, civic, and religious responsibilities—often prevent adequate preparation for class or contribute to frequent absences. Nontraditional students commonly display test anxiety, a lack of confidence in their writing and mathematics skills, and hesitance in using computers and other technology.

On the "up side," many nontraditional students make it all work somehow. Those who overcome the initial obstacles of attending college and achieve a measure of success frequently become quite self-directed—thirsty for the knowledge they didn't get when they "should have." They are motivated first to "pass," then to achieve high grades. Adult learners often become "overachievers" who will rewrite entire papers to gain an extra point or two. While traditional-age students demand their "right," many older students won't ask for the smallest extra consideration, e.g., to turn a project in a few days late.

As their success as students builds, older students often become highly motivated to serve as a role model for their children in school. They often proudly speak of posting their successful exams and assignments on the family refrigerator! While "Gen X'ers" often mask their disappointments behind a blank countenance, the devastation older students perceive from failure is often painfully displayed on their faces and heard in their voices. Older students are far more likely to stay after class to share their frustrations with an empathetic instructor or to discuss stimulating concepts from the course material. In the process, it is not uncommon for emotional reliances, even "crushes," to develop, which require careful attention to prevent possible hurtful ramifications.

Most older students learn best by doing, by applying the theory of textbooks to the rich set of experiences they have accumulated over the years and to the reality of tomorrow at work and home. They have a great deal they want to share, and in an informal environment they will do so, in the process making connections for themselves with the learning goals of the course. They tend to be problem-centered, rather than content-centered, and will often lose focus (and patience) with an instructor who is intent on "covering the material." Adult learners, recalling the classrooms of their childhood, tend to respond most effectively when the classroom environment is organized and relatively quiet and when they perceive they have ready access to the instructor, even though they might not frequently take advantage of it.

In recent years, much has been written and spoken of a "generational gulf"—an inability or unwillingness of those in one generation to understand, value, and adapt to the significant differences that shape the way those of markedly different ages perceive and react to the world. An ineffective professor accepts the gulf as a "given," contributing to the development of a fragmented classroom environment in which individuals work at cross purposes. The enlightened professor proactively manages the classroom so that, regardless of the course or discipline, diverse students learn to work cooperatively, in the process creating a synergy that intensifies the rewards both students and the professor receive from the class experience.

EMERGING INFLUENCES

Besides the generation to which students belong, other factors significantly impact their perceptions of college and their learning styles. Today, a fourth of all undergraduate students are members of minority groups—doubling their enrollment in the last twenty years. While enrollment growth among African Americans has exceeded that of white students, the sharpest percentage growth in minority enrollment in recent years has occurred among Asian Americans, Hispanics, and Native Americans. In many metropolitan colleges and universities, recent immigrants represent an especially significant student population. Obviously, ethnicity, language, religion, culture, and sexual orientation are each significant issues to which an adjunct professor must be sensitive, for each shapes the paradigm toward learning that each student brings to the classroom. The successful professor sees these differences as an opportunity rather than a threat to learning.

Seek continuously to understand more fully the perspectives of the types of students represented in your classroom through reading and discussions with colleagues, but more interestingly by listening intently and nonjudgmentally to individual students themselves. Identify well in advance the differences among students in your classroom and manage the ramifications. Incorporate your growing knowledge base into the richer environment that is created in your classroom when diverse perspectives are expressed. Although your job is identified as teaching a particular course, you could more appropriately define your role as creating an environment and providing appropriate stimuli for students to master a particular set of concepts, skills or attitudes. As stated before, our long-term goal is to equip students to become their own lifelong teachers.

In the past several years, a steadily increasing number of students with physical and mental challenges have begun to pursue an undergraduate education. Often, additional resources are made available so that visually disabled students can enroll in a computer science class, for example, or hearing disabled students can complete courses that largely employ a lecture method of instruction. As have other "minority groups," students with disabilities (and their families) have become politically active and assertive in recent years, expecting the educational community to more fully address their specific needs. You are legally and professionally mandated to accommodate such reasonable requests.

While it is important that you identify and impose high standards for all students in your class, it is also critical that you seek to understand the backgrounds of all your students and adopt a degree of flexibility in your interactions with them. The willingness to first understand the special conditions that influence your students enables you to treat each as an individual. Research of recent years tells us that there is not a single form of "intelligence."

When only the traditional definition of "intelligence" is accepted, a competitive classroom culture is fostered which ensures that some students will fail. In recent years, the concept of "multiple intelligences" has emerged to create a contrasting paradigm. Seeking to broaden the scope of human potential beyond the traditional IQ score, Howard Gardner developed the best-known theory of multiple intelligences. He challenged the validity of determining people's intelligence by taking them out of their natural learning environment and asking them to complete isolated tasks they have never done before. Gardner said intelligence has more to do with solving problems and creating products in a context-rich environment. His research yielded seven comprehensive categories of "intelligences":

- Linguistic intelligence—the capacity to use words effectively
- Logical-mathematical intelligence—the capacity to employ numbers effectively and to reason
- Spatial intelligence—the ability to visualize the visual-spatial world accurately
- Bodily-kinesthetic intelligence—expertise in using the entire body to express ideas and feelings
- Musical intelligence—the capacity to perceive, discriminate, transform and express musical forms effectively
- Interpersonal intelligence—the ability to perceive and make distinctions in the moods, motivations, and feelings of other people
- Intrapersonal intelligence—self-knowledge and the ability to act adaptively on the basis of that knowledge

In the traditional paradigm, students were either intelligent or they weren't. In Gardner's paradigm, students have more or less of a wide variety of intelligences. Our intention is not to introduce you to a complex concept in a "quick and dirty" way, as much as it is to sensitize you to the fact that each student has a gift that is worthy of nurturing. In the process of helping each student in your class develop to his or her fullest potential, not by imposing a preconceived limitation but by proactively soliciting students' individual input into learning decisions impacting them, your part-time job and heightened role in the human development process will become far more rewarding.

DEALING POSITIVELY WITH COMMON PROBLEM SITUATIONS

Regardless of their demographics, consistently encourage, in a positive and nonjudgmental manner, self-direction and responsibility in all students. In recent years, our society seems to have fostered in both overt and tacit ways a sense of victimization among those who face challenges. Many students have been affected and will judge your standards and procedures accordingly. Be intellectually prepared and emotionally willing to share quietly why it is in your students' best long-term interest to rise to your high expectation of quality in their assignments and examinations. While they will often dispute your words initially, most will finish the term thanking you for pushing them to turn out their best work.

Some students, especially those with low self-esteem or especially difficult histories, will challenge your best-intended words as discriminatory. At such times, you will be buoyed by following the suggestions in Chapter 5 for proactively building your understanding of your students early in the course. When preparing each class meeting, it is critical that you think through your words prior to addressing topics that have a gender, racial, political, or related sensitivity, so that if challenged, you can accurately share exactly what was said.

Given the nature of your students' lifestyles, you can assume some common problems will inevitably affect your classroom: tardiness, absence, being ill-prepared for some examinations, occasional lack of focus, and perhaps others. Rather than becoming upset and taking punitive action, we suggest you plan for the situations and build a solution into your design of the course. For example, since students will occasionally be late from work or family obligations, we suggest you minimize the impact of their tardy entry into your classroom by reserving a section of the room for late-arrivers. Should you find, several weeks into the course, that the overwhelming majority of the class is a few minutes late, you might delay the beginning of the class ten minutes and reduce the length of your break by a commensurate amount of time. Be creative, yet conservative, and seek feedback from your discipline leader in advance whenever you have questions.

We have always believed that if an effective learning environment were established in each classroom, absences and other student motivation problems would largely take care of themselves. While there will always be a minority whose behavior is inconsistent with your acceptable standards, it is critical not to punish the entire group of students for the actions of the few. The key is timely, unemotional, and frank confrontation of the problem. Ignoring the problem, hoping it will "fix itself," will (as in most other arenas of life) lead to unsatisfactory results. In Chapter 7 we highlight a technique called "transactional analysis" that many college professors have employed to promote positive results in such situations. Beginning with the first class meeting, it is critical to demonstrate structure, establish your standards, reinforce them through consistent behavior, and take action promptly when warranted.

LEARNING STYLES

In recent years, mountains of data have been gathered to help educators more conclusively understand how students learn. Presenting a great deal of that information at this stage in your development as an instructor would probably be counterproductive, but a sample might provide insight to aid you in your initial teaching assignment.

One of the most interesting efforts, commonly referred to as "brain-based" research, seeks to understand learning from the perspective of where and how certain types of information are processed. It suggests there are two major types of learners—those in whom the "right brain" is dominant, and those with a dominant "left brain." Right-brain learners tend to be intuitive, imaginative, and impulsive; they prefer to start with a broad idea and then pursue supporting information. They learn best by seeing and doing in an informal, busy, and somewhat unstructured environment. On the other hand, left-brain learners tend to be analytical, rational, and objective; they prefer putting together many facts to arrive at a general understanding.

Right-brain learners prefer group discussion, simulations, panels, and other activity-based learning, whereas left-brain learners prefer traditional lectures, demonstrations, and assigned readings. Although there are many exceptions, females tend to be right-brain dominant, while males tend to be left-brain dominant. The traditional lecture/demonstration approach is typically more effective with male learners rather than female students. At the same time, research indicates females are more effective in utilizing left-brain approaches than men are in utilizing right-brain approaches, and that females are more successful in transitioning from left-brain to right-brain approaches, and vice versa, than males are.

Another view of learning styles categorizes learners by the types of activities from which they derive the greatest payoff. It yields "tactile learners," who respond to physical objects that can be handled while studied; "visual learners," who facilitate their learning through use of charts, maps, and graphs; "auditory learners," who respond more effectively to the spoken rather than the written word, and others.

In this and other discussions related to teaching styles, the enlightened instructor probably will ask which of two major strategies is most effective. That is, should the professor initially adapt to the preferred learning styles of students or expect students to first adapt to his or her preferred methods? It is a highly complex issue with no instant answers. Each situation requires some study and individualized decisions to arrive at the "best" approach. Some professors can flex themselves quite effectively to the learning styles of students, while others would lose so much confidence in themselves in trying to do so that they might become totally ineffective in the classroom.

Having said all of this, remember that each student in front of you is in many ways unique. While it is useful to make yourself aware of the wide variety of issues impacting students today, there is risk in ever assuming you have heard or seen enough. Get to know each one of your students as well as you can, first by speaking with each one in the initial class, then asking each to complete the "Student Profile" form, located in Appendix 6-1. Later, build an ongoing dialogue with diverse students that will markedly increase your insights and create an accessibility to you in the students' minds that will markedly improve their motivation, attention levels, and understanding of your perspective. One of the greatest rewards of teaching is allowing yourself to be sufficiently vulnerable that you empower students to share more of themselves with you and their peers than might at times be comfortable. It is critical that you regularly assess your values and predispositions, talk with veteran instructors from whose experiences you can learn, and reflect upon your teaching experiences.

WHAT STUDENTS WANT FROM COLLEGE INSTRUCTORS

While each student subgroup has particular characteristics that affect the dynamics of a college learning environment, students consistently need the following from their college instructors:

- Expectations of student performance that are reasonable in quantity and quality and are consistently communicated
- Sensitivity to the diverse demands on students and reasonable flexibility in accommodating them
- Effective use of class time
- A classroom environment that values students' input and protects their dignity
- A classroom demeanor that includes humor and spontaneity
- Examinations that address issues properly covered in class, are appropriate to the level of the majority of students in the class, are punctually scored and returned, and are used fairly to determine final class grades
- Consistently positive treatment of individual students, including a willingness to spend extra time before or after class meetings to provide additional support

While these needs may represent a marked shift from the college environment of several decades ago, they approximate those which most contemporary employees have of their employers, taxpayers have of government, or customers have of businesses they frequent. While many of the trappings of higher education will no doubt remain, this new paradigm of "colleges and universities as service providers to consumer-oriented students" is now firmly entrenched. The successful adjunct professor will do well to embrace it.

THROUGH THE ADJUNCTS' EYES

Margaret:

As I prepare myself to teach, I've reflected back on my past few years of working and some of the values and habits of the younger employees. I recall sensing a reduced loyalty to the company, a reduced attention span, an unwillingness to come in a little early or stay a little late to complete a big assignment, and an inability or unwillingness to invest time in building relationships with their co-workers. Since those employees and many of my students will be in the same generation, I expect to see some of the same. There are reasons I don't fully understand that explain why today's young people tend to be this way. I really need to understand rather than judge this behavior, or my time in the classroom will become misery.

Karen:

Mr. Jackson and I were talking yesterday about changes he has seen among students in recent years. There are many more "nontraditional" students who are often reluctant to objectively evaluate their long-held beliefs. Since I will be focusing on political and legal issues which have been questioned extensively through some high-profile court cases of the last few years, and because I lack the age and perceived wisdom of Mr. Jackson, it may be especially challenging for me to get my students to look at issues analytically. While I'll probably be a little more understanding than Mr. Jackson with younger students, I am concerned that I will lack patience for those who come to class late or want extra consideration because of work or family demands. Getting through law school and establishing a career took a lot of focus and commitment on my part. Maybe it's as important for me to teach such values to students as it is to teach about the political system.

Juan:

As a teaching assistant at the university, I seldom have a student question much of anything I say in a significant way. Oh, they'll challenge me on due dates for assignments and things like that, but those are rather easy to deal with by focusing on the course syllabus which the professor gave them. In the class I will teach for the community college at night, many of the older students will be much more willing and able to freely discuss things from a set of deeply-held values. Many have worked in some very responsible jobs, have served in the military, and had other significant life experiences. Baby Boomers tend to value genuineness and relevance, so I need to be sure to provide that. One of the other teaching assistants at the university who taught at the community college told me about being "eaten alive" one night by an older student who had read and experienced some things related to a topic for which my friend had not prepared very well. I realize things will not turn out very well for me unless I am able to establish my credibility to teach the course material early in the term.

Most community colleges students are somewhat older, and the percentage who are female and minority is typically higher than in universities. Some are "late bloomers" who, though bright, did not apply themselves well in high school. Others have been "re-engineered" out of their jobs and require more sophisticated academic skills. It apparently won't be uncommon for me to have students in my class who are older than I am! Since many have been out of school for a period of time, "nontraditional" students often lack confidence in their academic ability and need encouragement and information about tutoring resources. Nearly all community college students work full-time or close to it and have limited time to do reading and homework. Therefore, my assignments need to be perceived as relevant and practical so that students will be able and willing to complete them. Community college students are commuters, which requires me to be more sensitive to issues like childcare, family finances, and transportation problems. This will be very different from teaching at the university, where most students live on or near campus and have their tuition and other expenses paid by parents.

TIPS FOR THRIVING

While we typically think in terms of teaching accounting, world religions, or another "course," or of teaching "night students," athletes, or some other "group," those adjunct professors who derive the greatest reward from their part-time teaching careers have adopted a different paradigm. They think in terms of the rich mosaic of individuals in their classrooms—each with a unique background of academic, occupational, family, social, economic, military, recreational, and other categories of experiences. Such teachers are energized by students who "don't get it," rather than judgmental of their shortcomings. These professors view differences of opinions as adding richness to the classroom, rather than challenging their authority. They view themselves as "facilitators of learning," rather than "sages on stage." Finally, they realize that, more than anything, their students thrive on feedback that is FAST—frequent, accurate, specific, and timely.

REVIEW OF KEY POINTS

- Today's college and university students are far more likely to be older and part-time than those of previous times.
- For very understandable reasons, many traditional-age college students lack self-discipline and academic foundation.
- Older students typically have many lifestyle challenges to overcome in order to attend college.
- Once oriented to college and with some measure of success behind them, adult learners are typically highly motivated to succeed.
- Common student success problems should be anticipated prior to the class, with solutions designed into the course.

SUGGESTED READINGS

Coulter, M. W. (1993, January–March). Modern teachers and postmodern students. *Community College Journal of Research and Practice*, 17(1), 51–58.

Howe, N., & Strauss, B. (1993). *13th gen: Abort, retry, ignore, fail?* New York: Vintage Books.

Knowles, M. S. (1980). *The modern practice of adult education: From pedagogy to andragogy.* Chicago: Follett.

Knowles, M. S. (1989). *The making of an adult educator.* San Francisco: Jossey-Bass.

Sheehy, G. (1995). *New passages.* New York: Random House.

Upcraft, M. S. (1996). Teaching and today's college student. In R. J. Menges & M. Weimer (Eds.), *Teaching on solid ground: Using scholarship to improve practice* (pp. 21–41). San Francisco: Jossey-Bass.

5

PLANNING YOUR COURSE

Focus Questions

- How do you design quality into the course you will teach?
- Why is the syllabus critical to the success of your course?
- What elements and characteristics should an effective syllabus possess?
- What resources should you consider incorporating into your course design?

As the beginning of the new term draws near and you increasingly expect your assigned course to become a reality, you must proactively intensify your preparation to deliver the course. We can all recall being in a situation where there was a clearly formulated plan in evidence and we could feel the security and confidence the planning engendered. We can also probably remember the sense of frustration evident in situations where no plan was evident. Your students will perceive, within a very few minutes, the presence or absence of a sound plan for your class. This chapter is designed to guide your preparation of a plan to provide students with an optimal learning experience within the context of the overall mission of the department and its established curriculum. The strategy underlying the design of a plan for your initial teaching assignment should be to maximize your strengths and minimize the impact of any weaknesses you bring to the course. The time and energy you invest in the planning effort will pay both short- and long-term benefits for you and your students.

DESIGNING AN EFFECTIVE COURSE

As an adjunct professor, your role in actual course design can vary between two extremes. If yours is a standard course you might be provided a detailed outline, syllabus, textbook, and other course materials, while you are expected to do little more than embellish the course material through your personal experiences and insights. Increasingly however, adjunct professors with recognized expertise in a critical field are being asked to develop and deliver courses that have not previously been taught by the institution or that cannot be taught by anyone else on the faculty. Though the demands of designing a course "from scratch" may seem daunting, the rewards can be substantial. Regardless of your position between those two extremes, it is critical to understand the basic process of course design. Because it tends to have a long-term impact on students, effective course design can repay the investment of time and energy it requires many times over.

An understanding of the process of course design requires an orientation to the concept of *learning domains*. The *affective* domain includes attitudes, character issues, appreciation of beauty, and the like. Evaluating learning in this domain might require students' developing something artistic, such as the writing of an essay, or the compilation of a portfolio of their creations. The *psychomotor* domain refers to physical skills and dexterity, and evaluation typically requires the demonstration of a particular skill at a clearly prescribed standard of performance. Lastly, the *cognitive* domain refers to the thought processes, whose development can be assessed in a number of ways that are addressed in Chapters 10 and 11. Of the three domains, the cognitive is likely of the greatest concern to most readers of this book.

In the 1950s, Benjamin Bloom published his renowned taxonomy of educational objectives for the cognitive domain—a concept critical to the knowledge base of a teacher. The taxonomy delineates six levels of cognitive complexity, ranging from knowledge level (lowest), through comprehension, to application, then analysis, followed by synthesis, and ending with the evaluation level. Introductory college courses typically emphasize the lower levels of *Bloom's Taxonomy,* while capstone courses tend to focus on the higher levels. The second or third courses in a sequenced curriculum likely focus in the lower middle of the range.

After you have determined where the course fits in the program curriculum, you must identify the specific goals of the course. For existing courses, a variety of resources are available to help, including your instructional leader and those who have previously taught the course at your institution. Collect several syllabi and carefully compare course design and strategies. For new courses, begin again with your instructional leader, but consider also the input of leaders of other disciplines at the institution whose curricula might include the course, discipline leaders at other institutions who have developed similar courses, employers or clients of students who complete the course, and perhaps others.

Once the overall goal of the course is formulated and a course description is reviewed (or, in the case of a new course, developed), you need to identify specific learning objectives. You will probably find it useful to think in terms of what educators call *behavioral* objectives, i.e., what you want students to be able to demonstrate at the conclusion of the course. Stating objectives in this fashion encourages use of action verbs such as *identify, contrast, explain,* and *analyze*—rather than *understand* or *know*—thus creating a sharper focus for both instructor and learner. The goals and objectives of the course will provide the overall course structure and drive such other decisions as the selection of effective learning activities, choice of required readings, methods of assessing student learning, etc.

Next, continue your planning with a thorough analysis of the personal resources you bring to the course. One especially helpful method for helping us understand these factors—SWOT analysis—might be borrowed from the business world. Thoroughly mull over the following questions as they relate to the course you have been assigned, then write down the specific points each elicits:

1. What are your particular *strengths* for delivering this course? Focus on your professional experiences likely to be valued by those who will later enter the field, not simply your longevity.
2. What are your *weaknesses*—in knowledge base, communications skill, etc.? Every instructor has some, so you will want to recognize them in order to develop a course plan that minimizes their impact.
3. What *opportunities* are presented to you from teaching this course? Does it provide a way for you to get a particular message to a group of people who might not otherwise be made aware of it, or to discuss issues that affect the success of your "regular job"?
4. What *threats* accrue from your teaching the course? If it will significantly reduce the time you have available for essential activities, you should plan course assignments and the number and nature of examinations—all of which require extensive time to evaluate—accordingly.

As you plan your course, your strategy should be to maximize your strengths and opportunities while minimizing your weaknesses and threats. For example, if organizational and writing skills are among your strengths and dynamic speaking is one of your weaknesses, you would be wise to structure your course with a significant amount of student-participation activities rather than extended blocks of lecture or demonstration. If you view teaching the course as an opportunity to interest students in careers in the industry that employs you full-time, you might want to incorporate a brief face-to-face appointment with each student early in your course, to more effectively maximize your stated opportunity.

A second highly effective course planning tool is the Personal Practical Theory (PPT), closely akin to the mission statement that has become so popular and useful to many individuals and organizations. Your PPT enables you to identify and develop your personal beliefs about learners, the instructor, the subject matter, the classroom climate, and learning.

In turn, the PPT serves as a guide to more effectively planning a course that achieves your personal goals.

Using the same five major categories, we suggest you actively engage in the process of developing your own Personal Practical Theory of teaching. While we have provided a model PPT in Appendix 5.1, resist the temptation to accept the beliefs in it as your own. Instead, use the model as starter for articulating your own grounded beliefs. The process of developing the PPT as well as the document produced will guide you in formulating a comprehensive plan for your course, help you organize individual class meetings, aid you in developing assignments that are better received and completed by students, and guide you in establishing an effective process for evaluating students. In short, the PPT helps you create a course that embraces your values and style and enables you to make more effective decisions as the course evolves over the term.

The time and energy invested in these two activities, prior to developing your plan for the course, will make your first teaching assignment much more rewarding. Students will be more engaged in learning, conflict will be reduced and problems avoided, and you will achieve a much greater sense of fulfillment. Give yourself at least several days to process these issues before attending to the development of a plan for your specific course.

IDENTIFYING POSSIBLE INSTRUCTIONAL RESOURCES

Throughout the planning of your course, be sure to carefully review key sections of the college catalog and adjunct faculty handbook that might impact your course. While you will no doubt need to return to these documents for clarification of policies and procedures as your course progresses, it is critical to begin your teaching with a clear understanding of official guidelines toward attendance, grades, withdrawal from courses, etc., so that your approach dovetails appropriately.

As your teaching assignment becomes more firm, acquire the assigned course textbook and its ancillary materials (instructor's manual, test bank, etc.) from your instructional leader. At the same time, request any course examinations used by a previous successful instructor of the course—even if they are dated or based on a previously used textbook. Besides saving you the time it would take to develop your own exams, these will enable you to better gauge the level of your evaluation practices. Remember that instructor-developed materials require a great deal of preparation, so thank their

providers appropriately. Later you might reciprocate with teaching resources you acquire or develop that your colleagues are likely to value.
Through this process, you may well nurture a mentoring relationship that
will be mutually rewarding throughout your teaching career.

From conversations with your discipline leader or mentor, you should
have a clear understanding of how the course fits into the flow of the entire
curriculum and a clear perception of the nature of students you can expect.
Clarify also the degree of latitude you are permitted in delivering the course:

- Must you cover every chapter in the book?
- Which concepts are considered the most critical and challenging for students to master?
- Which assignments are standard operating procedure for this particular
  course?

As you review the syllabi (at least two!) of previous instructors, focus
especially on:

- Textbook chapters covered and any deviation in sequence with which
  they were covered
- The nature, length, and complexity of course assignments
- The number, format, and length of examinations
- The overall scheduling of the course

If possible, talk with the providers of the syllabi to ensure your understanding of their strategies. As you note ideas for your syllabus, be conservative
about deviating too widely from the syllabi you have reviewed in terms of
assignments, reading requirements, number of exams, etc. An appropriate
maxim to embrace is "Seek to fit into the department before standing out."
The exception would be to include modifications that might be specifically
suggested by your discipline leader.

Next, review the textbook as thoroughly as possible. Although your initial perception may well be that the book is not as effective as the one you
used for this course while an undergraduate student, try very hard to find
much about the book you can embrace. If students are required to purchase
the book, avoid the temptation to minimize use of the book and thus risk
students' perceiving their money has been wasted. Many adjunct professors
have jeopardized relations with other faculty members, as well as made their
own teaching time very difficult, by criticizing the textbook to students. Veteran faculty members openly question the ability of a new colleague to effectively evaluate the appropriateness of a particular book for a particular
setting; students often interpret such remarks as reasons why they need not
keep up with assigned readings. If you become convinced after the term con-

cludes that the text is not a good fit with your course, quietly solicit and review those used by other schools. If you find one that you believe is clearly more appropriate and you perceive that your input is valued, share your findings with your instructional leader.

At a minimum, you should have read the first four or five chapters completely and the summaries of the remaining chapters before developing your syllabus. This textbook review should permit you to have identified the one or two chapters that might be of the least value. With the discipline leader's concurrence, you might be able to omit these from your syllabus. The course might also call for supplemental readings, which you must review and evaluate in a similar vein.

DEVELOPING YOUR SYLLABUS

As you draft your course syllabus, keep in mind that it should provide the increasingly overextended students who will populate your class with a complete and detailed course overview and agenda. Remember as well that you are not preparing simply to deliver a single course, but also playing a role in the future learning of students. As such, one of your goals should be to challenge students to assume greater responsibility for their own learning. A well-developed syllabus contributes to achieving that goal. It should be a thoroughly conceived, effective, and appropriate communication tool for the specific type of student your course is designed to serve.

Although some instructors provide overly lengthy syllabi for their courses, the one- or two-page syllabus that leaves common questions unanswered is a far more serious concern. To ensure that your syllabus is a good fit for your particular teaching assignment, continue to seek additional syllabi for courses similar to yours, especially for courses taught by instructors with glowing reputations. If your assigned course is a new one, continue to seek syllabi from institutions that have previously developed a similar course. Developing a syllabus with insufficient regard for what other professors have done lends itself to creating a plan that is out of touch with the department strategy, contributing to redundancy within courses and other potential problems.

Since your major goal is to facilitate your students' mastery of the course content, your syllabus should eliminate barriers to learning by anticipating nearly any reasonable question that a student might have about the course. Be aware however, that in recent years the syllabus has become more than the course plan. In our ever more consumer-oriented and litigious society, the syllabus has evolved into a *binding contract* between the instructor and the student, with all the implications we typically associate with that term. In your draft syllabus, provide answers to the questions you might ask as a student, such as "What's in the course for me?" If you intend to impose penalties for attendance you consider unsatisfactory, for assignments that are submitted after their stated deadline, or for similar situations, your policy should be consistent with college and department guidelines and must be spelled out clearly in the syllabus. Since it is not uncommon for today's students to question authority, the astute professor will always safeguard him- or herself against common challenges by investing sufficient time and thought in the development of each coure syllabus.

Given the factors described above, a model syllabus is included in Appendix 5.2 for your consideration. It is not designed to supplant any guidelines your discipline leader might have provided, nor to address all aspects of every teaching assignment. Instead, it seeks to help you develop a "grounded" syllabus, prompt you to consider critical points that may not have been obvious, satisfy the perspective of "consumer-oriented students," and save time and energy you might invest in other aspects of planning your course. The rationale behind each section included in the model syllabus is discussed next.

Class.   This section enables students to confirm basic information about the course, such as course number, meeting place and time, etc. Students who are actually registered for another class can easily excuse themselves to pursue their correct course without having to waste their time or disrupt the classroom environment after the focus has become more intense.

Description.   Providing students with a brief summary of the overall goal of the course—how it fits into the program curriculum and what role or status they will occupy upon its completion—will enable them to reconcile their sometimes incorrect expectations of the course with your paradigm. Make sure the description is consistent with the one in the official college catalog.

Textbook.   Sometimes colleges or universities allow professors to adopt textbooks for their particular sections of the course, while other institutions embrace a universal adoption for all sections of the same course. In addition, textbooks are sometimes adopted for only one term or a single academic year. The philosophy varies from department to department and school to school. Therefore, it is very possible that students might have bought, borrowed, or traded for an inappropriate book. (In recent years, many professors have developed "course packs," a collection of instructor-developed materials and articles from journals that are more current than the material included in the typical textbook.) This section of your syllabus clears up any text-related questions and theoretically provides a "check" for the bookstore should an exchange or refund be appropriate.

The textbook section might be extended to include supplementary readings; if those are extensive, an additional section might be added. If you are arranging for reserved readings to be available in the library, critical information about library policies and procedures should be included in your syllabus. When additional readings are assigned, provide students with a brief rationale, such as currency of information.

Related Courses.   This section provides the names and numbers of specific courses students should have completed prior to yours; these might be called "prerequisites" if they are specifically mandated in the college catalog. Seeking to communicate the rigor of their course, some instructors identify "unofficial" prerequisite courses and, in the process, dramatically limit enrollment in their course. Increasingly cost-conscious instructional leaders are not likely to approve tactics that reduce enrollment below reasonable projections. Contemporary educators view this section of the syllabus as a tool for helping students make their own more well-informed decisions on whether their enrollment is likely to lead to success.

Instructor.   This section is designed to establish the professor's credibility—academically and professionally. Your credentials and background should be stated rather briefly, then embellished in more detail during the first class meeting.

Office.   While adjunct professors typically are not provided individual offices, it is accepted practice to make oneself available to students on a regular basis in a secure place near the classroom. A quiet, semiprivate area in the student union or a vacant classroom, where students can feel comfortable sharing problems related to their progress in the course, is a frequent choice. In this section of the syllabus or in another logical place, provide a telephone number where students can reach you between class meetings. Establish times when you are available that ensure accessibility for students and convenience for you. Many instructors also include email addresses in their syllabi, promoting an ongoing reflective dialogue with students throughout the term.

Teaching Methods.   Students want and deserve a clear idea of the instructional methods you intend to employ, especially if those methods are likely to be perceived as somewhat unusual. Listing your methods also serves as good protection should a student later criticize your methods to a discipline leader.

Concepts and Skills.   This section may well be entitled "learning objectives," "class goals," or a similar term. Its primary purpose is to give students a clear idea of the specific concepts they will acquire in the course. A secondary purpose is to reinforce the perception in students' minds that you are organized and focused. Your list should probably include at least one objective for each of the textbook chapters you will cover in class. These objectives are typically listed in the course outline provided by your discipline leader or in the textbook or its ancillary materials.

Attendance Policy.   Since students will likely question this section for clarification, your classroom attendance policy should be developed only after thorough research. You first need to know the college and department policies, if any exist, as well as the common practices of the majority of full-time and veteran adjunct faculty members. You also should consider the lifestyles of your students, which might be quite hectic, as well as your own values. The important thing is to formulate language that is as specific as possible without eliminating all flexibility. It is difficult for your discipline leader to defend a punitive action against excessive absences if that policy is not spelled out succinctly in the course syllabus.

Grading Criteria.   Perhaps the most critical component of your syllabus will be its grading criteria. Therefore, its formulation should consider a number of factors. As stated earlier, students will compare your course to others in their degree programs. Especially in your first teaching assignment, your grading criteria should be consistent with that of other professors in the department. To give only two examinations when other professors are giving four, or essay examinations when others are giving primarily "multiple choice" or other "objective" questions, may well be perceived as highly risky to students fearful of failure. To require significantly more, lengthier, or more complex assignments would give many students a reason to drop your section and add an "easier" professor's section, or to not enroll in your course the following semester. After you have established your reputation, you might give another look at such factors and "raise the bar" if appropriate. This section should also spell out your policies on course withdrawal as well as the awarding of incomplete grades; this will provide support at the end of the course when you might take an action that a student regards as unfairly punitive.

Grading Scale.   When formulating this section, first determine any institutional or department policy that might exist. Some schools or departments mandate 90 to 100% is an "A," etc., while others view the development of the scale as a prerogative of academic freedom. Some schools also have policies—both formal and informal—on the distribution of final grades, such as no more than X% of students should achieve a grade of A, etc. Again, determine the common practice of full-time and veteran adjunct faculty members before formulating your scale.

Methods of Achieving Success.   This section simply outlines the time commitments and strategies for a student's obtaining satisfactory results in the class. It also identifies any potential resources that have been established to aid student success in your course.

Degrees and Certificates.   In the past few years, public institutions of higher education have been held increasingly accountable by their legislatures to ensure that the taxpayers' money that funds their programs is invested wisely. A similar perspective has also been seen in some private institutions seeking to ensure that supporters' dollars are wisely spent. The "bottom line" is that there is less support than ever for students to meander through their college experience, changing majors numerous times, accumulating excess credit hours and the like. This section is designed to influence students to complete in a timely manner the degree or certificate program(s) of which your course is a component.

Student Organizations.   This section promotes the development of students' social and leadership skills and their retention in degree programs by informing them of student organizations related to the curriculum that are available for them to join.

Tentative Schedule.   The final section of your syllabus should be a schedule of assignments, activities, and examinations. Stating it is "tentative" provides you flexibility should an especially unusual circumstance occur that might cause you, for example, to consider delaying an examination. Be reluctant, though, about changing your schedule once the course is underway. Doing so creates a potential domino effect by tacitly suggesting to students that there may be further deviations that prevent your completing the entire course.

Discretionary Sections.   Remembering that the syllabus is a binding contract with students and should anticipate the reasonable questions students might have about the course, you might want to consider additional sections in your syllabus. Many professors include a section called "Academic Dishonesty" that cites their own and the institution's policies on plagiarism and cheating on examinations. Others cite the location and operating hours of course-critical learning resources available to students—college library, computer labs, tutoring labs, etc. While these sections will lengthen your syllabus, they may well provide the essential protection for you and help for the student that will avert unpleasant outcomes in your course.

An old management axiom says "Plan your work, then work the plan," and apprentice carpenters are taught "Measure twice, cut once." A well-researched and formulated syllabus will make your job immensely easier and satisfying. It clearly outlines your expectations in all the critical areas of the course and protects you if ever challenged. As stated before, it is truly a contract that includes your offer to provide service, a tacit acceptance by students receiving it, and consideration for students' and the instructor's positions. Furthermore, it is enforceable.

In a society that emphasizes visual stimulation, also be mindful of the impact of the appearance of your syllabus on students. Modern word processors enable you to provide a document with excellent eye appeal, so use one or access the services of the college in using one. Typographic errors, poor photocopies, and the like communicate a lack of professionalism—not an image you want to create during the first class meeting and be forced to live with for the remainder of the term.

Your syllabus is so critical to your success that you should have your first one thoroughly reviewed, by your discipline leader, mentor, and perhaps a student, prior to having it printed for distribution to your class. If you follow the plan outlined here, you can be assured your discipline leader or mentor will be greatly impressed with your thoroughness and professionalism, which should help build your confidence as you embark on your new adventure.

PLANNING YOUR COURSE STRATEGY

Many new adjunct professors seem to view themselves and the textbook as the sole focus for delivering the course material. A more contemporary paradigm views you as a facilitator of instruction; first you must understand how students process information, then use a range of appropriate instructional methods and strategies to provide opportunities for students to learn material in a way that is most efficient and effective for them.

Recall that your students have probably been highly conditioned by a steady diet of electronic media; it is important to design stimulating elements into your class. Guest speakers, computer-delivered exercises, field trips, and videotapes are each potentially powerful vehicles for accomplishing that goal while also enriching the overall learning experience that your course provides students. Begin early to accumulate resources—through your professional and community contacts—to lend credibility and panache to your course and offer the opportunity for students to develop "real world" insights that textbooks and other traditionally employed materials cannot provide. It is critical to realize that the richest resources usually require significant lead time to arrange. Before committing to any specific opportunity, satisfy yourself that it effectively addresses one or more of your learning objectives and does not just liven up the class or fill up time. Many students, after being entertained, have in effect said, "That was fun and interesting, but what did it have to do with this course?" Effective guest speakers, field trips, and videotapes should provide material or perspectives that enhances, rather than rehashes, that which you have already delivered. They should be perceived as complementing and reinforcing your overall approach, rather than creating a perspective so divergent that the issue fails to be resolved in students' minds.

Is there a "magic number" of activities that can be effectively utilized in a course? Probably not—it depends on the subject matter, experience level of the students, and the passion the professor holds for the activities.

Before inviting guest speakers to your class for the first time, it would be wise to "clear" them with your discipline leader, to prevent a potential political conflict. Also remember that just because a potential guest speaker is an expert on some valuable subject does not necessarily mean he or she will be an effective presenter for your student audience. Never risk inviting a guest speaker who you are not sure will be successful—it can create problems that are difficult to overcome. Once you are satisfied those hurdles are cleared, identify specific points—topics that flow naturally out of the guest's area of expertise rather than items requiring their additional research—that you would like the guest to address. Provide those objectives to the guest speaker in writing and allow some time for that person to assess his or her ability to effectively address the issues in a presentation. Many guest speakers have been made to appear ineffective because they were provided unclear expectations by the instructor. Confirm in writing the exact date, time, location, content, and length of presentation you would like. In addition, request a resume or short biography from which you might prepare an introduction that energizes their presentation. Also request their supervisor's name and title so you can "c.c." them on the thank you letter you send to the speaker.

The cautions about guest speakers apply in even greater intensity to field trips you might plan. Be sure to clarify the institutional policy, and secure approval in writing from the appropriate administrator, before announcing any field trip to students. In addition, objectively evaluate the inherent risks of the field trip. Analyze if the rewards markedly outweigh the potential risks you will bear. As best as you can, determine from your discipline leader if your students are likely to benefit from the field trip. Consider also the very empty feeling experienced by a teacher who works hard to arrange a field trip only to discover during the trip that it was not perceived by students as a valuable opportunity. Some of the most effective field trips can be accomplished very close to or actually on campus—minimizing risk and inconvenience. A guided tour of an institutional facility administered by a terrific presenter, or a business with a special appeal located on the perimeter of the campus can be very worthwhile.

Contemporary videotapes also provide potentially rich learning experiences for students. Many of the same rules apply—relevance to the curriculum, acceptability in the eyes of the discipline leader, etc. Often, enthusiastic adjunct professors have shown a videotape in their class only to discover during the viewing that a full-time or veteran adjunct with whom the students have had or will have a class uses the same video in his or her course—so check out your plan in advance. A few other points should also be considered before you commit to including a particular videotape in your course plan. Generally, a video should not exceed a half-hour in length. (Feature films in a literature or social studies class are probably reasonable exceptions.) Always preview a videotape before showing it to ensure that the content, language, and complexity are appropriate for your students.

Include any guest speakers, field trips, or major videotapes on the tentative schedule of your syllabus to promote attendance at that class meeting and reduce problems inherent in students missing opportunities that are difficult to replicate. Integrate these enrichments fully into the context of the course and plan to evaluate students' retention of the concepts on exams or through reports. Avoid reinforcing the common student perception that these activities are time-fillers or unrelated to the course curriculum.

Finally, when using these enriched resources, always have a backup plan. Guest speakers get ill or stuck in meetings that make them unable to attend. Field trip sites lose their cheerful hosts to other firms or have power failures. Equipment sometimes does not arrive or has "technical difficulties" that prevent the showing of videotapes. When your plans go awry, students with high expectations sometimes demonstrate their disappointment in unpleasant ways.

A course with a sound plan (as communicated in your syllabus) and enriched with special learning opportunities will markedly impact your potential for success with students. Share your plan enthusiastically at your initial class meeting. Refer back to it on a regular basis throughout the course to provide students with the structure so many have failed to achieve in their previous schooling.

THROUGH THE ADJUNCTS' EYES

Juan:

As a teaching assistant at the university, I have found myself increasingly observing the small tasks of my senior professors, realizing my implementation of their plan will be far more effective when I more thoroughly understand its design. As I envision a time when I will teach full-time, I realize the importance of making my own first course the very best it can be. The Personal Practical Theory has been a particularly useful exercise. It has given me cause to question professors at the university about their beliefs, so I could better articulate my own. It has become a framework for me to create my own unique course—one I know I can explain to students and colleagues with passion and logic.

Karen:

In developing my course plan, I have not deviated from Mr. Jackson's much at all. As Anonymous once said, "If it ain't broke, don't fix it." Although the department chair encouraged me to talk with the full-time professor who teaches the same course, it seems to me that changing anything the first time out would not only open me up to criticism but would take valuable time which I really don't have much of right now.

Margaret:

The corporation for which I formerly worked employed an extensive, ongoing strategic planning process. Conducting the SWOT analysis as a function of planning my upcoming course has helped me realize that my strengths include organizing activities and conducting effective, interactive meetings. My greatest opportunity is to shape the style of some future managers. I also relish the chance to create a positive reputation within the higher education community locally that I might leverage into something greater than teaching a single course each term. Maximizing my strengths and focusing on my opportunities will create a more rewarding course plan, both for students and myself. My greatest weakness has always been "platform speaking," which I will minimize by lecturing only when absolutely necessary and then in very short time segments. The major threat in my course plan is having so many activities, videos, and guest speakers that I don't coordinate and integrate them all effectively, leaving students with a somewhat fragmented understanding of the major course goals.

TIPS FOR THRIVING

Regardless of profession, we are each in our own way becoming increasingly marketing-conscious. Those who seek to thrive in the classroom must contemplate the type of image they wish to establish in the minds of their students. We are not suggesting you attempt to be something you truly are not, but encouraging you to focus on the qualities you clearly possess in order to make your classroom efforts more effective and thus achieve a greater sense of personal fulfillment.

Recalling that today's students are highly visual learners, you should give special emphasis to the visual quality of the materials you provide to students. With desktop publishing software it is possible to incorporate graphics into your syllabus and other handouts with a minimum investment of resources. Such visuals are likely to create a perception among students that you are contemporary in a wide variety of ways.

In addition, you might want to contemplate color-coding your materials. For example, if you were to teach two separate sections of the same course, you might want to have all of the materials for one section printed on blue paper, while those of the other section are printed on yellow paper. Should you make minor modifications in materials, e.g. different versions of essentially the same examination, using color-coded copies will enable you to keep materials better organized.

REVIEW OF KEY POINTS

- Ask for specific teaching resources from your discipline leader.
- Talk with professors who have successfully taught sections of the course to which you are assigned.
- Conduct a personal SWOT analysis and Personal Practical Theory exercise to guide your course planning and to ensure that the course will be a good fit for your abilities and style.
- Develop a sound syllabus to serve as a complete plan and contract with students.
- Plan your overall teaching strategy well in advance, drawing on resources available from your full-time career whenever possible.
- Plan guest speakers and field trips well in advance, and implement plans only after thoroughly assessing all the inherent risks involved.
- Get organized from the beginning.

SUGGESTED READINGS

Diamond, R. (1998). *Designing and assessing courses and curricula: A practical guide.* San Francisco: Jossey-Bass.

Duffy, D., and Jones, J. (1995). *Teaching within the rhythms of the semester.* San Francisco: Jossey-Bass.

Eble, K. (1994). *The craft of teaching.* San Francisco: Jossey-Bass.

Grunert, J. (1997). *The course syllabus: A learning-centered approach.* Bolton, MA: Anker.

Stark, J., & Lattuca, L. (1997). *Shaping the college curriculum.* Needham Heights, MA: Allyn & Bacon.

APPENDIX 5.1   MODEL PERSONAL PRACTICAL THEORY (PPT)

Beliefs about learners

- Learners are responsible for their own learning.
- Learners should participate actively in learning opportunities.
- Learners should come to class prepared to learn.
- Learners should not limit the learning of other learners.
- Learners should learn for learning's sake.

Beliefs about instructors

- Instructors are facilitators of learning.
- Instructors should model good learning for their students.
- Instructors should actively plan for the diversity in their classrooms.
- Instructors should be consistent and objective in evaluating student work.
- Instructors should be frank, yet sensitive, with students.

Beliefs about subject matter

- Content should be examined critically for accuracy, currency, appropriateness for the group of learners, and so on.
- Course curriculum should dovetail with other courses.
- Course curriculum is continuously changing.
- The subject matter has a natural and professionally accepted structure.

Beliefs about classroom climate

- Classrooms should be interactive.
- Classrooms should be safe havens for the exchange of ideas.
- Student opinions count and should be validated.
- Classrooms should be nonthreatening.

Beliefs about learning

- There are a wide range of effective learning styles.
- Lessons should reflect varied student needs.
- Instructors must update their knowledge about learning, just as they update their knowledge of the course subject matter.
- Learning should be challenging, yet achievable.
- Appropriate feedback must accompany learning activities.

APPENDIX 5.2   MODEL SYLLABUS

Principles of Management
MAN 2021 Spring 20—

Class	Section B1, Monday evenings, 5:30—8:00 p.m. Mueller Center, Vero Beach
Course Description	This course provides an overview of the primary functions of management, challenges regularly faced by today's managers, and proven career-building strategies.
Textbook	*Management, 7/e,* by Tinker, Evers and Chance, available at Campus Bookstore, $82 (new)
Related Courses	Students should complete an introductory business course, or possess ample work experience in business, prior to enrollment in MAN 2021.
Instructor	Chris Lewis, Adjunct Professor in the Business Management Department, received his B. S. in Business Administration and M. S. in Human Resource Management from Western Michigan University. He has served as the Human Resource Manager at Sherwood Citrus since 1989, and prior to that managed a number of supermarkets. He has taught extensively in industry.
Office	The instructor will be available for consultation one-half hour prior to the beginning of class in V 117, and immediately after class. He can be reached by telephone at 462–4729 from 1 to 4 p.m. weekdays.
Teaching Methods	A wide variety of instructional methods are used to provide students with meaningful learning experiences. These include role play, group problem-solving activities, and self-analysis instruments, in addition to more traditional methods.
Concepts & Skills	Upon completion of this course, each student will be able to:

1. Describe the basic management functions, skills, and roles.
2. Discuss management's role in enhancing productivity and quality.
3. Identify and discuss the environmental factors that are influencing changes in the manager's role.
4. Make ethical decisions that satisfy diverse organizational stakeholders.
5. Summarize the basic concepts of strategic planning.
6. Explain the steps in making effective, nonroutine decisions.
7. Describe the use of commonly used decision-making tools.
8. Compare and contrast types of departmentalization.

9. Describe the dimensions and consequences of organizational culture.
10. Identify major legal dimensions of human resource management.
11. Identify critical leadership styles, characteristics, and behaviors.
12. Explain the manager's role in managing conflict and encouraging teamwork.
13. Explain the primary theories of motivation.
14. Summarize the different types and strategies of control.
15. Explain the role of budgetary controls.
16. Identify the factors influencing poor job performance.
17. Identify and explain principles of Total Quality Management.
18. Explain techniques for improving personal productivity.
19. Assess your personal potential for success in a management career.

Attendance Policy

Although the instructor is providing opportunities for each student's achievement of course objectives, students should realize the value their experiences offer others, as well. Therefore, it is critical that you attend class regularly to be a full partner in this enhanced learning environment. Roll will be taken at each class meeting. Your participation will be taken into consideration in case of a borderline final grade. It is each student's responsibility to personally contact the instructor in advance, if class is going to be missed, regarding missed assignments. The instructor will not accept late work without valid reasons. Students are encouraged to contact the instructor any time they are not achieving their intended level of success, before taking any other action. Students who need to withdraw must complete an official form and submit it consistent with college policy, *no later than April 5.* "Incomplete" grades are given only when an emergency prevents a student from completing a minor portion of the assignments of the course.

Grading Criteria

3 units exams @ 20%	= 60%	
Mini project	= 20%	
Final Exam	= 20%	

Grading Scale

90–100%	A
80–89%	B
70–79%	C
60–69%	D
Below 60%	F

Methods of Achieving Success

Achieving success in this course will require a time commitment outside of class that averages four hours per week. It is vital that you read textbook assignments *prior to* their being covered in class, and actively participate in class discussion, activities, and review.

Degrees & **Certificates** The contemporary workplace has come to greatly value formal credentials. Degrees, certificates, and licenses of all sorts have been widely embraced in many industries as a "ticket for upward mobility," and their significance will no doubt continue to grow in the future. This course is a requirement of several certificate and degree programs. We strongly encourage all students to consider the advantages of completing a 30-credit Technical Certificate and a 64-credit Associate of Science (A.S.) degree.

Delta Epsilon **Chi** Students enrolled in management and marketing courses are encouraged to participate in the local chapter of the national student organization Delta Epsilon Chi. The college's chapter has a rich history of success in state and national competitions, as well as service to our local communities. For further information, contact the Department Chair, Alan Roberts, at 462–4267.

(Note: Accounting, Computer Science, and Office Systems students are eligible for the co-curricular organization Phi Beta Lambda.)

Principles of Management
MAN 2021 B1
Spring 20—
Tentative Schedule

Date:	*Topics/activities/assignments*
January 8	Introduction, syllabus. Chapter 1.
January 15	**Martin Luther King holiday.**
January 22	Chapters 2 and 3.
January 29	Chapter 4. Review for exam.
February 5	**Exam No. 1.** Project overview.
February 12	Return/review exam. Chapter 5.
February 19	Chapter 6 and 7.
February 26	Chapter 8. Review for exam.
March 4	**Exam No. 2.** Chapter 9.
March 11	Return/review exam. Chapter 10.
March 18	Chapters 11 and 12.
March 25	**Spring Break**
April 1	**Exam No. 3.** Return/review exam. Overview of presentations.
April 8	**Project due, presentations.** Chapter 13.
April 15	Chapter 14.
April 22	Chapter 15. Review for final exam.
April 29	**Final Exam**

6

CONDUCTING AN EFFECTIVE
FIRST CLASS MEETING

Focus Questions

- What are the practical, specific objectives for the first class meeting?
- How do you create an effective classroom environment?
- What are the rewards of conducting an effective initial class meeting?

One of the basic truisms of life is that truly successful enterprises of any sort nearly always seem to have gotten off to a really effective beginning. The same holds true in teaching a college course. Success in achieving a great start is almost always directly attributable to the quality and quantity of planning that has been invested by the course professor. At the first session of a course, most students can quickly and effectively differentiate the teacher who stands before them highly prepared from those who are "flying by the seats of their pants." Unfortunately, too many professors, both full-time and part-time, conduct an abbreviated first class meeting accomplishing little more than introducing himself or herself to students and distributing a syllabus. They fail to realize that the problems they frequently encounter during the course could have been prevented if a more thorough and effective initial class meeting had been conducted. If the first meeting of your class is to be successful, you should strive to achieve seven distinct goals. This chapter features those in a sequence which will enable you to launch your course in a most effective way.

CREATE A POSITIVE FIRST IMPRESSION

If first impressions are truly lasting ones, they are worthy of your time and energy. Renowned communications consultant Roger Ailes claims you have less than 10 seconds to create a positive image of yourself. In the perception of the student, you are, in many ways, synonymous with the course in which they have enrolled. Students are greatly influenced by the visual component, therefore you must first look the part of the professional professor. How you should look might vary somewhat with the culture of the institution, the discipline area, the season of the year, and a number of other factors. But in general, you will dress semiformally and conservatively, as you would for a professional job interview. Avoid bright colors and unusual patterns, over-accessorizing, and clothing that makes a political statement.

Your classroom and materials must also create a positive first impression. Well in advance you should have prepared a comprehensive and attractive course syllabus as well as other printed materials to share with students at the first meeting. Arrive early at the classroom to ensure that the learning environment is neat and clean and that furniture is arranged effectively. Students will draw conclusions about your competence based on their first impression of the classroom. Depending on the nature of your course, the number of students you expect, and other factors, consider arranging the chairs in a circle or a "U-shape." (At the end of class, be sure to return furniture to its original position, erase the board, etc. so that the professor following you is not surprised.) Neatly print the course title, section number, and your name on the board before students arrive, so that anyone there by mistake will be prompted to their appropriate classroom. Be aware of other classes scheduled nearby so you might direct wayward students if they mistakenly enter your classroom.

Greet each student entering the room—shake hands, give your name, and ask for theirs. Be approachable and genuine. At the time scheduled for beginning class, move to the front of the room and begin by introducing yourself, identifying the course and section number, and asking if everyone is in the correct place. Assuming you have been provided an official class roster, you will want to call roll. Pronounce each familiar name and ask for help, without humor, for any that are difficult for you. Demonstrating an appreciation for another's name is critical to creating a dignified environment and rapport with students. Note absences and plan to follow up appropriately after class. Also identify those present whose names are not on your roll, then talk quietly with each one to clear up these situations before proceeding.

INTRODUCE YOURSELF EFFECTIVELY

Next, communicate to students in a few humble moments who you are and why you are credible as the teacher of the course. Dale Carnegie said we must each *earn* the right to speak. Remembering that today's college students are sometimes cynical toward authority figures, often deficient in self-esteem and extremely time conscious, state only the major reasons they would likely accept as demonstrating your expertise. Avoid what might be perceived as excess—students will discover more about you later in the class meeting and the term. Also seek to establish your approachability by "building common ground," such as stating your understanding of students' hectic lifestyles or their common negative preconceptions toward the subject matter. Clarify the measures you are taking to make yourself accessible, such as providing convenient telephone number(s) and making yourself available before and/or after each class meeting.

In this same vein, let us warn you about one of the most frequent traps into which adjunct professors, especially new ones, frequently step. As stated before, it is quite common that last minute shifting on the department chair's or dean's part may have assigned you to a particular course on very short notice. Anxious adjunct professors often cannot resist making students aware of this fact, by saying something like, "I didn't find out I would be teaching this course until yesterday afternoon," as if students will forgive them if at least the first class meeting doesn't progress smoothly! In the process, many students will discount the abilities and motivation of the teacher. Few will sympathize with the professor's "misfortune." As a result, most students invariably lower their expectations of the course and fail to manifest the enthusiasm so necessary to make it an optimal learning experience. Students lose by not having their intellectual needs met. The adjunct professor loses throughout the term by not gaining the emotional commitment from students that makes the teaching experience as rewarding as it should be. Your department colleagues lose by having to make excuses when students repeat the incident to them—which they will do! The institution loses because the perception is created that its instructional leaders did not manage effectively. What positive payoff is there for doing it?

CLARIFY THE CLASS GOALS AND EXPECTATIONS

The third goal of that first class meeting should be to clarify the course goals and your expectations of the students, and explain your role and philosophy. Since contemporary students typically have developed a consumer's mind-set, you may want also to identify the limitations of the course, i.e., what you will not be able to accomplish because of time, space, or other constraints. All of these can be accomplished largely through a structured and embellished review of the course syllabus. The payoff of the hard work you have invested in developing your course plan is the students' clear understanding of your strategy and their emotional buy-in that must be achieved if the course is to be a truly rewarding experience for everybody.

For understanding of your course plan to take place, you must effectively manage the focus of students during your review of the syllabus. We encourage you to make a quality transparency of each syllabus page for display on an overhead projector and, using a cover sheet, expose each section as you explain it. Provide clarification and elicit questions before moving on to the next section. You should also address less formal issues, such as your expectations of students who arrive late to class (again, you might want to reserve specific seats near the door so late-arrivers will not have to disturb others), and perhaps ask students if there are particular procedures important to them that they would like to incorporate into the class. We suggest you distribute printed copies of the syllabus to students only after reviewing it completely, promoting a more thorough analysis and potentially more complete acceptance. If you expect to have especially mature students, you might want to provide the syllabus as they enter the classroom, allowing them to review it while they wait for the scheduled beginning time of class. Regardless of the procedure you choose, ask for questions at several key points throughout the review of the syllabus. State also that you will begin the next class session by answering any questions about the syllabus, and that you will also use that opportunity to pose some questions to the class to ensure their understanding. Because the syllabus serves as a contract between you and students, as well as an agenda for the entire term, its complete understanding by students is essential to the overall success of your teaching efforts.

CONDUCT AN ACTIVITY THAT INTRODUCES STUDENTS TO EACH OTHER

To this point, you have created a positive visual impact, effectively introduced yourself, and thoroughly reviewed your syllabus—activities that together require probably 30 to 45 minutes. Students are typically quiet and contemplative during this time. They are likely performing a "cost-benefit analysis" of the course in their minds—feeling some pressure, perhaps some doubt as to whether they have made a good decision. You should continue to manage effectively by enabling them to discover a positive answer to that question, while releasing their pent-up energy. Most of us, including your students, rely on others' feedback to help us answer the important questions we face. But your students are likely to have come to this class meeting knowing few, if any, of the other students present!

As stated in Chapter 4, today's students are diverse and often somewhat lower in self-esteem than we might anticipate. Without some prompting, many of your students would likely complete the entire semester without becoming truly familiar with any other student in the class. Students reap great rewards by forming study groups, working on projects collaboratively, and simply feeling comfortable enough with each other to participate actively in classroom discussions. Given the external pressures of jobs, family concerns, and related matters, students' chances of being able to complete a course effectively is enhanced if each comes to perceive the classmates as a "support network," potentially able to supply emergency transportation, courier, and related services when asked.

Thus, your fourth goal for the initial class meeting is to provide students with the opportunity to meet some of their classmates in a nonthreatening and enlightening manner. Many teachers have students introduce themselves to the class from their seats, but that process fails to involve the emotions of the students in a way that might make the retention of information more effective. Planned icebreaker activities have a far greater potential to deliver the desired objective. You might recall participating in an icebreaker activity you could adapt to your classroom. If not, you might ask your department chair or other full-time professor, consult with someone who conducts industry training, or check with your local library or bookstore for proven resources.

If you are beginning the course on especially short notice, we have included a highly effective icebreaker activity in Appendix 6.2 that will require only a few minutes to finalize and photocopy. As the directions indicate, the goal of the activity is to have each person in the class meet every other person, share an interesting fact about himself, and perhaps have a little dialogue about career or family. (Emphasize to students that the goal is not to see who can complete the activity first!) If you anticipate an extremely large or small group you might modify the wording of the directions somewhat. At the end of this activity, each student will have met several new people with whom to chat and will have a tool for recalling the names and other key facts about everyone else. The small amount of time you invest in the icebreaker will help create a positive classroom atmosphere and pay additional dividends throughout the remainder of the term.

We suggest you follow the icebreaker activity with a break, enabling students to nurture newly formed relationships. Be helpful by identifying the location of the nearest rest rooms, water fountains, campus bookstore, or other important resources. When breaking, clearly print on the board the time when class will resume, and stick to it! Delaying the beginning or resumption of class for other than valid reasons, e.g., extreme weather conditions, leads to students' continually being late.

LEARN STUDENTS' NAMES

Following the break, or at the next class meeting if periods are brief, invest several minutes in de-briefing the icebreaker. Ask "Why did we invest class time in doing that?" and solicit their responses. From this, allow the conclusion to be drawn that their fellow students are valuable resources and identify some of the benefits which might accrue from assessing those resources, e.g., establishing study groups, etc. End the debriefing by asking if anyone can remember all the classmates' names. This activity facilitates the achievement of the fifth goal for the initial class meeting—your learning each student's name.

In addition, you might provide students self-adhesive name tags or tent cards made by folding 5" × 8" index cards lengthwise. Being able to draw upon the fresh experience of both the roll call and icebreaker and using each student's name as you address them for the remainder of the class meeting should markedly improve your ability to learn names effectively. Many instructors facilitate the learning of students' names and attendance-taking by asking students to select a designated seat for the entire term, and developing a seating chart. Other instructors feel that required seating stifles social interaction throughout the term. This decision is somewhat a function of the primary teaching method employed by the instructor, the number and maturity level of students in the class, and other factors. Regardless of your strategy, remember that a student who is addressed by name regularly feels more valued, is invested more effectively in classroom discussion, and will typically approach the professor more readily to have individual questions and concerns addressed. If you intend to develop a seating chart, be sure to warn students that you will do so based on their position at the following class meeting; this gives them a chance to adjust for improving their vision or hearing, or other factors.

This would be an excellent point for distributing copies of the *student profile forms*, found in Appendix 6.1. Depending on the nature of your course, you might want to add an additional question or two, such as "Which computer software packages do you use?" Before the next class meeting, review the completed forms closely. They will aid you further in learning students' names, as well as provide insightful information. They might also trigger follow-up questions, addressing issues that might impact students' success in your course. Some questions/directions on the form might need clarification. For example, "special situations, course" is intended to deal with such issues as whether the student has conflicts that will regularly delay their arrival to class or cause them to miss a particular class session. The "special situations, career" might provide students an opportunity for telling you they are looking for a job, etc. Reassure students that all student profiles are completely confidential. If time allows, have students complete the forms during class. If not, ask them to return the completed forms at the following class meeting.

WHET STUDENTS' APPETITE FOR THE COURSE MATERIAL

Depending on the time available and the nature of your course, you should at least whet students' appetite for the material you will cover during the course. Since students who may "add" your class later are not yet present, you might want to focus on contextual information and minimize your coverage of material that will appear on the first examination in the course. Some experienced teachers believe in delivering a more significant amount of material, not wanting to indirectly encourage students to "cut" the first class meeting or to waste any opportunity to impart valuable concepts to students. If yours is an advanced course for mature students close to the completion of their program, you especially might want to heed the later piece of advice.

If time allows, the first class meeting lends itself especially well to showing a brief video segment or discussing a current newspaper clipping that enhances the relevance of the course material in students' minds. Refrain from showing an extended video that might be perceived as your being unable to manage the class or cause concern about your "filling time." Reinforcing its role in your course plan, refer back to the syllabus to remind students of the assignment for the following class meeting. End the segment by asking an open-ended, nonthreatening question about the material you have addressed.

The textbook or course pack (see Chapter 5) adopted for the course is critical to your success as the instructor. It typically provides much of the structure, as well as the knowledge base, on which you must rely. Therefore, your first class meeting should include a review of its approach, features, and sequencing, with an eye toward helping students understand how the content, layout, and approach contribute to their mastery of the course material.

You can usually assume that few, if any, of the students have read any of the course material at this point, so it would serve no positive purpose to ask if they had. In addition to your brief overview above, try to provide some colorful information about the textbook that might encourage student reading. Your goal is to influence students to begin the establishment of a scaffold in their minds for the material that will follow in subsequent class meetings, and the text is a valuable tool for achieving it. Because of time or financial limitations, some students may not have been able to secure the book prior to the first class, so we would recommend you not begin detailed coverage of the text materials until the second class meeting. If you teach an evening class, determine the operating hours of the college bookstore or other source of textbooks or course packs prior to starting class; if necessary, you can take a break or dismiss class sufficiently early to enable commuting students to obtain their materials.

Because of previous experience with a competing textbook, the failure of the book to address issues critical to the course, or other valid reasons, you may prefer that another book had been adopted for the course. However, for you to be successful as the instructor, it is important that your students not perceive your low regard for this text. Criticizing aspects of the book to students, collectively or individually, contributes to their procrastinating in completing their assigned reading and to their failing to become fully engaged in processing the book's content. It also potentially encourages consumer-minded students to discount the value of the course itself. If solicited by your instructional leader, you might provide constructive comments related to the textbook. But be aware there are a number of factors that effect adoption decisions, and this text was adopted for reasons he or she probably supported.

REASSURE STUDENTS OF THE VALUE OF THE COURSE

Whenever people make a big decision, a condition psychologists call *cognitive dissonance* invariably follows. It's the state of mind that questions the wisdom of decisions. Marketing professionals call it *buyer's remorse* and they invest lots of time and money to reassure customers that their purchase was in fact a wise one to encourage repeat purchases.

Students frequently develop this state of mind after they invest what they perceive as large amounts of money and alter their schedules to take a particular course. Therefore, at the close of your first class meeting, reassure students that the course will be a valuable learning experience and a wise investment of their time. Review the reasons why the course is a good investment: important and relevant content, interesting classmates, and a dynamic classroom environment. Ensure that they leave the classroom after your first class meeting feeling they will get their money's worth!

THROUGH THE ADJUNCTS' EYES

Karen:

My law school training and courtroom experience have helped me hone solid presentation skills, which I know will be required to win over the Generation X and Generation Y students in my class. At the first class meeting last night I wore my navy blue courtroom outfit and made, from the nonverbal feedback received, a very positive first impression of competence and confidence. My key points were delivered in a graphic presentation utilizing my laptop computer and portable projection screen, which I set up and tested 30 minutes before the class started. I scripted my presentation like a summation to a jury and covered each point succinctly, yet thoroughly. In short, when we left for the evening, I felt like I had "knocked their socks off."

Margaret:

Although I had prepared as much as I knew how, I still felt like my opening class last night was a little "tight." I felt especially uneasy with the way in which I related to the half dozen young students enrolled. I thoroughly reviewed the syllabus section-by-section using transparencies on the overhead projector, and the limited dialogue that took place between the students and myself told me they understood the plan for the course. When I gave a brief overview of the textbook, I sensed some tension among the students, mostly from those who did not have the book with them. I've heard some students can't afford to buy all their books and will attend each class once before deciding which textbooks are most critical for them to purchase. If I had last night to do all over, I would have conducted a bit more energetic "icebreaker" than having the students stand and introduce themselves to the class.

Juan:

I conducted last night's first class meeting with the community college students in the same way that my favorite professor at the university conducts hers—and did I ever learn a lesson! After introducing myself and reviewing the syllabus, I asked the students to write a paragraph for me on the most significant news event of the past week, simply so I could get a sample of their writing style. University undergraduates seem to expect such assignments and complete them rather willingly and quickly. The nontraditional community college students really acted offended, as if I was insinuating that they couldn't write at an acceptable level. I held the class for the entire class period, only to have one student say on his way out that the college bookstore had closed and that students would have to make an extra trip to campus to purchase their textbook. I've got some "damage control" to do when the class meets the next time.

TIPS FOR THRIVING

It is critical that students leave your first class meeting understanding your plan for the course. If your syllabus is somewhat complex, you should consider investing 15 to 20 minutes following your review of it in a group exercise. First, divide the entire class into groups of two or three students. Have each team review the syllabus thoroughly and formulate three "What if" questions related to the policies and procedures outlined in the syllabus that could arise during the term. Once that task is completed, call on a spokesperson from each team to present one of their questions and solicit responses from those in the other groups. Call on each team sequentially until you are satisfied that everyone sufficiently understands the contents of the syllabus.

A thorough evaluation of your first class meeting is especially critical, for it enables you to assess "where you are" at the single most critical milepost for retaining students. It also helps you focus on predictable critical factors, with an eye toward fine-tuning your policies and procedures. There are several methods you might employ—we would suggest you use the following three in your very first teaching assignment.

First, provide students with a small piece of paper, something perhaps with a humorous image such as a cartoon character. Write three questions on the chalkboard and ask students to provide a response to all three and to place their responses in a container you have placed near the exit door. This procedure clearly demonstrates that students' anonymity will be protected and that you fully encourage a broad spectrum of perspectives. The questions might include:

- What do you think you will probably benefit the most from in this course?
- What aspect of the course concerns you most?
- What questions or issues need further clarification?

Collect the responses and take them home before reading. Other feedback/assessment efforts are addressed in Chapter 13.

Next, engage the few students who will typically linger after the first class meeting to talk with you further. They may want to address the points you sought to solicit in your first evaluation activity, to provide you information on their personal situation, or to give you feedback on your teaching style. Resist the inclination to pack your briefcase unless students and the professor for the following class are literally already entering the classroom. Invest this time to fully listen to students, reinforcing your image of approachability. You can be assured these students will tell others how friendly and helpful you were! If time and the situation permits, close your discussion with each of these students by asking for any final thoughts. Each will probably embellish their previous response with some useful information, but you want all of the data you can get at this key juncture—positive or negative.

Lastly, take a few quiet minutes when you arrive home to construct a "Ben Franklin" analysis. Divide a sheet of paper into two columns. In the left column list the strengths of the first class meeting; in the right column, list things that went less than ideally. If your planning was as thorough as we expect and your students were typical, you will no doubt have many more notations in the left than in the right column.

Then, and only then, will it be time to look at the notes the students wrote you. You probably will want to skim these soon after the class, but be sure to return to them later for a more reflective analysis. Seek to identify patterns: Did several students say essentially the same thing, either positive or negative? Prior to your second class meeting, prepare some summary feedback for the class based on their comments. This will demonstrate clearly that you value their opinions and, we suspect, contribute to the development of a much healthier classroom environment than you would otherwise have had. It will also give you a chance to check the validity of your perception at a time when the stakes are relatively low. Later, at midterm or at the end of the course, the stakes will involve students' grades and perhaps your continuation as an adjunct professor. It is much more effective to get useful data early in the course, enabling you to avoid making assumptions that create semester-long problems.

This informal evaluation process recognizes a very critical paradigm that has been embraced in the business world in recent years called "total quality management" (TQM), also known as "continuous quality improvement." As this course and your career in teaching progress, use opportunities provided by the natural rhythm of teaching, e.g., the beginning or end of class and immediately following activities or exam, to gather feedback on your performance. It is much more effective than waiting for formal measures mandated by others. We can all keep getting better at teaching—there is always some new technique for communicating a key concept, a student perspective to better understand, an obstacle to learning which can be eliminated. Embrace this mindset as you begin your career in teaching and you will increase the rewards both for yourself and your students.

REVIEW OF KEY POINTS

- Since first impressions last, create a positive visual image for your first class meeting.
- Earn the right to teach the course by introducing yourself convincingly, yet humbly.
- Clarify your goals and expectations by thoroughly reviewing the syllabus and embellishing it with other critical information.
- Introduce students to each other through a planned, enjoyable icebreaker activity.
- Learn and begin using students' names early in the course.
- Whet students' appetite for the course by sharing a pertinent current event relevant to the course.
- Provide students an overview of the textbook or course pack.

- Manage your class time effectively to signal your preparation and consideration for students.
- Reassure students that the course will be a wise use of their time and energy.

SUGGESTED READINGS

Ailes, R. (1996). *You are the message: Getting what you want by being who you are.* New York: Doubleday.

Heller, S. (March 1, 1996). "Bowling alone." *The chronicle of higher education.*

Jones, K. (1991). *Icebreakers.* Pfeiffer.

Marchese, T. (1991, November). "TQM reaches the academy." *American Association for Higher Education Bulletin.*

Margolis, F. M., & Bell, C. R. (1986). *Instructing for results.* San Diego: Pfeiffer and Associates.

APPENDIX 6.1　STUDENT PROFILE FORM

Completing this form is completely voluntary. It seeks information that will enable the professor to more effectively meet your learning needs. All information provided will be maintained in strict confidence by the professor.

Name _____ Course No. _____ Term _____

Mailing Address _____

Day Telephone _____ Evening Telephone _____

Goal in taking course _____

Ultimate educational goal _____

Special situation, course _____

If employed, position _____

Ultimate career goal _____

Special situation, career _____

Personal accomplishments _____

Hobbies/interests _____

Memorable learning experience _____

How do you learn best? _____

Learning challenges _____

Other questions/comments:

[Optional]　　　　　　 _____
　　　　　　　　　　Signature (denotes receipt of syllabus)

APPENDIX 6.2   MODEL ICEBREAKER ACTIVITY

The goal of this activity is for you to meet each person in the group, find or create a fact that is true of them, and have them print their complete name in the blank beside it.

1. Has spent significant time in uniform   _____

2. Speaks a "foreign" language fluently   _____

3. An avid reader of Stephen King novels   _____

4. Moved to present home within the last year   _____

5. Has shaken hands with a governor   _____

6. Has parachuted from an airplane   _____

7. Travelled outside of U.S. within last year   _____

8. Has attended a rock concert within last year   _____

9. Regularly "surfs" the Internet   _____

10. Has two or more children   _____

11. Has a parent born outside of U.S.   _____

12. Is an avid tennis player   _____

13. Has owned their own business   _____

14. Has seen the movie (title)   _____

15. Has been SCUBA diving within last year   _____

16. Got married within the last year   _____

17. Has read (title of book)   _____

18. Regular viewer of (title of TV show)   _____

7

MANAGING THE COURSE ENVIRONMENT

Focus Questions

- How do you get and stay effectively organized throughout the course?
- What are some useful communications techniques for dealing with challenging students?
- How do you retain students in your course for the entire term?
- What ethical standards are expected of adjunct professors?

Having met your students for the first time and gathered some data on which to evaluate your design of the course and your initial classroom performance, you are probably experiencing some significant relief. As you look ahead however, you can likely envision some challenges later in the course—the time required for preparing for every class session and dealing effectively with students who are not as motivated as you would like. It can be a little overwhelming, especially if there is no one to provide insight about effectively managing the context of a course. In addition to the analysis of the information provided by students at the end of your first class meeting, there are a number of other steps you might take to help yourself become even better organized and prepared for the remainder of the term. While some of these might initially sound like a significant expenditure of your time, we believe this investment of effort will yield a significant payoff later in the course and throughout your teaching career.

ORGANIZING YOUR COURSE MATERIALS

First, obtain an oversize three-ring binder and three-hole punch. In the binder, insert a copy of your syllabus, the initial official class roll, your dated class notes/agenda for the first class meeting and the completed student profile forms in alphabetical order. In the back of the binder, perhaps following a divider of some sort, insert extra copies of your syllabus. Invariably, new students will add your class and previously registered students will lose the first syllabus you provided them. Having an extra copy always at your fingertips makes you more "customer friendly" and self-confident. Subsequently, insert each week's lesson plan/agenda in your binder, along with the draft and an answer key for the final version of each of your examinations. Also insert the examination study guides, as well as a single sharp copy of each handout you give students. This procedure will not only help you remain organized throughout your initial teaching assignment, but will facilitate the preparation and delivery of your course a second time. It may also have some transference to another course as your adjunct teaching career evolves.

Next, carefully review the student profiles you had students complete during the first class meeting. Seek to fit a face to each name, focusing on where the student was sitting in class, statements made or actions he or she took during the first class, other students with whom each student associated during the "icebreaker," etc. In short, try to learn every student name possible before attending the second class meeting. Your ability to address students by name, quickly and confidently, will send students a strong signal about your expectations of them. You are more likely to see them well-prepared for class by modeling such behavior for them. Students will also likely follow your lead in calling their peers by names, contributing to the creation of a more positive classroom environment—"a community of learners."

On the student profiles, carefully note such things as learning disabilities, schedule conflicts and other challenges you may need to research prior to meeting the class a second time. Be especially aware that in recent years, federal and state legislation has been widely adopted to provide full access to all educational resources to people with a wide range of disabilities. Learn and implement the appropriate practices early in your teaching career to ensure accessibility for all students, while prudently protecting yourself. If necessary, plan to clarify students' needs in private at your second class meeting. Most actions, such as ensuring that students with sight or hearing disabilities are reserved seats in the front portion of the classroom, or that those with ambulatory disabilities are reserved a seat close to the doorway, require little additional effort. Other needs might require additional intervention by a third party. In either case, be proactive in promptly seeking appropriate remedies to such challenges.

As stated before, you might also want to reserve a section of the class-room near the doorway for those who arrive late, to minimize disruption of the classroom. You should also make any universal changes to your policies and procedures, perhaps with student input, at the beginning of your second class meeting. Students need to leave the second class meeting feeling secure that all of the critical decisions regarding launching the course have been made and that they can confidently begin to assume full responsibility for their success in the course.

If you have not already done so, conclude your extensive review of the course textbook or course pack. At a minimum, you should be thoroughly familiar with the material which will be included on your first examination. Prior to the second class meeting, use the test bank and any examinations of other instructors you have collected to begin a draft of your first examina-tion. Although it has been a topic of heated debate for years, most successful professors would agree that truly prepared, effective teachers, at least to some extent, "teach to the test." The degree to which you adopt this practice should depend on the level of the course and whether the content had pre-viously been broached in a required survey course, the difficulty of the con-cepts, the goal of the course and its role in the larger curriculum, the maturity of the students, and your personal values. You can be assured stu-dents will ask "Is this on the test?" and you should have processed in advance the type of response you want to give. "I haven't decided yet what will be on the test" is not the type of response that helps students feel secure or motivates them to maintain their reading and study throughout the semester. Students' knowing you have prepared the exam well in advance encourages more thorough learning and minimizes the last-minute cram-ming which so often spells disaster for their test scores.

MANAGING YOUR COURSE PLAN

To ensure that the allotted time of each class meeting is managed efficiently and effectively, it is critical to have a lesson plan and agenda. We recommend that your agenda include the approximate time requirements for each com-ponent, so you can effectively pace yourself while addressing every item. Many successful instructors even write their agenda, without time require-ments, on the board in their classroom before class so that students can orga-nize their thinking in advance. This procedure provides students a sense of direction and a mental scaffold upon which they can build their understand-ing of the material. An agenda might look something like:

1. Reflections on activity conducted at end of previous class meeting (10 minutes)

2. Review of homework (20–25 minutes)
3. Overview of Chapter X, using overhead transparency (10 minutes)
4. Introduction, viewing of video, Presidential news conference (8 minutes)
5. Debriefing of video, focus on Cokie Roberts' question (10–15 minutes)
6. Lecture on text pages 141–148, using prepared notes (20 minutes)
7. Break (10 minutes)
…etc.

Having an agenda on the board also prompts you and the students to move proceedings along, rather than get bogged down in long, unproductive discussions.

While such preparation may require the investment of several hours, it will foster an appreciation for your style on the part of your most-prepared students. On a personal level, such preparation will enable you to more effectively experience the sense of self-satisfaction that you need during your first term as an instructor. From a management perspective, your thorough preparation creates a momentum that should enable you to deal more effectively with the interpersonal aspects of teaching.

INTERPERSONAL COMMUNICATIONS WITH STUDENTS

Without rehashing ground already covered, suffice it to say that you can expect, during your first term of teaching, a rich set of challenges with students. Having a strategy from the outset not only enables you to be more effective in dealing with issues that arise but also increases your potential for building your own knowledge base about people. A few rules of thumb are important:

- Inside the classroom, listen at least as much as you speak.
- Perception is paramount: It is more important how you are heard than what you actually say. Regularly test your words in advance, through the emotional filter of those who are different from you in age, gender, race, sexual orientation, etc.
- Be extremely careful about interpreting college or department policy unless you have researched the specific issue under discussion. "I'll check and get back to you at the next class meeting" is a perfectly acceptable answer to nearly any such question.
- All criticism and most praise of an individual student (or of anyone else, including public figures) is more effective when delivered in private, rather than in front of the entire class.
- Maintain control of your emotions; in the long run, no teacher ever wins an argument with a student.

An especially effective tool to employ in managing your communications with students is transactional analysis (TA), an approach developed years ago by psychotherapist Eric Berne. TA assumes we each have an internal video-camcorder that records all the significant experiences of our lives, beginning prenatally. Those experiences enable us to form three distinct and sequentially developed ego states that determine the communications patterns we employ in everyday life.

The first ego state that formed was our "child." It is totally emotional, self-absorbed, and dependent on others for satisfaction of its physical, psychological, and emotional needs. The internal dialogue (self-talk) of the self-centered child is restricted to "I/me statements"—"I want," "Give me," etc. Regardless of age, we all retain a bit or more of a child in us. Our child laughs and cries to process emotions, and occasionally pouts and throws angry tantrums as well.

Modeling parents, grandparents, and other authority figures, a person develops next the second ego state—the "parent," which was reinforced through looking after younger siblings and playing with pets or dolls. Also emotional, the parent can be either judgmental or nurturing. The parent makes primarily "you" statements, e.g., "You make me so proud," "You'll never amount to anything," which sometimes linger on the "memory tapes" of others for a lifetime.

Lastly, each person develops the objective, analytical ego state which Berne called the "adult." This is the ego state in which critical thinking occurs and which effective professors will most often seek to activate.

At any point in time, only one of the three ego states is in control. The normal pattern is for each person to react to a situation based on the pattern of reactions emulating from the experiences recorded on his or her memory tapes. The closer the circumstances, tone of voice, etc. match the recorded experience, the more likely a similar reaction will be elicited. The proponent of TA says it is not enough to say one human being communicates with another, but instead one ego state of a person creates a "transaction" with an ego state of another. Some transactions, e.g., a parent to another's child, create complementary transactions that sustain themselves throughout a conversation and often throughout the life of an entire relationship. Others are less natural and will "cross" and breakdown very quickly. Conscious correction is required to continue the dialogue. The effective professor, employer, spouse, and holder of other key roles will monitor reactions carefully, and short-circuit those that are ineffective for any particular situation. Over time, thoughtful people learn to react more often from the adult ego state, since there is often some sort of negative payoff for reacting from one of the emotional ego states. Communication from the adult ego state is likely to activate the adult ego state of the other person and increase the objectivity of the dialogue.

In the stress of the classroom, an inexperienced faculty member is likely to react emotionally to an occurrence that would be more effectively addressed in an objective manner. The scenarios below are all typical in a college teaching environment. Each can be reacted to from either the child, parent, or adult ego state. The question becomes which choice would provide the most constructive resolution of the situation.

Transactional Analysis Exercise

Select the most effective response in each scenario.

1. At the third class meeting, a student arrives 15 minutes late to class and allows the door to slam behind him. At that moment, the instructor says:

    a. "Whoa, musta' been a major traffic jam!"
    b. "I'd appreciate everyone getting here on time and respecting their classmates!"
    c. Nothing at the moment, but at the end of class says, "Now that we're up and running, let's all plan to arrive promptly for each meeting. If you are late, please enter the room quietly and take a seat in the rear. OK?"

2. While the class is reviewing the results of an exam, a student accuses the instructor of having included a "tricky question." The instructor says:

    a. "Tricky? If you really knew the material, you wouldn't say that!"
    b. "I used the test bank. You'd think they'd phrase the questions more clearly."
    c. "There's something about that question that you consider unfair?"

3. At the end of a class during which a scored exam was returned, a single-parent student, known by her professor to be overextended, lingers to talk about her grade. The professor speaks first, saying:

    a. "I know how disappointed you must be."
    b. "You look miserable. Cheer up, it's only one test!"
    c. "You think *you* feel lousy. I spent a lot of time getting that test together, and you all were clearly unprepared!"

4. A struggling student catches on to a difficult concept quickly. The professor says:

    a. "You're picking up on this more quickly than most people do."
    b. "I'm really proud of the way you caught on to that so fast!"
    c. "Wow, you're really fast!"

5. During the second class meeting of the term, the professor states a well-developed opinion on a controversial matter. A student heatedly disagrees and offers his diametrically opposed opinion. The professor says:

  a. "It's clear you need to do some more research!"
  b. "Well, let's take a vote to see who is right!"
  c. "You've presented a viewpoint that many others share. Although I strongly believe in what I've said, I appreciate hearing your opinion. That's what being a critical thinker is all about."

Exercise Answers and Discussion

Experts in interpersonal communications tell us that only 7% of the impact of a message is attributable to the words being used; 38% is attributable to the tone of voice and 55% to the body language. Since we only have the words to go on, there may be some disagreement on the "most effective" response, but we believe the "adult" responses are: 1—c, 2—c, 3—a, 4—a and 5—c. In most cases, the adult answer is probably the most effective in contributing to a positive learning environment, influencing students to analyze the situation objectively rather than to react emotionally. However, we would argue that in problem 4, the "adult" response may be the second best choice. If the student is struggling to learn the material, it would probably be most effective to give the "nurturing parent" response—b.

Transactional analysis is a practical tool that can help you effectively deal with the array of challenging situations you can expect in your classroom. Mastering this technique will minimize emotional student reactions, enable you to maintain momentum in the classroom, and build your self-confidence.

Kenneth Blanchard, famous author, educator, and management guru, consistently emphasizes the importance of providing feedback to learners, calling feedback "the breakfast of champions." To be effective, he says, feedback must be immediate, specific, and disproportionately positive (1982). Successful college professors support that position by regularly providing students quiet, individual feedback—orally and through comments written on assignments returned to students. Providing regular positive feedback enables you to be more effective also when a constructive comment is required to correct less successful results.

MANAGING CLASS TIME EFFECTIVELY

Earlier in this chapter we emphasized the importance of having an agenda for each class meeting that includes the approximate amount of time you will spend on each item. In today's busy society, most students have become very time sensitive and, as we have said before, are increasingly value-conscious. Students fully expect you to make wise and effective use of class time.

First, begin each class precisely on time. Even if you are missing a few students and decide to begin by reviewing your previous class meeting for a few minutes, beginning on time sends the clear message that you are sensitive to all students—especially those who adhere to accepted policies. Many instructors have made the mistake of delaying the beginning of class for 5 minutes—"until the rest of the students arrive"—only to have even more students be 10 minutes late for the following class meeting. Your most motivated students typically will be on time, and their behavior should be rewarded. Unexpected severe bad weather and power outages are among the only reasonable exceptions you might make to this rule.

Adhering to an agenda you communicate to students will enable them to organize their thought processes and maximize retention of the material presented. Developing the agenda for each class meeting reinforces to you the importance of delivering instruction in segments, through diverse methods or activities. One of the most common student complaints about their professors is that they "ramble" too much—typically an indicator of overdependence on lecturing. The attention span of students has grown increasingly shorter in recent years, and that fact needs to be recognized in your preparation and delivery.

Depending on the length of your class periods, you may well need to schedule a break to provide students an opportunity to attend to their needs and to refresh their minds for subsequent instruction. We suggest that breaks never exceed 10 minutes, unless some especially unusual situation exists. State clearly that you are taking a break and write the time you expect students to return to class on the board. Breaks longer than 10 minutes encourage students to become engrossed in extrinsic discussions that contribute to their losing focus on learning objectives. Breaks also provide students, especially younger ones, with an excuse to skip the remainder of the class meeting, so be proactive in rounding up students following the break. If some do not return, during the following class meeting address the need to return after break by stating specific important or interesting activities that will follow their return. Restart the class after break at the exact time stated on the board, even if everyone has not returned to class, thus reinforcing your commitment to effective time utilization.

Learn to close off nonproductive activities or discussions positively. While you certainly want students' full mental engagement in classroom activities, you don't want to allow one or a few students to slow the pace of the class meeting. As you prepare to move to the next segment, address individual students quietly about your strategy and invite them to see you at the end of the class meeting to bring their effort to closure.

Energize your mentally fatigued students throughout the class meeting. Ask frequent rhetorical questions. Integrate the news of the day into your presentation. Provide vivid, everyday examples of the concepts being discussed. Move throughout the entire classroom, stopping for a few moments at several key spots. Recall memories from your past that put a smile on your face and relay the story if it fits the moment. If people have said you were funny, tell an occasional joke or story—but avoid them if they are too big a stretch from your natural style. Look for props in your daily life that enable you to relay "object lessons"—you can do a lot with a tool kit, one gallon jar, or a flashlight. Appeal to the visual by projecting occasional cartoons through an overhead projector. Speak in an especially dramatic way. Give your students a wrapped piece of hard candy or fortune cookie. Have fun!

Since students paid for an entire course, utilize the entire class period, even if some are vocalizing the desire to "Let us go early!" Letting the "tail wag the dog…" in this way only pressures you to repeat the action and relax other standards throughout the remainder of the term. The dedicated students will quietly rebel, to each other as they leave the class or on the class evaluations at the end of the term. Occasionally—depending on the nature of your course and the number of students enrolled—consider blocking out a period of time for one-on-one tutoring with students in need. If you do this, you probably want to encourage students not taking advantage of the personal tutoring to "pair up" in the library, student lounge, or other appropriate area to work together on some specific learning activity.

Before dismissing any class meeting, provide students with a brief overview—another form of advance organizer—of the next class meeting. This has the potential to get students energized for the activity and organize their thoughts and materials more effectively, so that the subsequent class meeting yields a better result. Although their faces might not show it, students want to be excited about school. So be especially enthusiastic when the following class meeting includes a guest speaker or other special activity. Their energy will feed the occasion.

Lastly—end each class meeting in a timely fashion. Many students have child care, work, or similar obligations to keep after class, and making them late does not contribute to a positive learning environment for the following class meeting. At the same time, it is critical to plan sufficient learning activities that the allotted time frame is fully utilized. Discipline leaders view adjunct professors' excusing their classes early as an indicator of a lack of preparation or commitment to the assignment.

RETENTION OF STUDENTS

As stated previously, those making funding decisions that affect colleges and universities have, in recent years, sought to hold institutions increasingly accountable for the percentage of students completing programs. Each professor—adjunct or full-time—shares an inherent obligation to participate actively in the effort to retain students. Most discipline leaders would agree that three major mileposts account for the overwhelming majority of withdrawals from college courses—the first class meeting, the first examination, and mid-term activities. Each of these mileposts must be managed creatively to ensure that retention of students is maximized.

Students arrive at the first class meeting with a set of expectations—some realistic, others perhaps not. The protocol outlined in Chapter 5 was designed to ensure that students' expectations are effectively addressed, that social bonds are built within the group through a planned activity, that students develop a positive perception of the professor, and that they are reassured of the reward they will receive for the time and money invested in the class. A primary goal of a truly effective instructor should be to have more students at the second class meeting than the first, because happy students will recruit their peers to join them in an experience perceived as valuable.

The second prominent milepost at which students are lost is typically when the results of the first examination are announced. Invariably, some students in the class probably "added" rather late, perhaps missing a class meeting or two. Some will have had financial or logistical problems that delayed (or prevented) their purchase of the textbook, contributing to insufficient preparation for the examination. Others will have experienced a challenge in their work or family lives and simply lacked the time to adequately study. In Chapter 8 we outline a strategy that provides unsuccessful test-takers with an opportunity to redeem themselves, while rewarding students who were adequately prepared and successful. In the meantime, clarify your personal thoughts about giving students a second chance.

A final point at which students are frequently lost from the class occurs at about mid-term, when typically a major assignment is due or a major examination is administered. The key to managing the timely submission of major assignments is to break them into smaller chunks that are more manageable to students. This might entail their submitting a project proposal (which requires narrowing of the topic, preliminary planning, and research of the assignment) well before the entire final project comes due. A similar tactic might be adopted with major examinations, in which a portion is administered at one class meeting, while the remainder is given at the following session.

A proven tactic for managing the impact of these mileposts is to require an office session with each student in the class. You can schedule it by developing a simple matrix that you circulate during a class meeting early in the term. Building on the information gathered through the icebreaker exercise of the first class meeting and the completed student profile forms, solidify your relationship with each student in the class. Busy students might be provided a reward for attending, such as a review of several questions on the first examination or a look at resources that you consider especially valuable for completing major assignments. Since office space is often in short supply, you might need to use the classroom, library, or other convenient location to hold your sessions.

PROFESSIONAL PRACTICES

Most would agree that any enterprise is more effectively managed when the key players trust the motives and behavior of the leader. The college classroom presents many potential ethical challenges that should be contemplated prior to their being faced. Following are four scenarios you are likely to face early in your teaching career.

Exercise: Evaluate the ethical behavior of the adjunct professor in each scenario.

1. Employed full-time as a governmental administrator, John recently began teaching at the local college. In the fourth week of the term, he administered the first exam. Mary, a traditional-age student, was a "no show" who had also missed the previous week. After the exam, John telephoned her at the number she had provided on her student profile. A middle-aged man answered the phone. John identified himself as Mary's professor and asked for her. The man identified himself as Mary's father, told John that Mary was not home, then asked the nature of the call. John replied that Mary had missed the test and went on to speculate about its impact on her grade.

2. The sales manager of a real estate agency, Michelle is teaching "Introduction to Marketing" for the second time. She regularly applies concepts from the course to the real estate industry only, and each time mentions her agency and its high standards of performance. At the final class meeting she stopped each student entering the classroom, shook hands, and gave the student a business card while saying, "If I can ever help you out, give me a call."

3. Joan's class had been especially enjoyable to teach—a diverse group of traditional and nontraditional students. Many of the students were working professionals, highly motivated and fun-loving. At the beginning of the final class meeting, one of the students announced that everyone was going to a nearby cocktail lounge following class and that Joan was expected to join them. A fun-lover herself, Joan joined them, but limited herself to one drink.

4. Student Sam struggled the entire term in Janet's class. Janet provided him extra support and tutoring after class, and by the final class period it appeared he would get a satisfactory grade. Sam was genuinely appreciative, saying, "No instructor has ever gone out of their way like you!" As Sam came into the room for the final exam, he handed Janet a small bag with a wrapped gift. Janet was quite surprised when, after all of the students had left, she opened the package to find a pair of gold earrings.

Answers: While these scenarios describe seemingly innocent behavior, each involves a rather serious ethical mistake by the professor.

1. John was on solid ground initiating a call to Mary. Since she had willingly provided him the telephone number, a reasonable person would justify his using it in this situation. However, John had no authority to provide anyone other than Mary such information, in spite of her age and the real possibility that her parent had paid at least part of her tuition. John could be held in violation of the Privacy Act by an unhappy Mary.

2. Since hers is a general marketing course, Michelle's behavior in relating all concepts to the real estate industry is, at best, less than effective teaching and, at worst, "tacky." However, she clearly overstepped her bounds in the way she promoted her firm, and especially in the way she distributed her business cards. Obviously, one of the Michelle's primary motivations for teaching the course is "rainmaking" for her full-time job. However, ethical practices would limit her to identifying her employer and providing business cards only to students who voluntarily requested them. Her style may well have communicated to students that they were obligated to refer business her way and thus created uneasiness likely to be reported to college officials.

3. Drinking with students is an especially thorny issue. Some would probably condone moderate social drinking between professors and mature graduate students, especially in a campus pub when the students reside near campus and walk to class. However, among undergraduate students, where clearly there is a strong chance that at least several of the students are underage, drinking is not appropriate. In the litigious climate of today's society and with the strong possibility that students drive to class, Joan is putting herself in a riskier situation than many might first realize. In a class of adult students, there is also a strong chance that at least one would have a substance abuse problem. Contributing to students of any age being placed in such a personally threatening situation could have disastrous results. As an alternative to the cocktail lounge, Joan might explain her reluctance and suggest a family restaurant or coffee shop where alcohol is not served. Barring that, she would be well advised to "beg off."

4. Janet's acceptance of the gift (signified by her opening it) runs the risk of being perceived as a bribe for a grade. She should have genuinely acknowledged Sam's generosity but explained that it would be inappropriate for her to accept any gift.

The consistent display of high ethical standards will immeasurably benefit all aspects of your teaching. Students will provide you more of the respect so critical to success inside the classroom, while discipline leaders will come to view you as an exemplary member of their faculty team.

SURVIVING WHEN YOU'RE NOT
PREPARED FOR CLASS

Despite your thorough course planning, your concern for students and commitment to the institution and its instructional leaders, situations will arise—illness, family emergencies, overwhelming projects within your full-time position—that prevent your being fully prepared for every class meeting. Golfing friends sometimes allow each other a "Mulligan," and most students will excuse one flawed performance during a term. Prior to experiencing a situation in which such indulgence is needed, develop some contingency plans you can employ on short notice. These might include:

- Recruiting a guest speaker from your circle of colleagues who you know has previously delivered a presentation on a topic of probable interest to your students or who could answer questions about his or her area of expertise.
- Conducting a *carousel brainstorming* activity, in which a course issue is examined from several perspectives. Section off the chalkboard, identify the perspective above each column, divide the total group of students into the same number of sections as perspectives, then have them rotate through each section listing appropriate facts. For example, you might conduct a SWOT analysis (see Chapter 5) of a particular organization, public figure, or practice. Debriefing the activity is an excellent opportunity to not only help students develop a more grounded perspective, but identifies ideas upon which you can "piggyback" during the remainder of the class period.
- Dividing the students into groups of three or four and asking them to develop several questions that would be appropriate for inclusion on your next exam.
- Assuming you can typically obtain a VCR on short notice, identify a video (one your students are not likely to have seen) at your local rental store or through another source that embellishes material from your course.
- Assign students roles, e.g., press, governmental figures, etc. and conduct a focused analysis of a late-breaking news story that is related to your course content.
- Divide students into groups to work on an assigned course project or upcoming exam, perhaps even excusing them to go to the library, computer lab, or other appropriate campus resource.
- As a last resort, admit your inability to prepare and allow students input into formulating a strategy for best utilizing class time.

In each case, the key is to shift the initial attention away from yourself (to permit you to gather your thoughts) and onto an activity that engages students in a new and significant way. If you permit yourself to relax, you might be surprised how a wise use of class time might rather naturally emerge.

Should an emergency not permit your attending class at all and you can recruit an appropriate substitute, you might combine several of the above activities to salvage the class meeting. If that is not possible, give your instructional leader(s) a call as early as possible and ask for suggestions. He or she might be able to identify an appropriate substitute instructor or suggest another contingency plan. If you are unable to reach an appropriate decision maker and must cancel the class, do all of the following:

1. Contact someone in a position of authority at the college to say you will miss class and ask them to have someone meet the class or, at a bare minimum, post a sign on your classroom door.
2. Telephone as many of the students as possible (numbers should be on student profile form) and ask those you reach for their help in contacting others.
3. Continue to pursue contact with your instructional leader until you are able to supply appropriate details.

When you next meet your class, apologize genuinely and make appropriate changes in your course plan to minimize the negative impact on students.

THROUGH THE ADJUNCTS' EYES

Margaret:

My class met for the fourth time last night, and upon reflection, I can see some ineffective patterns emerging in my classroom management. Integrating the reading assignment and some current events, I was able to move the class into a very effective discussion. Feeling very good about our progress, I let two particularly vocal students drone on too long. That delayed our break, and I failed to encourage students to get back in a timely manner. The bottom line is that we didn't adequately cover the planned content and our first test is next week. I could tell from students' faces that some were frustrated, probably about our not reviewing the study guides that I had earlier provided. I have learned the "hard way" the importance of developing an agenda for each class meeting, which includes some time parameters for each component. Also, I should have reminded the entire class that they could call me, as indicated on the syllabus.

Karen:

Our class has now met four times. The first meeting established the structure and culture of the class very effectively, and students have responded well to the lectures and activities I've scheduled. Mr. Jackson has repeatedly said that his biggest reward from teaching was the private questions students would pose before and after class and during breaks. I've yet to get any of those and wonder if I've created a barrier that prevents such dialogue from developing.

Juan:

Now that I've met the class four times, I must admit that the differences between the university and community college teaching environments have proven to be more substantial than I expected. While there are clearly some academically deficient students in my class, there are at least as many or more very bright and educationally hungry students. Some of the classroom rules that are commonly accepted by university students—such as students being in their seats when the class is to begin—are totally disregarded by these community college students. I have tried to make an appointment with my department chair and even left a message on her voice mail asking her to visit my class to give me some feedback and guidance. She has no secretary. She left a message on my answering machine saying she teaches five class sections herself and has a direct conflict with my class meeting time. She offered to see me a week from Friday afternoon, but I'll be involved in a workshop at the university then.

Out of frustration, I have starting turning to a couple of my graduate student friends and we have devised a plan for them to visit my class. In two weeks we are going to videotape one of my class presentations and critique it together afterwards. This should give me another perspective to help me plan more effectively for the remainder of the semester.

TIPS FOR THRIVING

This chapter has dealt with the "management" of your teaching assignment, but modern organizational theorists emphasize the key differentiation of "management" with "leadership." In recent years, institutions of higher education at all levels have adopted increasingly sound management and marketing principles for their institutions to survive the turbulent changes being experienced in their "industry." Regardless of your discipline, your adjunct faculty career will benefit markedly from your staying abreast with such contemporary concepts as "total quality management," "niche marketing," "productivity," "accountability," and "students as customers." An understanding of these concepts will better equip you to adopt to the continuing changes within higher education.

REVIEW OF KEY POINTS

- Organize your course materials in a single binder.
- Proactively discover the uniqueness of each of your students.
- Use the concepts of "transactional analysis" to deal effectively with challenging situations.
- Give all your students immediate, specific, and positive feedback.
- Begin each class on time, follow an agenda, and end at the scheduled time.
- Anticipate and try to prevent student withdrawal at the typical points—first meeting, first exam, and mid-term.
- Promote and consistently display highly ethical standards in your classroom.
- Plan thoroughly for those times when you might be underprepared for or must miss meeting your class altogether.

SUGGESTED READINGS

Berne, E. (1964). *The games people play.* New York: Ballantine Books.

Blanchard, K., & Johnson, S. (1982). *The one minute manager.* New York: Berkley Books.

Blanchard, K., & Peale, N. V. (1988). *The power of ethical management.* New York: William Morrow.

Harris, T. (1967). *I'm O. K., you're O. K.* New York: Avon Books.

8

INSTRUCTOR-DIRECTED
LEARNING METHODS

Focus Questions

- How do you create an environment in your classroom that is conducive to learning?
- How can you enhance the effectiveness of lectures with today's undergraduate students?
- What special measures should you take to maximize the rewards of video presentations and guest speakers?

One of the primary goals of this book is to help you begin to develop a teaching style that is effective with students as well as personally rewarding. Early in our teaching experience, we "teach as we have been taught"—it's the only skill base we have. Unfortunately, those models and techniques are less than fully effective with today's students. As we discussed in Chapter 4, your classroom is likely to be populated by a far different type of person than those who sat beside you during your student days. Achieving success with such individuals requires a well-grounded understanding of your own philosophical base. It also requires familiarity with diverse teaching methodologies built on sound principles, as well as an understanding of how students perceive and process the information flow that you create within your classroom.

This and the following chapter address seemingly opposite ends of a teaching methodologies continuum. At one end (upon which this chapter focuses) are methods that place the primary control of learning activities in the hands of the instructor. Such methods are those upon which most novice adjunct professors naturally rely. Their strength lies in their potential to provide structure, organization, and sequence to the large number of students who have had little of it provided in their backgrounds.

TODAY'S TEACHING AND LEARNING PARADIGM

As you begin to conceptualize how you will approach the teaching of your course, you will likely reflect on your own undergraduate student experiences. You might recall the first meeting of a class when the professor somewhat boastfully said something akin to "Look to the left, then to the right—at the end of this course one of the two students you see now will not be here." This effort, designed we assume to stress the high standards of the professor, was symptomatic of what was accepted as common practice not so long ago in higher education. It no doubt lingers deeply in the minds of some traditional professors. Their paradigm views the professor as the sole intellectual resource in the classroom, imparting knowledge to students, characterized by Professor Kingsfield of *The Paper Chase* as having "minds of mush." Simply stated, "teaching" entailed having students, regardless of their pre-existing mindsets, embrace the professor's perception of the course material, integrate that perception into the formulation of an "enlightened" view, then regurgitate that view in carefully crafted essays—"or else!"

There is, no doubt, still a degree of merit to this approach in certain courses today, and our purpose is not to denigrate any particular position on teaching. However, most college and university instructional leaders would state that a rather significant paradigm shift has taken place that makes that traditional position untenable in the contemporary environment.

As relayed in Chapter 4, students over recent years have changed significantly in the way they process information and images. It serves little purpose here to debate whether those changes are good or bad—they are fact. Television, with its influential visual images and rapid pace, as well as computers and other forms of technology that provide instant feedback to users, have rendered ineffective the dependence on the lecture as the exclusive vehicle of instruction.

A contemporary approach to developing teaching strategies seeks more thoroughly to understand how the human brain processes information, then uses instructional methods that are likely to be more efficient and effective in achieving mastery of course concepts. The healthy human brain has a virtually inexhaustible capacity to learn—to detect patterns, to remember, to self-correct from experience, and to create. Conceive for a moment of your students' learning systems as computers, with input devices that include all five of their senses, a wonderful central processing unit (CPU) and a variety of output devices that enable us to evaluate the quality and quantity of their learning. No effective learning can begin to take place until the CPU is "booted up." Learning cannot continue unless the CPU remains actively engaged in processing the information and feelings that flow freely through your students' stimulated input devices. Achieving the learning outcomes which we have established for our courses requires an ongoing understanding of, and attendance to, students' learning systems.

For success in the new millennium, your students need to synthesize information *meaningfully*—one of Bloom's higher-level objectives—rather than acquire the *surface* knowledge that education has so often emphasized. To facilitate students' fullest development within your course:

- "Start where the learner is"—intellectually and emotionally—whenever possible, making connections to students' existing knowledge bases and maturity levels.
- Establish learning goals they are capable of achieving and that extract meaning for each student.
- Give regular, specific feedback on their demonstrated learning achievements.
- Evaluate frequently, and at the level of Bloom's taxonomy in which the material was delivered.

Your overall objective should be consistently to create win–win relationships with students. You, your instructional leaders, and the institution are successful only when students achieve a level of learning that all stakeholders perceive as appropriate.

CREATING A POSITIVE LEARNING ENVIRONMENT

The effectiveness of student learning begins with the creation of a positive learning environment, in which students are sufficiently relaxed to permit the full functionality of their learning systems. Some words or phrases we might use to describe such an environment include:

- Warm, friendly, accepting, safe
- Stimulating, curiosity-creating, engaging
- Shared responsibility, cooperative spirit
- Trusting, safe, secure sharing of diverse ideas
- Professional, ethical, high standards

Assuming you followed the recommendations in Chapter 6 for getting your course off to a successful start and those in Chapter 7 regarding managing the course climate, the seeds of this environment have been sown. You now simply need to nourish it through regular, personalized, positive comments to students, to demonstrate respect for diverse viewpoints, and to attend to the small details that so often contribute to the perceptions formed in the minds of impressionable students. If you find yourself several weeks into the term without having attended to these points, give them your immediate, full attention so that the remainder of the term maximizes its payoff for both your students and yourself.

A related issue that you might need to address is the course structure. Many students are likely to be affected by dysfunctional home or work lives and may arrive at your class meeting with a plethora of issues running through their minds. To achieve effectiveness with your instruction, you must employ methods that enable such students to leave their problems outside your classroom and focus on the learning objectives that your course is designed to deliver.

One especially effective tool for achieving structure is the "advance organizer." Simply stated, an advance organizer is an image or set of information, often already known to a learner, that is used by an instructor as a bridge to learning new material. It provides the structure, that is, a section of the scaffolding in the mind of the learner, upon which new learning can be built. Examples of advance organizers include:

- An agenda written prominently on the chalkboard that students can scan prior to the beginning of a class meeting
- A rhetorical question posed by the instructor to create focus on an issue; for example, "Have any of you ever been awakened in the middle of the night by a terribly loud noise?"
- A large photograph or other visual prop that can be easily seen by all students in the class, used to focus a discussion
- A popular song—from today or yesterday—played to create an appropriate context for facilitating learning of an important concept
- A short activity or game that gets students involved physically, then is transitioned to a learning objective
- A story, metaphor, or analogy to which students can easily relate
- A video clip from a popular television show or news broadcast

Advance organizers are most effectively employed when you begin to cover a new concept, start a new time block, or when students seem to be losing their focus. The best advance organizers are easily developed, requiring only a sensitivity to students' perspectives and a bit of creativity. They are most effectively employed when used in variety—some oral, some visual, some funny, some profound.

TECHNIQUES OF EFFECTIVE
TEACHING PRESENTATIONS

An effective instructor learns to think of himself or herself as a craftsman. Like a carpenter or stone mason, the instructor must develop a tool chest that includes the wide variety of aids required to complete the total job most efficiently and effectively. Each large job is then divided into subtasks, and specific tools are selected to most effectively complete each task. Traditionally, many professors relied nearly exclusively on only one instructional tool—the lecture. While traditionalists and revisionists vary widely on the value of lecturing, the following are widely accepted as potentially effective uses of lecturing:

- Establish the broad outlines of a body of material
- Set guidelines for independent study
- Model intellectual attitudes you hope to encourage in students
- Encourage learners' interest in a topic
- Set the moral culture for discussions (Brookfield, 1990)

Given that today's students may have limited attention spans and are highly influenced by television, computer graphics, video games, and related stimuli, for you to rely primarily on a straight lecture for most class meetings is likely to be ineffective. Therefore, when you must lecture, employ grounded procedures and techniques for maximizing its impact. First, limit the length of your lectures to 15 to 20 minutes. Employ an alternative teaching method or two before returning to lecturing again. Use a variety of visual stimuli during your lectures. Besides the visual props mentioned earlier, a wide range of related tools permit you to display not only written words, but the diagrams, charts, and tables that have become such integral mental processing tools for us all.

The overhead projector, employing either transparencies or computer-generated graphics, is an especially effective tool when correctly managed, because it enables you to organize your presentation in advance and permits you to face students and gauge reactions as you lecture. Publishers of popular textbooks often furnish vivid coordinating transparencies. Ask your instructional leader if those are available for your course or ask for permission to contact the publisher's sales representative to obtain them. If you produce your own transparencies or graphics, keep phrases short and simple, using "bullets" (•). You can embellish these brief points through your lecture. Always have an extra projector bulb available, as well as materials for keeping the glass free of fingerprints and other distracting imperfections.

Flip charts (pads of large sheets of paper) can be employed spontaneouly and also enable you to prepare presentations in advance and face students when using. From a psychological perspective, flip charts provide an emotionally warmer tone and seem to facilitate greater student participation. They are especially effective in courses that focus on interpersonal issues and skills. From a logistical perspective, flip charts enable you to tear off sheets which can then be thumb-tacked or taped around the classroom, providing students the chance to refer back to previously covered material and sequence their learning. Since they do not require electricity and are portable, flip charts are especially convenient and reliable.

The chalk or marker board is best used in situations in which spontaneity is critical to the success of your lecture—for example, when involving students in identifying material for class review. Avoid writing long passages that require you to keep your back turned to students for extended periods. You would be wise to print in letters viewable to those furthest from the board and to keep extra chalk or board marker pens and erasers in your brief case.

Professionally produced visual materials (maps, charts, globes, or other props and video clips) enhance your lectures as well. By thinking through in advance whether these materials can be easily viewed by students from their normal seating positions, you will be prepared to reposition chairs or make other adjustments to the classroom that will maximize the effectiveness of these learning aids.

The impact of a lecture is also largely influenced by your communications techniques. Be careful to make effective verbal transitions and to establish the appropriate context for your lecture. For example, simple phrases such as "You will recall that in our last meeting, we were discussing X and its impact on…" enable your students to get on common ground with you. Throughout your lecture, observe students' body language to assess their mental engagement in the material and their level of understanding. Avoid moving on until you are convinced that the overwhelming majority are "with you." To check out their understanding, pose one or two appropriate agree/disagree questions, asking students to respond with "thumbs up" or "thumbs down." This tactic reinforces your nonthreatening classroom culture and permits you to clear up confusion before progressing. Make the lecture more interactive by prompting student mental engagement and application of the material by asking rhetorical questions. These might include "What would happen if I…?" Follow up with "Would it…or…?"

A classical style of lecture that has received renewed interest in recent years for its ability to promote critical thinking is the Socratic method. Frequently used in law schools, the Socratic method was showcased by the character Professor Kingsfield in the film (and later television series) *The Paper Chase*. The Socratic method typically employs assigned readings, then roots out values held by students through the pointed questions of the instructor. Once a student response is given, the lecturer probes further through increasingly more pointed questions. The effective use of the

Socratic method requires mature and secure students and a classroom culture of trust and mutual respect.

Regardless of how well "produced" it is, lecturing has limited potential for effectiveness with today's students. First, lecturing is limited in its abilities to fully engage the learning systems of students, especially if the seating arrangement puts them at a great distance from the lecturer. Second, the lecture environment does not typically encourage the widespread participation by students in the classroom dialogue. While it is not possible, or even desirable, to totally abandon lecturing, the effectiveness of student learning requires the employment of additional instructor-directed techniques.

VIDEO PRESENTATIONS

Many instructors have realized the potential of video presentations for contributing to the richness of their courses. However, videos need to be selected carefully to ensure an appropriate fit with the curriculum and to prevent their being perceived as time fillers. In some courses, videos are not appropriate at all. Their use tends to be most effective in the introduction of units of instruction by providing appropriate contextual information and in the conclusion of units by providing applications of course concepts.

Instructional leaders have commonly responded positively to the value of videos by purchasing them for libraries and resources centers, as well as providing the necessary equipment for their showing. When preparing to effectively use videos in your classrooms:

- "Clear" the video program with your immediate instructional leader to ensure that it is not commonly used in another course within the curriculum.
- Limit video presentations to 20 to 25 minutes, or if it is critical to show a longer work, divide its showing into segments with debriefing sessions interspersed.
- Preview the video program shortly before using it in class, to ensure its viewing quality and that the content is appropriate to the instructional unit and your particular group of students.
- Order viewing equipment far enough in advance to ensure its availability during the class period in which you intend to show the video.
- Check equipment immediately prior to using it in class, to ensure not only that it is working properly but that you understand its controls.
- Introduce the video to class, providing an "advance organizer" of its contents and the specific things you would like students to look for as they watch.
- After the showing, discuss the video, synthesizing its content with the other elements of the instructional unit.

As convenient and professional as they are, it is especially important that you not overuse videos in your class. There is a risk in developing an image among students and fellow faculty members as an instructor who is taking short cuts and failing to provide sufficient rigor to the course. Unless your class is directly related to the film, news-gathering, or related industries, you probably want to limit yourself to showing no more than two or three videos during a term.

GUEST SPEAKERS

Occasionally having a guest speaker is potentially an excellent way to increase learning and the perceived value students develop of your course. As in the case of video presentations, be careful not to overuse this tactic. Observe the following guidelines in using a guest speaker:

- Clearly identify your objectives in inviting the guest speaker, e.g., addressing an important issue in which your knowledge base or the textbook is relatively weak.
- Clear the guest speaker with your immediate instructional leader to ensure there is no reason why he or she should not be invited to speak.
- Obtain a resume or biographical sketch in advance to prepare an appropriate and enthusiastic introduction which energizes the speaker.
- Clarify explicitly with the speaker, well in advance, exactly what you would like addressed in the presentation and your time parameters.
- Clarify the speaker's posture on accepting student questions, including any areas that are "out of bounds"—the last thing you want is for the speaker to be embarrassed.
- Confirm by telephone the guest speaker's presentation several days in advance.
- Develop a contingency plan in case the guest speaker is a "no show"— meetings get called at the last minute, traffic accidents occur, etc.
- Play an active nonverbal role during the presentation, maintaining consistent eye contact with the speaker and encouraging students to do the same.
- Prompt appropriate questions when appropriate, adhering to his or her imposed limitations.
- If the speaker exceeds the time parameters markedly, simply stand and move from your seat in the rear to the side of the classroom.
- At the conclusion of the presentation, thank the speaker for specific content items and insights that were provided.
- Provide the students a short break during which you walk the speaker to an appropriate location for a more personal thanks, and clarify who should receive a copy of a thank you letter.

- Discuss the presentation with students to positively reinforce instructional objectives.
- Deal positively with any student criticism of speaker.
- Mail the guest speaker a professional letter of thanks promptly, with a photocopy to his or her designees (usually work supervisors).

Afterwards, talk with a key student or two to determine their perception of the guest speaker's effectiveness. If you decide to ask the speaker to return for subsequent terms, be somewhat protective of his or her availability. Many guest speakers feel an obligation to serve their local communities in this way, but each has their limits. Clarify what those limits are before saying anything to your colleagues that might encourage their invitation of your guest speaker to one of their classes.

This chapter has provided only the most essential information on the major instructor-directed methods available for delivering your course. Many articles and even entire books have been written on these methodologies; over time, you will want to review some of these. It is especially critical to talk with your instructional leader, mentor, and other colleagues in this formative stage of your development as an instructor, to ensure that you continually improve the quality of the "product" you deliver to students. In this way, you will also increase the personal rewards you receive from teaching.

THROUGH THE ADJUNCTS' EYES

Margaret:

Largely because of my uneasiness as a public speaker, my course plan has included using a video nearly every class period to provide context to the issues and concepts we address. All have been borrowed from people whom I know in the training departments of two local companies—so they're more current than the ones available in the college library and instructional department. I have also had four guest speakers. During last night's class, as I was introducing the video, I noticed one of the students roll her eyes and look at one of her friends as if to say, "Oh no—not another video!" It sent a shock wave through me because I thought the television generation would respond overwhelmingly positively to using videos. I've thought since last night that I should be providing a better introduction and conducting a more thorough debriefing of the videos and guest speakers, so that students can make a better connection to the material they're reading in their text. Maybe I should take a few minutes at the end of the next class meeting to conduct a brief informal evaluation of the course to this point, so I can gauge the impact of my teaching methods.

Karen:

I have had the sense that there is a great deal of commonality between the skills involved in courtroom and classroom presentations. It's very important to vary the pace, volume, and tone of my speaking, use rhetorical questions to prompt thinking, and dramatically emphasize key phrases. As in the court room, I have incorporated appropriate and diverse visuals—overhead transparencies, chalkboard, large charts, and graphs—to help the television generation more effectively digest information.

I have yet, however, to sense a personal connection to any students. They are all polite and participate well in discussions, but they seem in a hurry to leave the room at the conclusion of each class meeting. I would really like to find a way to improve that situation.

Juan:

One of my students met me prior to last night's class. She had a frustrated countenance and an anxious tone in her voice as she asked if we could speak in private. We found a place removed from the traffic flow, and she paused to gather herself. Slowly she shared that she was frustrated in her ability to follow my class lectures. She relayed that mine was her first class in many years and that the vocabulary I used in class was confusing to her. Many of the words I seemed to use so easily in my lectures were not in the reading assignments. Although she had bought a small dictionary to bring to class, she often was unable to find the word quickly and found herself becoming disconnected even more from my lecture. She had had a conversation with one of her classmates, who was also challenged to process the lecture. He thought I was going out of my way to impress students and was intentionally "talking over their heads." I first felt defensive, but after a few moments I realized that there was some truth in what she was saying, given the level of the students. I also realized that it had taken courage for her to approach me and thanked her for bringing the situation to my attention. I hereby pledge to be more careful.

One of my graduate student friends from the university told me about a technique for improving students' ability to follow my presentations. It is designed to reduce the frustration students often feel when too much material is presented too quickly. It was an acronym—SUE—for using the chalkboard more effectively. "S" stands for say it before writing, "U" for check understanding, and "E" for erase energetically before introducing new material. I employed the concept during last night's class and sensed a positive reaction among students.

TIPS FOR THRIVING

There is something very special about watching a true professional work, be they a physician, carpenter, or teacher. In many ways, teaching is a craft that, like so many others, requires the development of a core set of values and vision of a desired outcome. It also requires the mastering of a growing kit of tools. Each tool has a specific purpose, but when used in situations for which it was not designed, it loses its effectiveness. The carpenter who uses a wrench to drive nails will find that he not only loses efficiency but also damages the wrench in the process, causing it to slowly lose its effectiveness in the tasks for which it was designed. Instead of relying on straight lecture, "the hammer" of many professors, learn to employ other teaching tools. In the process, you will develop a far more effective and rewarding teaching style. Keep thorough notes throughout your course, evaluating the strengths and weaknesses of teaching tools you employed in each component of your course. Like a good carpenter, continually look for new tools, from the books listed at the end of this chapter as well as from peers; this will not only increase your efficiency, but will create in you the pride of a master craftsman.

Become invested also in developing the communication skills that differentiate the truly effective instructor from others. Vocal energy and variety (such as changing the pace of your delivery) are qualities you can develop when your focus in sensitized. Carefully observe, and where appropriate, begin to model the effective behaviors you notice are especially effective.

REVIEW OF KEY POINTS

- Form learning partnerships with the students in your class.
- Focus on how students learn before formulating your strategy of presenting material.
- Employ Bloom's Taxonomy to guide your teaching and evaluation strategies.
- Create and nurture an environment within your classroom that removes fear and engenders cooperation and trust.
- Use advance organizers to help students prepare their minds for learning.
- Limit lecturing to the objectives for which it is best suited.
- Use visual materials effectively to enhance student retention of lecture material.
- Employ questioning techniques that engage students' minds without creating fear.
- Follow prudent procedures when using videos to maximize learning effectiveness and minimize potential negative ramifications.
- Manage the use of guest speakers carefully to ensure that learning objectives are attained.

SUGGESTED READINGS

Brookfield, S. (1990). *The skillful teacher.* San Francisco: Jossey-Bass.

Caine, R., & Caine, G. (1991). *Making connections: Teaching and the human brain.* Alexandria, VA: Association for Supervision and Curriculum Development.

Cashin, W. E. (1990). Improving lectures. In M. Weimer & R. A. Neff (Eds.), *Teaching college: Collected readings for the new instructor* (pp. 59–63). Madison, WI: Magna.

Kindsvater, R., Wilen, W., & Ishler, M. (1996). *Dynamics of effective teaching* (3rd ed.). White Plains, NY: Longman.

9

STUDENT-DIRECTED LEARNING METHODS

Focus Questions

- How do students benefit from learning activities that they largely direct?
- Why are well-planned classroom discussions especially effective for undergraduate students?
- How do you effectively incorporate cooperative learning and other contemporary strategies into your teaching?

This chapter continues the discussion of learning begun in the previous chapter by focusing on the methodologies largely directed by students themselves. It is understandable that many instructors, but especially those new to teaching, question employing such methods. After all, Chapter 4 highlighted common learning challenges that suggest the need for a great deal of structure in the classroom. Supporters of a highly structured learning environment might ask, "If students are so capable of directing their own learning, why are colleges and universities even needed?" The contrasting perspective suggests that the ultimate goal of higher education in today's world is to enable students to access and process rapidly changing information effectively—in effect, to become their own lifelong teachers. Against this complex philosophical context, keep an open mind as we seek to explore the potential benefit of incorporating an appropriate measure of student-directed learning activities in your course.

THE CONTEMPORARY VIEW

We have stated several times that the successful teacher must "start where the learner is," and further suggested that many learners are not where we would hope they would be. At the same time we should remember that in the years since our own undergraduate days, the learning environment has changed a great deal. Television and other forms of rapid-turnaround information-delivery systems have greatly expanded the amount, as well as enhanced the currency and realism, of information to which students have been regularly exposed. In the 1940s, people read newspapers or listened on radio to accounts of World War II battles days after they occurred. Today we watch real battles on live television, complete with instant analysis by commentators well-researched in the strategies of each warring party. Personal computers—in schools, in homes and in the workplace—have empowered college students to pursue information of their own choosing and at their own pace. Such searches are far more efficient than the library visits that fueled the curiosity of older generations.

Several decades ago, most professors sought to shape and control the information flow that influenced their students, categorizing information into discrete compartments. Today, instructors typically face students whose greatest need is to sort out and make sense of a vast reservoir of information that can be assimilated into their everyday lives. This dynamic shift has fueled a movement toward emphasizing *natural* (or *genuine*) knowledge—making connections in the learner's mind between an existing knowledge base and new information or perspectives. This approach is consistent with achieving the higher-level learning within Bloom's Taxonomy—application, analysis, synthesis, and evaluation. Thus, in introductory courses in which students probably lack a significant knowledge base of terminology and basic concepts, a large ratio of instructor-directed learning activities employ analogies to related situations familiar to students. Advanced courses logically employ the more student-centered methodologies of this chapter, those that build upon the situationally-specific experiences the instructor can expect the students to have had.

Teaching exclusively as we have been taught may be comfortable for the instructor, but it is often not very effective with today's markedly different students. As you begin your teaching career, your success will be enhanced greatly if you develop a teaching style that regularly employs some student-directed methods. Getting to that point requires first an open mind to the methods outlined in this chapter, your willingness to experiment and subsequently analyze and reflect on your efforts, and regular discussions with colleagues more experienced in these methods.

ORCHESTRATING EFFECTIVE CLASSROOM DISCUSSIONS

Students learn best when their minds are effectively engaged. Research demonstrates that mental engagement during discussions is superior to that which occurs during lecture. When material is new to the majority of students, some degree of lecture, demonstration, or other instructor-directed method of introducing information and concepts is required. But for the information to take root in the student's mind, a brief period of discussion is especially effective. Discussion is appropriate for enabling students to do the following:

- Apply information delivered through instructor-directed means to situations they perceive as relevant.
- Evaluate the validity of their previously held beliefs.
- Analyze the diverse perspectives of other students within the class—a significant intellectual need among younger students, who (many would say) have largely been conditioned to be self-absorbed.
- Synthesize material delivered from diverse sources—textbook reading, the instructor, and other students from a range of backgrounds.
- Evaluate the evidence and logic provided by others against their own developing knowledge base.
- Gain motivation for pursuit of additional learning.

Students often retain information most effectively from classes in which the discussions were frequent, nonthreatening, lively, and constructive. Achieving such discussions is a significant challenge in contemporary classrooms, populated as it is by diverse students with varied experiences. Probably the major obstacle to orchestrating effective discussions is the large size of many classes. Because of fear of embarrassment, lack of knowledge, low self-esteem, reluctance to "stick out from the crowd," and other reasons, many students are reluctant to actively participate in large-group discussions. Many can cite vivid and detailed embarrassing experiences that prevent them from actively participating. You can probably relate to those situations from your own experience, so be sensitive to such feelings. To achieve an atmosphere in which classroom discussions achieve their fullest potential, employ the following common-sense practices:

- Early in the term, break the class into smaller groups of no more than five students (sometimes called "buzz groups") to discuss a critical question.
- Establish ground rules for discussion groups, including the valuing of all opinions and the expectation of some participation from each student.
- Before discussion begins, have students introduce themselves to each other and select a spokesperson for reporting their collective conclusions.
- Monitor the discussion within groups to ensure that "ground rules" are understood and followed.
- Elicit participation from all students by posing nonthreatening, "opinion" questions.

- Have each group report their findings in an orderly way, encouraging amplification of key points.
- Summarize the overall activity by citing appropriate points you heard within groups and asking for illumination from individuals making those points.
- In subsequent classes, expand group sizes somewhat.
- After an appropriate class culture of tolerance and openness is established, begin posing relatively broad, yet not overly abstract, questions to the entire class, then encourage them to apply course concepts through subsequent questions.
- Pause to allow students ample time to mentally process questions, encouraging their more grounded response which will build confidence and encourage heightened engagement.
- Call on a respondent who has raised a hand or who has through less obvious nonverbal signals indicated a willingness to participate.
- Scan the entire room so that you subsequently call on someone physically distant from the present speaker, creating a more dynamic atmosphere.
- Avoid calling on those whose body language indicates they are not mentally engaged—it will only stifle their future and others' present participation.
- Encourage involvement of nonparticipants out of earshot of other students.
- Provide feedback on the positive components of responses, especially from those who have heretofore been reluctant to participate.
- Be reluctant to directly criticize an "incorrect" response; instead, ask if someone "sees it another way," being sure to clarify the correct information before moving the discussion along.
- When discussion bogs down, summarize appropriate points before posing an additional question.
- Be extremely careful about providing the single, "correct" answer before students have had a chance to formulate their own responses. Premature explanations from the instructor condition students to wait for such responses in subsequent discussions and stifle their mental engagement.
- Close discussion positively by asking if someone would like "the final word" or by stating how the conclusions apply to the course objectives.

The best discussion leaders occasionally will experience challenges in achieving a free-flowing, highly engaged dialogue. Three of the most common problems are: lack of general participation, discussions that divert into areas inappropriate for your course, and highly personal or emotional reactions by students. Although these can be reduced when you thoroughly plan and anticipate the discussions you will hold, such problems, especially during the early stages of your teaching, are likely to occur nonetheless. Each requires that you employ a grounded strategy in order to achieve a positive outcome.

Even after you have achieved a positive environment for classroom discussion, you sometimes will sense passivity from much of the class. This is especially common as the course winds down the last few weeks and students are overwhelmed with assignments due, in addition to the normal challenges of their daily lives. First, remember your Transactional Analysis training from Chapter 7 and avoid the tendency to slip into your "judgmental parent"—punishing students for nonparticipation. Instead, build common ground by saying something like, "You look a little withdrawn," and give a student or two a chance to vent some emotion. You might shift the order of your lesson plan slightly and provide some instructor-directed activities. Later in the class meeting, you might elicit discussion most effectively by first employing the small-group strategy that you used early in the term and a more humorous and engaging debriefing than normal. Also, providing increased positive feedback to individual students, as well as comments of a classwide nature such as, "I'm really proud of the way this class has…" will likely pay big dividends.

Discussions that go far afield cause noncontributing students to become disengaged, and they take the focus off your learning objectives. Unattended, such discussions quickly establish a pattern in the class. In the interest of building a positive classroom atmosphere, many new instructors have been reluctant to assert the need to focus on a specific learning objective, then spent the remainder of the term feeling a loss of control. As in most problems, the best solution to wayward discussions is prevention. This is best achieved through a clarification of the parameters of the discussion—reinforced visually through use of a chalkboard or overhead projector. If the discussion starts to wander, a simple reminder of the parameters is usually effective and nonthreatening.

Occasionally, permitting a degree of wandering makes the discussion more lively and engaging. However, you must be proactive about stepping in early to refocus on your goals. Do so by first acknowledging the collective experiences of the wandering speakers, then asking a transitional question that returns the discussion to its proper focus. If such measures prove ineffective, remember the *Pareto Rule,* which warns you that 80% of your challenges will come from 20% of your students. For the student who repeatedly makes unrelated comments, you might say something akin to "That's an excellent point, one we will explore further when we get to Chapter 14," or otherwise seek to intensify their focus on your learning goals. Sometimes it is useful to speak with such students out of earshot of others—first thanking them for their involvement in class discussions but going on to ask their help in encouraging the less involved students by allowing you to seek their participation.

No doubt influenced by sensationalized news coverage and confrontational interview programs on television, students sometimes contribute highly emotional and frequently personal reactions during classroom discussions. They periodically evolve abruptly into arguments, dividing the class along gender, racial, political, or religious lines. More often than ever before, students are likely to directly challenge your opinion and authority. The key in such situations is positive anticipation, knowing your personal comfort level with such situations, and knowing your students' limits. If discussions become heated, stay appropriately involved with your most "adult" tone of voice, asking questions which return the focus to objective points made in the textbook, lecture, or other learning experience to which students have been exposed. Use the board or overhead projector to list points and summarize; this process will minimize the repetition of argumentative points and engender objectivity.

Like so many activities in teaching, orchestrating effective classroom discussions is a balancing act—between the costs and potential benefits of time invested, and the personal rewards and the damage that can accrue. Discussions are most effective when carefully planned with your learning objectives clearly in mind.

COOPERATIVE LEARNING

One of the more popular instructional developments in recent years is the widespread employment of "cooperative learning," which places students within small groups to pursue outcomes that are mutually beneficial. Although you may hear the terms "collaborative," "peer," or "group learning," which most practitioners regard as largely synonymous, cooperative learning contributes to an egalitarian environment in the classroom and shifts the role of the instructor to that of a facilitator of learning who draws on the existing collective knowledge base of students and integrates additional information when appropriate. It tends to engender a much more participatory and flexible learning environment in the classroom. Cooperative learning mirrors the movement within the American workplace toward utilization of self-directed work teams to solve problems more effectively.

Like any tool, cooperative learning has both strengths and weaknesses. Five advantages include:

- Actively engaging the learning system of each student, through positive interdependence
- Empowering each student to pursue learning that he or she perceives as relevant, thus creating individual accountability
- Building the interpersonal skills so necessary for success in the larger society

- Developing solutions that integrate more perspectives and the ground-edness that flows from group processing
- Providing the instructor with the opportunity to more effectively manage the learning environment

The major disadvantage of cooperative learning occurs among a typically small minority of students who will sometimes take advantage of the freedom of this approach to piggyback on the efforts of other group members. Therefore, it is incumbent upon the instructor to assume the following roles effectively:

- Before class, decide on group size and composition, arrangment of the room, and materials to be used.
- Monitor and intervene as needed; this includes assisting with the task, processing of discoveries, and bringing closure to the exercise.
- Structure win–win outcomes, individual accountability, and intergroup cooperation by specifying desired behaviors.
- Evaluate the quantity and quality of students' learning.

The time you invest in additional planning for cooperative learning activities is usually rewarded by the freedom you experience to monitor classroom implementation and the opportunity to provide individualized coaching for students whose needs are greatest.

Typically, groups of three to four students work most effectively. With fewer students than this per group, there is too little information and experience for them to develop good solutions. With larger groups, individual students, especially shy ones, have less opportunity to be fully engaged, and to contribute to the group solution. Larger groups also lend themselves to being dominated by one or two students, yielding a rushed solution, while providing weaker students a "free ride." Although it is somewhat more time-consuming, discussions are more lively and solutions are more broad-based when members are diverse in age, gender, race, and other factors. Thus, it is typically more effective to assign members to groups randomly, rather than allow students to form groups themselves.

To establish work groups, simply decide how many students you want in each group, count the total number of students in the class, then divide the first number into the second. That will yield the total number of groups you will need. Beginning at a convenient place within the class, have students "count off" up to the number of groups you need. Then have all the "number ones" stand up and move to a certain part of the room to conduct their discussion. Proceed with the "number twos," etc. You can also achieve randomness by having students draw numbers or items of a particular type or color from a container.

The effectiveness of cooperative learning largely depends on the quality of the learning materials you employ. Having students group together to answer the review questions at the end of the textbook chapter is typically only slightly more effective than assigning the same material as homework. Custom-designed case problems, using characters and situations with which students can easily identify, will provide a dynamic learning opportunity that cannot be duplicated at home or in the library. Materials that require students to explore their personal values and to talk with others of diverse beliefs create a truly synergistic environment.

When employing cooperative group activities, it is critical to monitor the progress of each group, ensuring that they are progressing adequately toward the achievement of the learning goal. First, move quickly throughout the classroom to gauge understanding of the assignment among all groups. Then, circulate more deliberately to provide an additional resource to groups that might get stuck. Rather than simply provide information, ask questions that will stimulate students to uncover clues enabling them to solve their own problems. You will undoubtedly see your stronger students emerge as teachers of their peers within each group, more firmly mastering their own understanding of the concepts. At the same, the learning of weaker students is enhanced because information and concepts are explained by their peers in terms they are more likely to understand.

Following completion of group activities, it is essential to lead a discussion that enables students to make mental connections to the learning objectives and to place their discoveries in proper context. Instructor-posed questions, both rhetorical and pointed, are especially effective in the debriefing process. Before class ends be sure to bring the activity to a satisfactory level of closure. This might include the assignment of additional out-of-class research that enables the development of a more comprehensive solution to the case problem at the opening of the following class meeting.

You are likely to feel uncomfortable in your initial attempt at employing cooperative learning, possibly to the extent of feeling guilty about not being "in charge" of the classroom. You might also feel you have misused time which could have been more effectively employed "covering" more material. Some students, imprinted by the consumer mindset mentioned earlier, might send signals that you have somehow shirked your responsibilities by not "teaching" the class. After objective reflection on the quality of the discussion, a monitoring of students' overall reactions, and perhaps discussion with experienced facilitators of cooperative learning activities, you will likely overcome your negative feelings in a very short time. Remember, your goal is to maximize the depth of students' understanding; we predict you will find yourself valuing the potential of cooperative learning and looking for additional opportunities to employ this most effective instructional strategy.

ROLE PLAYING

As a teaching methodology, role playing attempts to help students discover personal meanings within their social worlds and to resolve personal dilemmas with the aid of their social group. Through the risk-taking inherent in improvisation, the student will typically overwhelmingly validate the educational payoff of the activity. Role playing is more intensive and personal than other teaching–learning methodologies, and has the following benefits:

- Enables students to develop an understanding of others' perspectives
- Encourages students to work with others in analyzing situations and developing workable solutions
- Provides a rich, realistic environment for students to apply concepts they have learned
- Gives students insights into interpersonal challenges they are likely to face in their careers and private lives
- Enables students to effectively contrast problem-solving methods by role playing a situation several times from diverse perspectives
- Provides a constructive channel through which feelings can be expressed and feedback processed
- Enables students to build self-esteem and confidence
- Helps students realize that college courses can be fun

Whether the scenarios selected are deadly serious or light-hearted, focused on the *affective, psychomotor* or *cognitive* learning domains or a combination, role playing requires an instructor to do the following:

- Identify and introduce to the class a sufficiently explicit problem, including an appropriate context.
- Thoroughly explain the rules of the social system that will guide the role-play exercise.
- Match and orient students to their roles in the activity.
- Find appropriate methods of involving especially shy students, perhaps as chief observer/evaluators.
- Set the stage for students, including the establishment of observation tasks.
- Monitor the activity to ensure it pursues an appropriate direction.
- Afterward, hold a class discussion to assess the accomplishment of desired learning outcomes.

Role playing is an especially effective teaching–learning tool within the social sciences and occupationally oriented disciplines, contributing to long-term retention of fundamental concepts. What more effective way of promoting an understanding of the judicial system could be found than by having students with assigned roles conduct a mock trial? Or what more valid means of mastering an understanding of the role of entrepreneurship could be utilized than by having students develop a business plan, which is then presented to a group of potential financial backers? How better might one develop conversational foreign language skills than to role play an everyday situation staged in an appropriate location?

Many otherwise passive students will prepare extensively to deliver an authentic representation of a role that will be so closely scrutinized by their peers. When prompted early in the process, such students will go on to ask themselves all sorts of "what if" questions as they move toward their presentation, continuously improving the quality of their learning up through and including the presentation. Such learning activities clearly have the potential for enriched learning unmatched by other instructional methods.

EXPERIENTIAL LEARNING

Subject to multiple interpretations, we use the phrase *experiential learning* in its more narrow sense to include activities that require students to react to a situation extemporaneously. Some are "games"—requiring students to toss a ball or maneuver through a "spider web." Others are self-analysis activities. The "learning payoff" in each case, however, is not so much the activity itself, but a skilled debriefing that engenders personal reflection and an expansion of natural knowledge. Such activities were popularized in the 1980s by Outward Bound, an organization with roots in the wartime training of British sailors. Various "initiatives" are designed to enable students to discover, in a very grounded way, the nuances of sensitivity, teamwork, and leadership.

Effective debriefing requires the facilitator to share his or her observations and to solicit increasingly more insightful responses from participants. Students are encouraged to make connections between the initiative and the environment for which they are being trained. Experiential training holds significant potential for enlivening a wide range of courses and should be investigated by instructors seeking a truly memorable experience for students.

DISTANCE (OR "DISTRIBUTED") LEARNING

In recent years, electronic teaching technologies have dramatically changed the learning environment in higher education. Each of these—instructional television and the personal computer most notably—enable the individual student to access learning materials far more conveniently. Freed from the extensive classroom attendance requirements which electronic courses offer, more students than ever before—those who live in remote areas, are employed in jobs with irregular hours or must juggle multiple tasks—are able to pursue a college education.

While distance learning methodologies have been largely dominated by the full-time faculties of colleges and universities, adjunct professors increasingly are becoming involved in computer-based instruction. Electronic mail is being widely employed by adjunct professors to communicate with time- and place-challenged students, to collect and return assignments, and even to administer quizzes and examinations. Increasingly, personal web pages are being employed by instructors to continually update and customize learning resources for students. More than ever before, students are interacting with each other through these electronic means, pursuing knowledge of their own, rather than the instructor's choice. As technology becomes more sophisticated and its adoption becomes more widespread, increasing numbers of instructors will employ it in some measure to more effectively deliver their courses. Adjunct professors who possess highly specialized knowledge and employ these methods will see their value to colleges and universities increase even more.

Technology is markedly shifting the relationship with undergraduate students so the instructor becomes a partner, resource, coach, and facilitator rather than merely a presenter of information; provides more individualized, rather than mass, instruction; deals with students more actively engaged in self-directed learning; and assesses student achievement based more on projects than on examinations.

While distance education delivery systems initially focused largely on occupational, especially technical, education, it has since been widely embraced by those in other disciplines of the college and university. Creative writing, for example, is more effectively and efficiently learned when the professor's feedback is provided in a much shorter turnaround time than has been traditionally possible.

In short, distance learning is extremely student-directed and student-paced, providing adjunct instructors opportunities to markedly increase their impact on higher education. You are encouraged to explore the wide range of resources available for integrating its use into your teaching.

FIELD WORK

For decades, institutions involved in preparing students for occupations have employed *cooperative education* (not to be confused with "cooperative learning"), such as internships and externships, to place students in actual work settings and, in the process, link course content to the demands of the business world. Many can attest to the learning value of those experiences and to the accompanying opportunities it provides for students to make valuable career-building contacts.

Since the late 1960s, when student idealism led to the demand for increased relevance in higher education, field work experiences have become a significant part of the curricula in other discipline areas as well. In fact, there has been a resurgence in *service learning* in very recent years to rival that of the "peace and love generation." Field work is highly motivating to many students and provides a rich opportunity to develop the higher level learning of Bloom's Taxonomy. It has the potential to provide insights that will markedly influence students' perceptions of their communities and their roles within them, and it assuredly aids in making more informed career and lifestyle decisions.

The challenge with field work lies in ensuring the legitimate role of each experience in achieving predetermined learning objectives. While students will value the independence inherent in field work and the personal satisfaction they receive from it, we must strive to ensure that the experiences they pursue contribute to learning that is transferrable to a wider arena. Thus, not only must learning activities be carefully selected, but opportunities for reflection and analysis must be built in to the field work experience.

If you plan to include a field work experience in your class, one tool you should strongly consider using, to ensure the learning value of the field work, is an individual *contract* with each participating student. This process generally involves a three-step procedure:

1. Develop parameters of the experience, including the product you expect students to generate (such as reaction paper, journal, video, and/or oral report), its evaluation criteria, and related logistical requirements. Provide a printed copy for each student, with a list of possible topics for stimulating their thinking.

2. Create a proposal form for students to submit for your review before their actually beginning the experience. This will give you the opportunity to provide some direction and minimize the chance that students will waste time employing ineffective or inefficient tactics.

3. Review the student proposal and provide written comments. This becomes a binding contract when returned to the student. That is, for a certain body of work, submitted within stated time parameters and performance standards, you agree to award a particular grade.

A model student field work contract is included as Appendix 9.1, but you may want to consult your mentor or instructional leader before finalizing your plan to ensure that it meets commonly accepted standards of your situation. Field work experiences, although potentially extremely valuable to students, need to be examined for their impact on the overall curriculum and the goals of the department and institution.

STUDENT PRESENTATIONS

As you will see in Chapter 11, students master and retain learning very effectively when they present their work to others. Anecdotally, we each can remember details from a school presentation made many years ago. Regardless of the discipline area, your students will likely benefit from making presentations as well—as long as sound practices are followed.

First, recognize that most people of any age experience anxiety over making presentations and need some degree of reassurance to be successful. One key form of reassurance that many professors overlook is providing students with an adequate overview of the assignment. As a result, students commonly make unfocused, disjointed presentations that contribute to their feeling ineffective. A series of such presentations makes your managing classroom time problematic, leading to some students not having adequate time to make their presentations. Well in advance therefore, students should be provided in hardcopy the goals and objectives of the presentation, as well as a detailed rubric that will be used in its evaluation. A model is provided in Appendix 9.2. If your course has an especially large enrollment, or building teamwork is an especially desirable goal, you might consider having students make presentations in a group setting, e.g., as members of a forum or panel discussion.

If yours is an introductory course or if students voice considerable anxiety, provide coaching in techniques of effective presentations and consistently model excellent presentation skills for them. Emphasize techniques of gaining viewers' attention, effectively using visual aids, and vividly concluding a presentation. When you introduce the assignment ask a student with a proven track record in another professor's class to demonstrate effective presentation skills. Or, show and explain a video of an excellent presentation. A final, but far less desirable option, is for you to deliver a presentation yourself, emphasizing in advance the key points which students should observe. Some students are likely to have trouble objectively separating such a presentation from your regular lecture or demonstration, while others might view such a presentation as *the* model and work so hard to duplicate it that they appear unnatural.

For both viewers and speakers to derive full value from presentations, feedback must be plentiful, objective, and consistent. We recommend providing viewers input into the evaluation of their peers using the rubric as a guideline. One frequently used method is for viewers to be given 5" by 8" index cards and asked to anonymously write three strong points and one suggested improvement for each presentation. These cards are returned to the presenter, attached to the evaluation form completed by the instructor.

Recalling an axiom of effective management practices, praise from the professor for student presentations needs to be delivered in public, while any constructive criticism should be given in private. Having your students present their work in a supportive environment markedly increases the retention of material they delivered as well as that presented by their peers. It also contributes to the enhancement of student self-efficacy and esteem.

Lastly, nearly any good idea can be overdone! Unless yours is a public speaking course, resist the increasingly common tendency to have students present the majority of the course content through various types of presentations. Consumer-oriented students are likely to perceive that such an arrangement denies them access to the expertise of a professor for whom they invested considerable financial resources. Discuss this issue with your mentor or instructional leader before finalizing plans for your course.

THROUGH THE ADJUNCTS' EYES

Karen:

In an effort to build a warmer classroom environment, I used a technique in class last night that one of the other adjuncts I have met told me about. She called it "cooperative learning." Rather than assigning the case problems at the end of the chapter as homework for individual students, I divided the class into groups of 3, then had each group develop a single response for which they would all get credit. I had a really good feeling about it initially, as the students got very involved in their discussion. Some students who had not asked a question or made a comment the entire term got pretty engaged. I need to rethink my strategy though, because at times I seemed to stifle, rather than promote, active participation. As I was circulating throughout the classroom, several students asked pointed questions to which I unfortunately gave them too quick an answer. That served to encourage others to ask questions of me, rather than solve the problems themselves within their group. Cooperative learning has great potential for helping students understand this material, but I need to let them explore on their own more, even make a few mistakes. I would be better to probe the groups through Socratic questioning like my law school professors did, rather than give them the answer.

Margaret:

At the end of last week's class meeting, I conducted an informal, anonymous evaluation of the course so far. Not surprisingly, the students said I had used so many videos and guest speakers that some didn't feel like I was really teaching the class. Afterwards, I committed myself to finding some additional methods that would help students better understand the often complicated material of this course.

Many of the training programs we conducted at my corporation used a workshop approach, in which employees would solve problems in small groups. Last night in class, I used some materials I had modified from some one of those workshops, and it went over great! It was the most personally satisfying class we have had all semester and, like videos and guest speakers, this teaching method didn't require me to be the "expert on stage." As I debriefed the activity I really liked the role I was playing. The students really gained some insights that the other methods didn't provide.

Juan:

Still feeling a little frustrated in my ability to engage the more mature students in my class as well as I'd like, I led the class in something very different last night. Borrowing an idea from one of my high school teachers, I developed some very basic scenarios and had students role play responses that reflected their understanding of the material we have covered in the last two chapters. I was amazed with the results! One fellow, probably in his 40s, who has been a grouch all semester, really got into his role. He was clever and funny, and at one point took his part up to, but not over, a very delicate line with a female student. She responded well to the "mental sparring," as did the other females in the class. I'm sure this activity helped students master the information in a much more effective way. Although I will use role playing later in the semester, I need to plan carefully and be careful not to overuse it.

TIPS FOR THRIVING

This chapter has exposed you to some of the more widely used student-directed learning methods, but there are dozens of additional tactics and strategies available for enabling students to "discover" things worth learning. Many of these are activities that students can complete in a relatively short amount of time, but which add considerable flavor to your course. Among our favorites are physical games, such as a ball toss and "hula hoop" exercise that enable students, when effectively debriefed, to discover the dynamics of teamwork and its role in the workplace. Another is the pencil-and-paper self-analysis activities commonly found in specialized magazines. Such activities stimulate students to discuss issues with family members and friends, providing reinforcement and the opportunity for added insights that flow naturally from explaining things learned to others.

Besides being the manager of the context of the class you deliver, perhaps your greatest role is that of "champion" of your discipline. Your passion and creativity are the spark that ignite the fuel imbedded in the minds of your students. When you demonstrate that mindset genuinely and persistently, your students will become far more effectively self-directed than you ever could have imagined.

REVIEW OF KEY POINTS

- Today's students are likely to possess a knowledge base you can build on through student-directed learning activities.
- Resist the trap of teaching only as you have been taught yourself.
- Students' minds are more engaged during classroom discussions and other self-directed learning methods than activities directed by instructors.
- For classroom discussions, use small groups until students attain a satisfactory comfort level.
- Use cooperative learning techniques to enable students to effectively process and apply material from your presentations.
- Resist accepting the few negatives of "cooperative learning"—it has far more benefits.
- Employ role playing to enable students to understand diverse perspectives.
- Experiment with experiential learning initiatives to enliven your class.
- If possible, use some distance learning methods to make your course more convenient and effective for students.
- Field work experiences provide students with a rich opportunity to develop higher level learning goals.
- Employ student learning contracts when using field work.
- Integrate student presentations into your course to increase retention of material and build self-efficacy of students.

SUGGESTED READINGS

Arreola, R. A. (1995). Distance education: The emergence of America's virtual university. In P. Seldin (Ed.), *Improving college teaching* (pp. 219–233). Bolton, MA: Anker.

Colberg, J., Desbery, P., & Trimble, K. (1996). *The case for education: Contemporary approaches for using case methods.* Needham Heights, MA: Allyn & Bacon.

Davis, B. (1993). *Tools for teaching.* San Francisco: Jossey-Bass.

MacGregor, J. (1990). Collaborative learning: Shared inquiry as a process of reform. In M. D. Svinicki (Ed.), *The changing face of college teaching* (New Directions for Teaching and Learning No. 42) (pp. 19–30). San Francisco: Jossey-Bass.

Magnan, R. (Ed.). (1990). *147 practical tips for teaching professors.* Madison, WI: Magna.

McKeachie, W. et al. (1994). *Teaching tips.* Lexington, MA: D.C. Heath.

Neff, R. A., & Weimer, M. (Eds.). (1990). *Teaching college: Collected readings for the new instructor.* Madison, WI: Magna.

Silberman, M. (1996). *Active learning: 101 strategies to teach any subject.* Needham Heights, MA: Allyn & Bacon.

Svinicki, M. D. (1990). Changing the face of your teaching. In M. D. Svinicki (Ed.), *The changing face of college teaching* (New Directions for Teaching and Learning No. 42) (pp. 5–15). San Francisco: Jossey-Bass.

Vella, J. (1994). *Learning to listen, learning to teach.* San Francisco: Jossey-Bass.

APPENDIX 9.1   MODEL FIELD WORK CONTRACT AND PROJECT PROPOSAL

MAN 2021 B1
Individual Field Work Project

Please use the following topics as a **guide** in your formulation of a project idea that will be relevant to your present job or future career. (Note: ABC Company is a fictitious name. It is assumed that all projects will focus on a **real,** not a fictitious, organization.)

A Training Needs Analysis for ABC Company

ABC Company's Employee Recognition Program

An Orientation Video for New Employees of the ABC Company

A Performance Appraisal Program for ABC Company

A Handbook for Employees of ABC Company

ABC Company's "Adopt a School" Program

A Training Manual for Clerical Employees of ABC Company

A Wellness Program for Employees of ABC Company

The ABC Company Compensation Program—An Analysis and Evaluation

The Merchandising Plan for the ABC Store

An Analysis of Customer Attitudes for ABC Company

The Management Development Program of ABC Company

An Employee Recruitment Program for ABC Company

"Burnout"—Its Impact on the Nursing Profession

An Analysis of the Leadership Style of P. J. Johnston

Projects should answer the standard questions of who, what, when, where, why, how, and how much. Narrative should be written in the "third person." When research sources of information are used, they should be cited according to APA standards. The project should be professional in appearance, and thus produced on a word processor.

After selecting your project idea, complete the attached proposal form, and submit it to the instructor **no later than the identified deadline.** Proposals will be reviewed and returned with comments at the class meeting following.

Proposals due: February 22, 20—

Final projects due: April 4, 20—

MAN 2021 B1
Project Proposal

Student _____

Identify the **product** of your project, e.g., a 15-page paper, a 10-minute video, etc.:

Identify the learning objective of your project, making a clear connection to the course objectives identified on the syllabus:

Provide a detailed outline of your strategy in completing the mini project:

Identify the number and nature of feedback session(s) you would propose holding with the instructor prior to final submission of the project:

Proposal deadline: **February 22, 20—**

Final projects due: **April 4, 20—**

APPENDIX 9.2   PRESENTATION EVALUATION SCORING RUBRIC

Goal of Presentation _____

Student _____

Opening   (___ points possible)   **Earned** _____
Did presenter effectively gain attention of audience?
Topic appropriate for this audience?
Presentation effectively "framed," i.e., parameters established?

Comments:

Body of presentation   (___ points possible)   **Earned** _____
Presentation remain focused clearly on topic?
Logical points developed to support topic?
Presentation follow a logical, effective sequence?
Sufficient evidence presented to support speaker's point of view?
Appropriate props, visual aids, utilized?

Comments:

Closing   (___ points possible)   **Earned** _____
Essential points effectively summarized?
Presentation end on a strong closing statement or question?

Comments:

Vocal Qualities   (___ points possible)   **Earned** _____
Pitch?   Volume?
Rate?   Articulation?
Tone?   Vocal variety?

Comments:

Non-verbal Qualities   (___ points possible)   **Earned** _____
Facial expression?   Gestures?
Eye contact?   Use of notes?
Posture?

Comments:

Additional Comments:

                                                 TOTAL SCORE _____

10

DEVELOPING, ADMINISTERING, AND ANALYZING EXAMS

Focus Questions

- What are the characteristics of an effective college-level course examination?
- How should the professor approach constructing the examination?
- What special precautions should be taken when administering a test?
- What are the critical follow-up activities to an examination?

Few activities of teaching cause the new professor as much concern as developing examinations that accurately evaluate students' learning. Although examinations serve to provide data upon which the professor formulates course grades, they play significant additional roles for both the instructor and students. Effective exams provide feedback for both students and professors to build assessments of their success, and for some students to make decisions that influence their continuation in the course and, perhaps, the discipline. Examination results can build students' self-confidence or inhibit its development. In discussions with their support network of peers and family members, students often reveal that test results can be either a great source of pride or of severe disappointment and embarrassment. Far more than many instructors seem to realize, the results of exams dramatically affect the morale of both students and teachers and contribute to the quality of the learning environment within the classroom.

EXAMINATION DEVELOPMENT STRATEGY

Most of us can probably cite horror stories from our own lives about a test-taking experience. One of the authors of this book recalls being asked on the final examination of a particular course to identify the author of the course textbook. Its author was not a person cited during the course or otherwise known to have made a significant contribution to the discipline. Few students studied that bit of trivia and consequently missed a question whose only purpose seemed to be to round out the total number of questions required to make the exam scores simpler to calculate. Clearly, the professor developing the exam should have invested a few more minutes in the development of his test, so that the final perception of his teaching was far more positive. As in this case, much of students' perception about the effectiveness of an instructor flows from how tests were managed. Probably the most common negative student perception is that the test was punitive in its approach, relying on tricky or trivial questions. As you begin formulating a strategy of test development, be especially mindful that tests:

- Are necessary for instructors to determine if students are learning
- Must be well-designed if they are to be effective
- Are only *estimates* of what students have learned
- Can be abused, even by well-intentioned instructors

Therefore, your approach to testing must incorporate several perspectives—the student's, your instructional leader's, perhaps the textbook author's, and your own. Students grow best when they receive appropriate, timely, specific, and positive feedback. Students suffer when tests are punitive, vague, disconnected to the material, or capricious.

Though we typically associate one overriding type of instructor decision with examinations—grade determination—there are others which are at least, if not more, important. Tests should accurately assess how well students are progressing toward the achievement of their overall educational goals. Exams should also contribute to making better instructional decisions, such as how much class time should be dedicated to concepts that students did not sufficiently understand. Finally, well-designed exams should contribute to diagnostic decisions related to directing students to resources that might contribute to their success. With so much riding on the results, the examination must be developed based on sound principles and a sensitive, constructive approach focused on long-term learning goals.

Often, the novice professor waits to "cover the material" to be included on a particular examination before beginning its development. Out of an effort to either save time or to ensure that all test items were covered, this practice typically leads to less-than-ideal results. Given the many demands on their time, adjunct professors are seldom able to construct effective test items, word process, and print the examination in the timeframe between finishing the coverage of the material and the actual administration of the examination. Waiting so late to develop the exam also provides insufficient time to de-bug questions and proofread the final draft, raising the possibility that errors will affect the results of the test, create problems for students, and embarrass the professor.

By developing the examination prior to covering its contents in class, the professor will be more likely to emphasize the most critical points at the appropriate time. In its most extreme form, this practice is referred to as "teaching to the test." Though it is often criticized by traditionalists, this practice might be understood best when positioned at the end of a continuum whose opposite end is "not giving students a clue to the content of a test." Based on your own values and the ability, motivation, and time availability of students, together with common practices of the department you must decide where to be on that continuum. Since the ramifications of test results are so great, you are encouraged to discuss this issue thoroughly with your discipline leader or mentor prior to developing your first examination.

QUALITIES OF AN EFFECTIVE EXAMINATION

Traditionally, experts in educational testing have emphasized the importance of three qualities of an effective examination.

- *Content validity* refers to a test's ability to effectively evaluate what it is supposed to measure. More specifically, did the test items, i.e., questions, elicit responses that demonstrated student mastery of a particular concept? A "comprehensive" final exam that derived 50% of its questions from a single chapter in a textbook that was covered in its entirety would lack content validity.
- *Reliability* refers to the dependability or consistency of students' scores. Stated another way, if the test were repeated, would the scores remain essentially the same? A test with questions that engender a great deal of guessing by most students would lack reliability, because results in a similarly prepared group of students would probably vary greatly.
- *Objectivity* refers to a test's score flowing primarily from the student performance being measured, rather than the idiosyncrasies of the instructor constructing the exam. Tests with many questions worded as if they were "fact," when they are actually the opinion of the test developer, lack objectivity.

These three general test properties should undergird your test development strategy. Also, in order to create fair and effective examinations, you should consider the following principles:

- An effective examination should be a learning, as well as an evaluative, experience. It should serve as a thorough review of the content addressed, enabling students to deepen their mastery of the concepts included.
- Each examination should be a win–win situation for students and the professor, rather than the battle of wits that has so often been the case. If many students regularly must re-read test questions several times to clarify what the wording of the questions seeks to elicit, students are losing.
- An effective examination should evaluate the most critical concepts and not blatantly trivial information.
- An effective examination consistently differentiates levels of students mastery by including a mix of basic, intermediate, and difficult questions. Your examinations should contribute to your teaching strategy of building *meaningful* rather than *surface* knowledge by including an appropriate ratio of higher-level questions.
- An effective examination has no significant surprises for the well-prepared student.
- A well-developed examination will reflect the time spent on the concept in class or otherwise emphasized by the instructor. As students, we all hated it when questions not covered at all in class appeared on the examination. Nearly as much, we felt cheated when an activity requiring a large chunk of class time was not included among the questions, and we probably paid less attention the next time such an activity was conducted.

Although the task of incorporating so many properties might seem a little overwhelming, you will be rewarded richly when you experience the results of your first well-designed exam. While students are known to commonly experience "test anxiety," it also is common for instructors to become anxious over the administration of an exam. Invest the extra time to develop a valid, reliable, and objective first exam so that after the test you experience the type of "rush" that successful students feel.

DEVELOPING OBJECTIVE TEST ITEMS

Novice teachers often wonder about the best format for their tests. As is often the case in teaching, there is no single "best" answer—it depends on the nature of the learning, the level of the students' knowledge and experience, and other factors. In selecting the appropriate format for your tests, first ask "Where does my course fall in the sequence of the curriculum?"

Introductory courses especially often employ *forced choice* test items, e.g., true–false, multiple choice, matching, and so on. The term *objective* test, defined somewhat differently in another context earlier in this chapter, is often used synonymously with forced choice. Perhaps the single most important thing to remember is to **test at the level you have taught.** Among students' greatest test frustrations is to be taught at Bloom's knowledge and application levels only, then to be tested at the application and synthesis levels. That is not only unfair to students but is inherently ineffective in the teaching and learning process.

On the surface, true–false items are easy for the instructor to develop and use in a test. However, to make a true–false question the least bit challenging, the instructor must employ tactics which are often regarded as tricky by students. This leads to heated discussions when scored exams are being reviewed in class, and reinforces the adversarial relationship we should be trying to avoid. Regardless of how well, or how poorly, written, true–false test items provide students with a 50% chance of success—even without reading the question! On balance, true–false questions are not as effective in most college course environments as other types of test items.

Well-written "matching-item questions can be very effective for evaluating students' mastery of vocabulary words or for linking knowledge items to one another. Typically they are not appropriate for more sophisticated levels of learning. The exercise found in Appendix 10.1 will enable you to refine your skills in developing matching-item sets for examinations.

"Multiple-choice" items are no doubt the favorite testing method for most instructors of undergraduate classes. When properly worded, multiple-choice items can be valid, reliable and objective in situations calling for knowledge, comprehension, application and even limited analysis learning situations. Therefore, it clearly would be in most instructors' best interest to develop their skills in creating effective multiple-choice test items. Some tips for creating effective multiple-choice items follow.

- Tailor (or adapt, if you are beginning with test bank questions) the difficulty level of the test item to the reading comprehension level of your students.
- Ensure that correct answers are objective, rather than opinions, unless you clearly indicate what famous person or recognized body held the opinion.
- To reduce guessing, offer 4 to 6 response options to each question, ensuring that the wrong choices ("distractors") are plausible responses rather than "throw-aways."
- Arrange the question so that the opening statement ("stem") includes all necessary qualifications needed for answer selection, creating response options that are relatively short.

- Ensure that both the correct response and distractors are approximately the same length, with similar amounts of detail and levels of complexity.
- Ensure that none of the wrong choices could be considered correct by someone truly knowledgeable in the field.
- Avoid "clangers," such as having the subject–verb agreement correct for only one option, or the last word of the stem being "an" when the correct response begins with a vowel.
- Omit nonfunctional words and trivial facts.
- Avoid negative constructions. For example, rather than "Which of the following is *not...*," use "All of the following are true, *except.*"
- Although limited use of phrases such as "Both A and B are correct," "None of the above," or "All of the above" might contribute to the effectiveness of a test, be careful that such items are not disproportionately the correct response. Too often in many tests, "All of the above" is the correct answer.
- Avoid response options that overlap or include each other. For example, "Less than 25%" overlaps with the choice "Less than 50%."
- Whenever possible, for *application* and *analysis* questions use situations to which students can easily relate, thus encouraging longer-term retention.

Since instructors are often anxious about developing effective exams, many rely on test banks provided by the publishers of their textbooks to generate questions for their exams. There seems to be an inherent confidence that questions included in test banks have been validated through extensive classroom use. While many test banks are valuable resources for effective questions as well as great time-savers, be aware that some have poor questions that have not been validated at all. Some test bank questions are totally unusable, while others require editing before they can be used effectively. Your students deserve a valid, reliable exam and have the right to expect you to provide it. Poor questions, whether from test banks, or any other source, are inexcusable. The exercise in Appendix 10.2 will equip you to develop more effective multiple-choice test items.

EFFECTIVE ESSAY TEST ITEMS

Although objective tests clearly are convenient to score, many observers attribute an overdependence on their use as a contributing factor to a marked decline in the writing and critical thinking abilities of students. In contrast, essay questions are relatively easy for the instructor to write and they eliminate student guessing and emphasize the sophisticated communications skills that society and the marketplace increasingly demand. When managed properly, essay writing is widely accepted as contributing to the development of higher level thinking, encompassing Bloom's application, analysis, synthesis and evaluation levels. More specifically, essay questions help students achieve the following learning outcomes:

- Establish meaningful connections between theoretical principles and practical situations
- Compare and/or contrast two or more approaches to an issue
- Explain the range of factors which contribute to a particular situation
- Integrate information from several sources to explain a particular situation
- Propose and defend a grounded solution to a problem
- Evaluate the quality or appropriateness of a product, process or action

In addition to the time required, scoring essay questions presents other challenges. Students often have been conditioned to equate "quantity of words" to "quality of response" in an essay—a perception that unfortunately has been reinforced in some classrooms. That paradigm of wordiness sometimes invades the minds of instructors who score longer essay responses higher even when they contain extraneous or "bluff" material. Scored essay question responses may also contribute to uncomfortable interchanges with disagreeable students. Let us offer some suggestions for minimizing these occurrences.

Before the exam, instructors employing essay test questions might invest some class time in teaching students to write an effective essay response. One effective way likely to be well received by students is to provide the class with an essay question that could plausibly appear on the first exam. On the chalkboard or overhead, succinctly write and explain the content and writing standards you will employ in scoring responses. Solicit feedback before moving on to ensure that your point was understood. Then, emphasize that each response will be scored beginning with "0" and that points will be awarded for positive achievement, rather than starting with "10" (or whatever the possible score is) and taking points off for making incorrect statements or writing improperly. Provide all the students written copies of your criteria to guide their preparation for the exam.

Then, divide the class into groups of two or three students, and provide them, one at a time, three written responses to the question. Based on the scoring standards you presented (leave the overhead or chalkboard display in place), they are to score each response. You probably would want to give them a clearly poor response, an average one, and an outstanding response—in that order. Following their analysis, discuss the experience and provide your score for each of the three. For the outstanding response, emphasize the key correct components and points awarded for each. Students are thus equipped to begin their preparation with a clear understanding of your expectations.

Your time in scoring essay responses will be made more efficient if you carefully plan your questions. First, compose essay items with clear parameters within their wording so students will not be tempted to write unnecessarily long responses. After writing your initial essay questions, you might want to have your mentor or other veteran instructor review them with this focus, as well as difficulty level, in mind. Next, based on the criteria provided to students, outline the specific content, organization, and process you expect to be included in each effective response and assign objective point values for their attainment. Be prepared to share this rubric with the class when you return their scored exams. To ensure your objectivity when scoring essay items, conceal the student's identity by covering the name or having them use the last four numbers of their Social Security number on the response pages. If you assign more than one essay on the same test, score all of the responses to the same question at the same time, before proceeding to score any of the responses to subsequent essay items. Minimize delays between scoring sessions to maximize your continuity of thought and minimize the impact of your mood.

Once your exam is fully developed, with its probable combination of objective and essay items, enlist the help of your mentor or other veteran instructor to give it a final review prior to printing. Develop your scoring key and use it to guide your exam review. Besides the correct answers, your key should include margin notes of why particular choices are correct or incorrect and the source of the question, e.g., page number in the textbook.

FACILITATING STUDENT SUCCESS

All instructors want students to accept full responsibility for their performance on tests, but enlightened professors realize they themselves have a stake, and therefore a role to play, in facilitating success. Several tactics are possible; as the instructor, you must weigh the costs and benefits of each tactic to arrive at a position that fits your values, the experience level of students in the course, and departmental and institutional standards. You might want to consider the following information as you formulate a position on this issue, especially as it relates to the first test in a course when students are often grappling to overcome anxieties.

Most instructors would agree that students have a right to enter each exam with a clear and accurate expectation of test content and format. At a minimum, the professor should clarify that expectation through a detailed review conducted the class meeting prior to the exam. An effective review can utilize varied formats, depending on the maturity level of students, the format of test items, the complexity of the material, and other factors. For example, if the exam is largely "objective," the instructor might take a sample of questions from the exam, reword them slightly, and provide a handout. Students can then be assigned to groups of no more than three (they should not form their own groups, which are likely to be comprised of individuals too similar to each other) and provided a single copy of the handout. Allow perhaps ten minutes for students to formulate responses to explain to the rest of the class. The professor can then debrief the collective responses, focusing on the concepts that give students the most difficulty. The handout can then either be collected, or each student given a copy from which to study.

For classes with especially anxious students, a week or so before the first exam you might provide a study guide with a simple listing of the concepts that will be included on the exam. In addition, you might want to divide the class into small groups during the last 20 to 30 minutes of class and encourage them to discuss possible responses while you circulate throughout the classroom. Since students have become acquainted somewhat with each other largely through your earlier icebreaker activity, you should once again encourage them to form study groups outside of class to prepare for the exam.

Before releasing students from the class meeting prior to the exam, describe for students your procedures for administering the exam, including:

- Supplies (for example, Scantron answer sheets or blue books) they will need for the exam
- Special seating arrangements or other procedures you plan to employ to ensure that a secure and quiet environment is created
- The schedule you will follow in administering the exam, including time parameters you will employ. If your class periods are long, plan to give the exam at the beginning of the period, rather than cover additional material. Also explain the activities that will follow the test administration, and any other critical information
- A restatement of penalties for not taking the exam (which should also be in your syllabus)

Reviewing these details in advance will contribute to a positive perception by students and increase their sense of confidence as they embark on the exam.

ADMINISTERING THE EXAMINATION

Arrive especially early for the class period during which an exam is to be administered, allowing yourself time to adjust the temperature and other factors, as well as meet students who might have arrived early with questions about the exam. Designate a seating area near the door for any students who arrive late to minimize disruption to students who will be engaged in the test. If you have not already done so, proofread the final copy of the exam carefully, marking any typos or factual errors that might have withstood earlier scrutiny.

When students begin arriving, it is critical to create an atmosphere of positive expectancy and trust. Greet students as they enter and ask each an open-ended question about their readiness, such as "How are you feeling about this?" and in other ways proactively deflate their anxieties. Avoid jokes or remarks that might be perceived as flippant, since these can contribute to an adversarial dynamic within anxious students.

When the scheduled time for beginning class arrives, ask the class as a whole if there are any final questions you need to clarify prior to starting the exam. If there are, answer them in a constructive manner, avoiding lengthy, highly detailed responses. Be patient and reassuring. Ask students to have only the materials required to take the exam on their desk and place everything else on the floor (or in some other specific out-of-the-way area). Direct them where to bring their exams and answer sheets when completed and remind them of time parameters and your procedures for scoring and returning the exams. If you found any typos or other mistakes on the exam, direct students to delay beginning the exam until all are distributed, then review the corrections that should be made on the test. Remind them once again of the time parameters of the test. Wish them good luck.

DEALING PROACTIVELY WITH STUDENT CHEATING

Perhaps the single most unpleasant aspect of teaching is dealing with cheating. We inherently feel we were fair in developing the exam and resist believing *our* students feel the pressure to make grades that fuels dishonorable behavior. When we allow ourselves to feel that way, we sometimes fail to take the proactive measures necessary to create the classroom security and clear positive expectations that can minimize, though not eliminate, the pressure to cheat. Students who perceive that their peers are cheating and that the instructor does nothing to prevent it often lack the self-discipline to resist cheating themselves at the next opportunity.

Peeking at other students' papers and using crib sheets continue to be widely employed as test-cheating methods. However, technology, larger classes, the use of machine-graded answer sheets, and the risk-taking mindset so common among students today have evoked more brazen methods, some of the which are described next.

- Students use calculators, micro-cassette recorders, and other electronic devices to store potential answers.
- Students well prepared for the exam write responses on a second Scantron answer sheet which they surreptitiously give to a friend as they leave the classroom.

- Students adhere potential answers to body areas that instructors cannot readily see and therefore are less likely to investigate.
- Students have someone else take an exam for them.
- Students accuse the instructor of losing an exam that was not submitted.

Clearly, prevention is the most effective strategy to minimize cheating. (Therefore, avoid having someone else proctor your exam because it increases the incidence of cheating.) It is critical to create a trusting classroom atmosphere where students know that you want them to perform well. Asking students in a positive tone and monitoring their placing of books and notes in secure places prior to distributing the exam will help. Having students disburse themselves throughout the entire classroom, rather than clustering in the same area, will also send the message that you care about ensuring the chances of success for the better-prepared students. For classes with large numbers of students, it takes little additional work for you to develop a second version of the exam that scrambles the order of questions.

Another preventive technique is to develop exams that are perceived as fair and secure by students. Often, the accusation by students that certain questions were tricky is valid, as it relates to ambiguous language and trivial material. Ask your mentor or other experienced instructor to closely review the final draft of your first few exams for these factors.

SCORING OBJECTIVE EXAMINATIONS

Since multiple choice and matching questions require a single letter answer, they are inherently easy to score. Traditionally, scoring of such items was facilitated through use of an answer sheet and a corresponding key that could be positioned next to it. In recent years, this process has been made even easier through the use of scoring machines and especially designed answer sheets. The most common of such systems have been developed by the Scantron Company. The machine first reads an answer sheet marked as a key, then scores each student answer sheet, marks incorrect answers (advanced models even print the correct answer) and prints the total number of correct responses. Obviously, this can be a great time-saver, especially when there are many students in the class. However, Scantron machines provide an even greater advantage by providing analytical information for the instructor.

Scantron systems enable the instructor to insert an item-analysis form into the machine following the scoring of all student answer sheets, providing a count of the number of times each question is answered incorrectly. Thus, the instructor can easily focus on questions missed most frequently, evaluate their clarity and accuracy, and contemplate corrective actions that might be taken.

The logical next step in analyzing the test results is to list the scores, from highest to lowest, and calculate the average score. Since the results on the first exam are so critical for both you and the students, you might want to meet with your mentor or other veteran teacher—ideally familiar with this particular course—to review the exam results. Resist the temptation to curve the test by adding a certain number of points to all scores. Curving grades discounts students' success on exams and places responsibility on the instructor. It also raises the expectation that future exams will be curved. Should you decide that one or more questions were poor, think about eliminating the question(s) and re-calculating the scores. While it might take a few additional minutes, this corrective action reinforces to students that they are being held responsible for their own success.

REVIEWING RESULTS OF EXAMS WITH STUDENTS

Since immediate feedback enhances effective learning, always review the results of exams no later than the period immediately following its administration. Do not allow a student who has missed the exam and not taken a makeup delay the critical review process. Instead, make arrangements for such students to take an alternative version of the test prior to rejoining the class. (To minimize possible negative reactions to this procedure, you would be wise to explain it during the pre-exam review.)

If answer sheets were used in administering the exam, initially return only the exams themselves and review each question thoroughly. Students therefore will more likely focus on their understanding of each question rather than which they answered incorrectly. Be prepared, from the Scantron or other form of test-item analysis, to identify how many times each question was missed. Thoroughly double-check the questions missed most often and dedicate extra time during the review to ensure that students leave with a clear understanding of the correct answers. Be prepared to deal constructively with argumentative or otherwise emotional students by building "common ground." If appropriate, be willing to lead them through the process of logically determining the correct answer. Compliment their effort and provide reassurance.

Before distributing the corrected answer sheets, write the scores in a ranked list on the board (without students' names), together with the class average, so students can clearly see where they stand within the group. Return scored answer sheets in random fashion, rather than from highest to lowest scores. Make eye contact with each student and make a quiet, constructive comment.

Realize anew that exam results are interpreted by each student through a very personalized lens. Affected by the expectations of employers (whose degree of tuition reimbursement may depend on the final course grade) and expectations of family members (who might prefer mom or dad not to be giving up limited time to attend school), students often put a great deal of pressure on themselves to perform. Schedule a break immediately following the review of exam results and offer to meet individually with students. In addition, extend an invitation for them to meet with you at the end of the class meeting to discuss their concerns. Employ the transactional analysis skills you learned earlier in the book to ensure that students leave the class meeting with as constructive a view of the test results as possible. Each of us retains for a long time the memories of those who influenced us during the periods of our lives when situations were most challenging. Students are very much that way with exams!

THROUGH THE ADJUNCTS' EYES

Juan:

In administering my first exam, I was struck again by the dichotomy between community college and university undergraduate students. The range of the exam scores was 42 to 98, and the average score was 74. The distribution of scores was nothing like the bell-shaped curve I had expected! There were more A's than B's or C's, no D's, and more F's than C's. I was flabbergasted! Upon reflection, I realize that university students largely study in groups—in the dormitories or, in a few cases, in fraternity and sorority houses. Community college students, who work and commute to campus, usually study alone. The overachievers do well, because they are motivated to improve themselves at work or prove something to their children, their spouses, or themselves. Those who get behind usually have no one at home who has gone to college capable of helping, and often find it hard time-wise to access the help that is available in tutoring labs.

The class period following the exam, when I returned and reviewed their papers, was more difficult than I expected. Several students were primed as soon as I walked in the room. Although they maintained their composure, I could see frustration built up in their eyes. As we reviewed the exam, some common complaints emerged. The first was that the test included a lot of material that wasn't sufficiently covered in class. When I responded that it was in their reading assignment, one student asked why she needed to come to class if the exam was going to be taken totally from the textbook. Several students then said that some of the things we spent a lot of time on in class were not included on the exam. While university students would probably not have verbalized any complaint, the community college students were vehement. Although their complaints were stinging, I listened closely, and upon reflection, have to admit there was a lot of truth in their complaints. I think the fact that I showed concern and listened carefully was a positive. I told them I would re-think the results of the test and develop some sort of remedy. They seemed to accept that—reluctantly.

Karen:

I gave my first exam last night—a mid-term. Mr. Jackson planned only two exams for the course, both of which I will be using. Each has 100 multiple choice questions and covers 8 to 10 chapters from the textbook. As students were taking the exam, I reviewed it closely for the first time. There were 6 or 8 questions that were challenging to me! A good number of the questions required an evaluation of actions taken by the courts—not a level at which I had delivered the material. Several questions had a convoluted format that tested the students' test-taking ability more than it did their knowledge of the material.

I dedicated the entire class meeting to the exam. When students left, several looked like they had seen a ghost. I left the classroom feeling like I had really let the students down. Having the exam cover so much material and waiting so late in the term to give the first exam were big mistakes. My not reviewing the exam earlier in the term, simplifying some of the questions, and making sure I addressed the material in my lectures were even bigger mistakes!

Margaret:

Two weeks before giving my first exam, I had the students work in small groups to provide input into its development. While a few made suggestions that were overly elementary, most of their ideas on what should be included were practical and appropriate. Since we had good results working in small groups to solve case problems, I included on the exam several case problems similar to the previous situations. In class the week before, I reviewed extensively for the exam, gave them a study guide that included the concepts I expected them to have mastered, and told them the number and format of questions. To me, the process should work just like it does at work, where you give employees a job description and performance appraisal form, show them what to do, then give them feedback on how well they are doing. I also encouraged students to study together outside of class.

When they came to take the exam, most students looked confident and relaxed. Overall, the results were outstanding, although a few students lack sufficient writing skills for this level. As we reviewed the scored exam, there were no complaints, even though three students got failing scores. Two of those saw me at the end of class and apologized for not having dedicated more time to preparing for the exam.

TIPS FOR THRIVING

As stated earlier, feedback on results is the most effective of motivating factors. Anxious students are especially hungry for positive feedback. You can quickly and easily provide it by simply writing "Great job!" or "Terrific" on the answer sheets or tests of students who did especially well. For students who performed less than ideally, a brief note such as "I'd love to talk with you at the end of class" can be especially reassuring. Again, the key is to be proactive and maintain high standards, while requiring students to retain ownership of their own success in the course.

Since your major goal is empowering students to achieve their own success and the first exam in a course is typically the major departure point for students dropping out of a course, you might want to develop a contingency plan to deal with disappointing scores. One which works quite well, while maintaining student responsibility for success, is "Plan B." On your syllabus, you outlined your grading procedure for the course ("Plan A"), similar to that in the model syllabus in Appendix 4.1. If you used a simple scheme, where each component was weighted at 20% of the final course grade, you can easily offer students not scoring up to their expectations a win–win alternative. If they choose, they may drop the score on the first exam only (*not* the lowest score of all their exams) by recalculating the weights on the remaining components to 25% each. Since there are many understandable reasons why students might get off to a slow start in a class (for example, added the course after the term began, were unable to purchase the expensive textbook in a timely fashion, and so on), "Plan B" is very defendable from the professor's position and protects the students' self-efficacy. In addition, this plan requires the student to intensify his or her commitment for the remainder of the course.

This chapter contains many tips for effectively developing, administering, and following up examinations. The common thread is that testing can and should be a rewarding experience for both students and you. With that idea solidly in mind, you can very effectively overcome for yourself, and help students overcome for themselves, the anxiety that accompanies testing.

REVIEW OF KEY POINTS

- Examinations contribute significantly to the overall perception students develop of an instructor.
- Develop a draft of your exam early to ensure that material on it is properly addressed in class.
- Ensure that your exams are valid, reliable, and objective.
- The test item format selected should dovetail with the learning domain and level within Bloom's Taxonomy.

- Well-written test items employ easily understood criteria.
- Essay test items encourage effective writing and critical thinking skill development.
- Proactively manage student success on exams by clarifying mutual expectations and holding a thorough, interactive review of material it will include.
- Meticulously organize every detail of administering the exam.
- Avoid having someone else proctor an exam for you.
- Thoroughly analyze overall exam results before returning them to students.
- Return scored exams no later than the next regularly scheduled class meeting.
- Demonstrate sensitivity to the anxiety that many students feel before, during, and after taking exams.

SUGGESTED READINGS

Jacobs, L., & Chase, C. (1992). *Developing and using tests effectively.* San Francisco: Jossey-Bass.

Kubisyn, T., & Borich, G. (1996). *Educational testing and measurement: Classroom application and practice* (5th ed.). New York: HarperCollins.

APPENDIX 10.1   MATCHING-ITEM EXERCISE

This exercise is designed to increase your sensitivity to the ineffective dynamics of many matching exercises. As you respond to questions, note any characteristics of the exercise that might create unfair disadvantages or advantages for students.

Directions: Match the name from the left column to the achievement in the right column. Enter its letter in the appropriate space. Each correct answer is worth 10 points.

_____	1. Madame Curie	a. Father of psychoanalysis
_____	2. Adolph Hitler	b. *Fuhrer* of the Third Reich
_____	3. Charles DeGaulle	c. Wrote *The Communist Manifesto*
_____	4. Peter Tchaikovsky	d. French inventor
_____	5. Karl Marx	e. Leader of France during World War II
_____	6. Sigmund Freud	f. Wrote *The 1812 Overture*
_____	7. Louis Pasteur	g. Developed process for purifying milk
_____	8. Nicholas II	h. His assassination led to start of World War I
_____	9. Georgi Zhukov	i. Last czar of Russia
_____	10. Archduke Ferdinand	j. Russian general, led WW II assault on Berlin

What situations did you find which might be problems for students taking the test, or the instructor who will base grades on its results? Check your findings against some of the faults listed below.

Incomplete Directions.   There are *two* "French inventors" in the list. Does the student put both correct answers down, or through process of elimination determine that since "g" goes with "7", then "d" must go with "1"?

Easy Guessing.   Two of the questions—2 and 7—were on the same line with their correct answers—"b" and "g" respectively. There are ten total items and equal numbers in both lists, making the overall "process of elimination" especially easy. If there were two or three extra achievements listed, the chances of guessing correctly would be markedly reduced.

Position of Lists.   The material would be more logical and less time-consuming for the student to process if the achievements, i.e. long phrases, were in the left column and the names, i.e. shorter phrases, in the right column.

Lack of Commonality in Lists.   The list includes politicians, royalty, writers, inventors, a physician, and a composer. The exercise would be much more effective if all were of very similar roles and if the historical period were more limited.

Order of Names.   While not a major problem in a list of ten names, the fact that names are not given in alphabetical order could make a longer exercise much more time-consuming and confusing for students to complete.

Clangers.   The use of certain terms contributes to a mental "clanging" clue for students, providing an extra, inappropriate tip to the correct answer. "Pasteur" and "milk," "DeGaulle" and "France," and "Hitler" and "fuhrer" produce such a clanging sound. "His" rules out Madame Curie as a possible choice.

APPENDIX 10.2   MULTIPLE-CHOICE ITEM EXERCISE

As you review each of the following questions, determine any obstacle it might create for students completing the exercise. For ease of focus, the content of each question is derived from material in this book.

Directions: Select the **best** answer to each of the following and enter its letter on the answer sheet. Each correct answer is worth X points.

1. Which of the following would a department chairperson and dean expect of you during your teaching of a semester-long course?

   A. Telling lots of "war stories" and actively promoting your full-time career
   B. Arriving a few minutes before to the scheduled starting time of each class meeting and staying a few minutes afterward

    C. Canceling a class whenever you had a business, medical, or personal reason

    D. Speaking up vehemently for the "one best way" on all issues within the course

    E. Assigning at least 20% of students a "D" or "F" as a final course grade

2. Which of the following is not true of an effective course syllabus?

    A. It serves as a contract between the instructor and the student.

    B. It includes a "tentative schedule" that the instructor should expect to modify.

    C. It provides answers to most reasonable questions students would have.

    D. It is especially clear on the issues of grading and attendance/participation.

    E. None of the above.

3. During the first meeting of your class,

    A. distribute your syllabus, but don't review it until the second meeting.

    B. the classroom and your handout materials should create a positive first impression.

    C. wait for 10 minutes before starting to allow all students time to arrive.

    D. take about 15 minutes to review your professional and personal background.

    E. be sure to tell students if the class was assigned to you on short notice.

4. During the first class meeting, avoid

    A. "heavy stuff," like reviewing the goals and limitations of the course.

    B. learning students' names, because if they drop the course you have wasted time.

    C. going into great depth with the material of the course.

    D. introducing yourself to individual students.

    E. gathering any detailed information about students.

5. Which of the following is the most important reason for conducting "icebreakers"?

    A. Break down barriers between students who are likely to be passive

    B. Give students a chance to have some fun as a balance against the "heavy stuff"

    C. Provide students a chance to satisfy their need to "fit in"

    D. Create a positive learning atmosphere

    E. Encourage students to begin relationships that might lead to forming study groups

6. Which of the following is true of "learning domains"?

    A. The psychomotor domain refers to the thought processes.

    B. The effective domain refers to attitudes, character issues, and appreciation of beauty.

    C. The cognitive domain refers to physical skills and dexterity.

    D. All of the above are true.

    E. None of the above are true.

7. Which of the following lists the correct sequence of "Bloom's Taxonomy"?

   A. Application, analysis, knowledge, comprehension, evaluation, synthesis
   B. Knowledge, comprehension, analysis, application, synthesis, evaluation
   C. Analysis, knowledge, comprehension, application, evaluation, synthesis
   D. Knowledge, comprehension, application, analysis, synthesis, evaluation
   E. Comprehension, knowledge, analysis, application, evaluation, synthesis

8. Which of the following are true of the effective use of "cooperative learning"?

   A. Students work in small groups to process information or solve problems
   B. Groups work best when members are alike in age, gender, etc.
   C. Students should work with the same group of students throughout the term
   D. Groups should include no more than 4 students so everyone is encouraged to contribute
   E. Both A and D are true.

DISCUSSION

These questions may well seem very much like some you have taken as a student, but let's analyze each more closely.

The correct answer to 1 is clearly B. That answer was easy to determine because "distractor" (choice) A (and perhaps others) was a "throwaway." Although many instructors believe the first question on any exam should be relatively easy, in order to relieve student anxiety and build confidence, this question is probably too easy for our intended audience, i.e., the readers of this book.

Questions 2 is messy. First, many test-takers would have difficulty focusing on the key issue in question, largely because of the negative nature of its stem. Rewording the stem to read, "All of the following are true of an effective course syllabus, *except:*" would prompt the attention of the student more effectively. In addition, given the stated choices, the "correct" answer is E, i.e., "none of the above." However, the pattern of the original question—"Which is…not" is "none…" is confusing to anybody, but especially to anxious students. Many bright students who otherwise knew the correct answer would probably not select E as the correct answer because of the flawed phrasing.

Question 3 looks pretty good doesn't it? The choices required you to process and analyze appropriate concepts for your level of teaching experience. Did you select the "correct" answer, B? Although you probably didn't need it, there was a clue. Notice all of choices except B began with a verb, which probably created a subliminal "clanging" in your mind. The question would be more valid if choice B were reworded to also begin with a verb.

Question 4 also requires an appropriate degree of analysis. But, it would confuse some students because the trigger word in the stem, "avoid," is negative. The human mind has a challenging time focusing on a negative, and thus the question has an uneasy feeling about it. "All of the following are appropriate activities of the first class meeting, *except:*" is a more effectively worded stem.

The purpose of question 5—encouraging recall of valid reasons for conducting an "icebreaker"—is appropriate in a quiz for a reader of this book. But the way the test item is written, the "correct" choice is largely the opinion of the writer of the question. Again, the question could be rewritten with an "all of the following, *except:*" stem. Or, the existing stem could be used if four of the choices were reworded to make them objectively incorrect.

To many people, question 6 has a "giveaway" answer. A and C are clearly wrong, so D is also wrong. While B seems like the correct answer, "affective" is the actual term for the described domain. Unless correct spelling of terms is critical in your course, students should not be evaluated with such relatively trivial choices. Such questions are perceived as mean-spirited by students, and they serve to stifle their motivation and increase their test-anxiety for the remainder of the course.

Were you tempted to look back to Chapter 5 before answering 7? The correct answer is D. While this question might be appropriate for a student majoring in education, it requires an inappropriate level of exactness for a reader of this book. It is very easy to make a similar mistake in exams you develop for your students. Such questions serve to encourage students to memorize facts that are forgotten soon after the exam, rather than develop an appreciation for the overall concept.

Like Question 3, the final test item also has a hidden clue. The plural verb "are" in the stem serves as a "clanger" for choice E. A number of students who did not fully understand the material would probably get this answer correct. In the process, the overall value of the exam is discounted.

Finally, did you notice the pattern of the responses? Three of the eight questions (not counting the "opinion" Question 5), or 38%, were correctly answered B. Since each question had 5 choices, B should be the correct answer on only about 20% of the questions in this multiple-choice exercise. Many teachers unknowingly fall into patterns in which they disproportionately use a particular letter as the "correct" response. Such patterns are discerned by some students, often those who were not necessarily the best prepared for the exam.

APPENDIX 10.3   MODEL STUDY GUIDE

Principles of Management
Exam No. 2, Study Guide

Chapter 5
1. Explain Gantt charts, uses
2. Explain PERT diagrams, uses
3. Calculate "break-even point"
4. Common ways of determining how much inventory to hold in stock
5. Explain "just in time" inventory system, when used

Chapter 6
1. Explain measurable characteristics of jobs that improve employee motivation
2. Challenges facing the job designer
3. Explain "self directed work teams"
4. Advantages/disadvantages of job specialization
5. Characteristics of enriched jobs
6. Compare/contrast methods of nontraditional job scheduling
7. Advantages/disadvantages of telecommuting

Chapter 7
1. Advantages/disadvantages of a bureaucracy
2. Compare/contrast types of authority
3. Explain function, applications of organizational chart
4. Methods of departmentalization
5. Advantages/disadvantages of flat organizations over tall ones
6. Explain components of delegation
7. Factors affecting size of span of control
8. Explain foundation, development of organizational culture

Chapter 8
1. Contrast "personnel management" with "human resource management"
2. Identify key shifts in workforce
3. Components of staffing function
4. Compare/contrast job analysis, job specifications, job description
5. Explain, cite cases of "reverse discrimination"
6. Explain the Americans with Disabilities Act
7. Compare/contrast types and examples of sexual harassment

11

ALTERNATIVE ASSESSMENT

Focus Questions

- What are the essential characteristics of alternative assessment?
- How do you encourage "genuine" rather than "superficial" learning?
- How can you effectively evaluate student projects?

The preceding chapter emphasized the importance of instructors developing examinations that accurately assess students' mastery of subject matter, but many contemporary educators are placing less emphasis on traditional "paper and pencil" testing and more emphasis on students' ability to apply information in real-life situations. This change in the way student achievement is measured is commonly called *alternative assessment*. Advocates of these methods stress the importance of ensuring that students are able to demonstrate, through a variety of means, what they have learned. Traditional testing told us what "facts" students may have memorized, but this rarely gave us insight into how well they could use that information in the real world. Alternative assessment, sometimes referred to as *authentic* or *performance assessment*, requires students to engage in activities in which they can demonstrate their new knowledge and can explain what they have accomplished. Alternative assessment supports and reinforces the student-directed learning strategies discussed in Chapter 9, while traditional testing methods are best suited for instructor-directed learning strategies.

PLANNING FOR ALTERNATIVE ASSESSMENT IN YOUR COURSE

John Dewey, generally accepted as the most influential leader in the history of American education, believed that the fundamental goal of education was to create "natural," or what some call today "genuine," knowledge. He stressed that the starting point for learning was in the everyday experiences of the student, and that the real test of mastery learning lay in the ability to apply what was learned in the everyday arena (1916). The best American teachers, at all levels of education, have firmly embraced Dewey's axiom and regularly incorporate activities that foster students' ability to connect the classroom to their everyday lives.

Today, proponents of Dewey's approach would agree that effective alternative assessment activities:

- Are open-ended, that is, they require students to construct a response or perform an activity
- Measure higher order thinking and complex skills, such as finding solutions to a local problem, engaging in a debate over a controversial issue, writing a response to a newspaper editorial, developing an advertising campaign or business plan, or writing a short story or poem
- Require extended periods of time for performance, frequently a span of several class meetings or longer, rather than the hour or so of a traditional exam
- Are often designed to be performed by groups of students, rather than individuals
- Provide the student with a choice of tasks from which a selection appropriate for individualized learning goals can be made
- Use judgmental scoring which requires providing students with appropriate, detailed guidelines prior to development of project
- Ask students to perform in ways appropriate to the standards of an environment outside the traditional classroom, e.g., those of a particular work setting

An assertion first made by D. G. Treichler (1967) and since refined by other authors states that human beings generally remember:

- 10% of what they read
- 20% of what they hear
- 30% of what they see
- 50% of what they both see and hear
- 70% of what is discussed with others
- 80% of what they personally experience
- 90% of what they teach to someone else

Traditional testing largely evaluates the reading, listening, and observing of students, while *alternative assessment* focuses on what students personally experience, what they share with their peers, and what they thoroughly embrace and advocate to others.

Each of us probably can remember countless examples of the wisdom of this approach from our days as students. The investigations we made into real situations affecting our communities, the promotional campaign for a product or service to which we were especially loyal, or the speech which we delivered in hopes of influencing others to embrace our point of view are all retained much longer than the feedback we provided on an objective examination. When we employ alternative assessment, we reinforce the axiom Dewey expressed and advocated.

The key to achieving genuine learning from student projects is to allow students' input into the selection of project topics and/or the criteria of evaluation. The degree of that input, however, must be carefully weighed. In analyzing the appropriate degree of student input, again envision a continuum with the right end identified as "instructor determined." At this point on the continuum, all of the decisions regarding the student project are established without input from the student. These decisions include the topic, form (e.g., written paper, oral presentation, video presentation, etc.), length, number and type of resources that must be employed, criteria for evaluation, weight as a component of the final course grade, and others. The strength of the instructor-determined method is that projects are theoretically consistent and easier for the instructor to evaluate. The downside is that students are likely to have little or no intellectual or emotional investment in the quality of the final product.

At the other end of the continuum all of those decisions are made by each student individually. The student's investment is theoretically maximized, since he or she is empowered to make all critical decisions on the project. In the process, students typically develop a more grounded understanding of the learning styles and learning strategies that are most effective for them. This is a key element in becoming an effective lifelong learner. Student-determined assessment obviously engenders a wide range of forms and lengths, which—while initially somewhat challenging to compare and evaluate—hold the potential of significant long-term value to students and increased personal rewards from teaching.

Logically, most college instructors using student performance as part of their assessment strategies select a method of project development somewhere between these two extremes. In an introductory course, in which students are likely to be intellectually unsophisticated in the subject area or with students likely to be undisciplined, an approach that adheres closely to the "instructor determined" end of the continuum should probably be employed. It is critical that you think through all aspects of the project—its overall learning goal, the format and length that are achievable for the type of student you are likely to have, and—perhaps most importantly—the exact criteria you will use to evaluate the project and the impact the project will have on the final course grade. You would be wise to have your mentor, a peer teacher, or instructional leader review your ideas and help you plan your activities and evaluation strategies, thus assuring reasonable expectations from your students.

You must avoid markedly changing guidelines or expectations after students begin their projects if you decide you did not adequately determine what your students were capable of achieving or what you really wanted them to do. Such actions not only frustrate and de-motivate students, but contribute to fostering uncomfortable classroom situations for students and the instructor alike. In the bigger picture, such actions stymie the instructor's ability to create an appropriate image and tend to inhibit enrollment in future courses he or she might teach.

Once the assignment is made, provide students several weeks to develop their ideas before seeking a commitment to a particular choice. Dedicate a few minutes at the beginning or closing of each class meeting to deal with questions that will arise in students' minds regarding the project. Students seem to be conditioned to expect the instructor to answer every question regarding projects with precise detail. Since you want to shift most of that responsibility to the students, you may want to refer them to sources that could provide answers to the questions. To avoid much of the minutia students like to deal with during class time, distribute explicit, written information and guidelines early.

In advanced courses, when students have some knowledge base in the subject area, a system closer to the student-determined end of the continuum should be employed. You might provide options along several points of the continuum, such as offering students the choice between completing a standard project that you would expect a large number of students to select or one which provides greater personal latitude. In that middle ground, you might provide students with a list of acceptable topics from which they might select a topic, or formulate a project that approximates one on the list. Or, you might conduct an open classroom discussion that leads to consensus building on a common approach. You could even have students work collaboratively on a topic and develop group presentations. If the latter is promoted, you will need to make some class time available for students to work in their groups. This is particularly true when you teach adults who have limited time outside of class. How much time you devote to group work in your classroom should be balanced against the value of the activity to overall learning of the course objectives. Of course, some time outside of class is expected, but "in class" time can ease the burden of students getting together to plan and work.

As you approach the student-determined end of the continuum, you are engaging in what is commonly called "independent study." Highly sophisticated students are not only going to work on their own, but will thrive on the opportunity to individually negotiate what they are going to do, how long it will require, and how they are going to demonstrate achievement of their objectives. Although you are still ultimately responsible for evaluating the students' work, you are providing them a great deal of control over what they do. When you have students engaged in learning at this level, you want to be certain that both you and each student are very clear about what he or she is going to do and the standards of performance and evaluation. This type of learning is widely embraced by those who view developing the life-long learning skills of students as one of the major goals of higher education.

Championed by Malcolm Knowles and other leaders of adult learning practices, learning contracts are designed to maximize the degree of student commitment and the relevance of the learning outcome. Such contracts are designed to identify learning goals, establish the criteria of the learning activities, and clearly establish the evaluation methods and standards before the student begins a learning project. For the student, a thoroughly developed learning contract provides direction and clarification throughout the activity and creates emotional security. For the instructor, the contract clarifies his or her role as a resource and reinforces the fact that responsibility for learning is upon the student.

OPTIONS FOR ALTERNATIVE ASSESSMENT

The type and nature of alternative assessment activities is limited only by your and your students' collective imagination. They include "products" that students can complete and in-class presentations—either individually or in collaboration with others—or a combination of the two. The following ideas are designed to provide insight into just a few of the rich possibilities.

In recent years, an especially popular method of alternative assessment has been the *student portfolio*. Long used by artists, photographers, advertising, and public relations professionals to demonstrate their skills to prospective clients, portfolios have been adapted by instructors increasingly concerned about the long-term payoff of their courses. Many believe the quality of student learning can be more effectively communicated through portfolios than test results and essays.

Portfolios provide students an opportunity to present a collection of their work that reflects their growth and understanding of the subject matter. The content of a portfolio should be inclusive of a variety of work performed by the student, but should not include all of their class work. Students should be held responsible for identifying the work that best exemplifies their increased competency. A portfolio could include written assignments, photographs of their own and others' created works, and so on. However, simply including these items does not constitute an appropriate portfolio. A well-conceived and effective portfolio should also include students' reflections and analysis of what they learned, focusing on their learning experiences and the feedback that you, and perhaps others, provided during the process. This reflection fuels the long-term, genuine learning that should be the major goal of the entire educational process.

Through the use of portfolios, students' perceptions of themselves as individuals are enhanced. As you review a student's portfolio, it is difficult not to recognize him or her as a unique individual who exists beyond the realm of your classroom. Since the personalized feedback you provide in this context is perceived as especially meaningful, you must take care to choose carefully the words and phrases that will fuel continued growth.

Effective portfolio assessment establishes a reiterative process within the instructional strategy. That is, students do an assignment, get corrective feedback from you, then react to that feedback and make alterations to which you in turn provide additional feedback. The process is personal, ongoing, and active. Not all students need to be doing exactly the same thing at the same time. Students who need or want more time to be reflective and corrective can be accommodated, as can those who desire immediate change in their performance. Thus, the learning cycle is made highly personal and more psychologically rewarding.

A major drawback to portfolio assessment is the time it takes to provide the necessary feedback to students—there is no denying that this type of assessment is intensive when done effectively. However, with good management skills on your part and a clear understanding of your expectations for portfolios, the benefits far outweigh the drawbacks. Rather than employ portfolios for the entire term, you may choose to use it for a single unit within the class. You are limited only by your own creativity in the way and extent that you employ portfolios as a means of assessing student achievement.

Because of their ability to aid the retention of material, classroom presentations are another especially effective method of alternative assessment. Besides the traditional individual speech and instructional presentation, these methods include several types of group presentations. Involvement in a forum or panel discussion encourages presenters, and to a lesser extent, listeners, to view a particular issue or work (book, movie, etc.) from a wider range of perspectives. Debates encourage intensive listening, critical thinking, and management of emotions. "Mock news conferences" encourage the development of all of the above and facilitate functioning under pressure—an increasingly more important skill in today's society. The keys to success in using any of these potential forms of assessment are making effective matches between the method and ability levels of students and ensuring a clear understanding of ground rules and evaluative criteria among students. Be sure to set students up to be successful, rather than to have an experience that stifles their continued development.

The video camcorder opens up a wide range of alternative assessment possibilities for the creative instructor and student. For example, a videotaped walk through a site as common as a cemetery or as rare as a castle, when accompanied by an in-class narration by the student, has great potential to demonstrate a student's mastery of an historical issue. While teaching a course in "Human Resource Management," one of your authors had a student demonstrate her appreciation for and understanding of the components of effective new employee orientation through a video orientation she had developed with the support of her employer. The accolades and "A" from the project she received in the class came in addition to the recognition from her peers and promotion consideration she received from her employer.

A final group of alternative assessment activities are those that require student writing. While traditional papers encourage grounded mental processing of course concepts, their effectiveness as learning tools can be enhanced through more contemporary assessment methods. Traditionally, papers have been graded with no opportunity for rewriting. Research indicates that when students are provided the opportunity to rewrite sections after receiving instructor feedback, with the opportunity to improve their grades, many will take advantage of it. In the process, they not only deepen their understanding of the topic, but improve their writing skills as well. Professors who embrace this approach often have students submit their papers in sections, each of which has a deadline and is graded. Students may either keep their grade on each component and submit only the remaining components, or declare their intent to rewrite. At the final deadline, students submit their previously graded components along with their final paper. The previously graded components are, in effect, re-scored in the context of the final completed paper. Increasingly, many instructors are allowing students to submit partially written papers via email, so they can receive more immediate feedback throughout the process of writing of a paper.

Whether written in papers or journals, presented orally, videotaped, or submitted in other ways, methods of alternative assessment are endless. The best relax the boundaries between the course itself and the environment into which students will be moving following the completion of the course—i.e., they are "real world." Such projects make that transition smoother and increase the richness of the educational experience both to students and to the professor committed to students' long-term success.

EVALUATING ALTERNATIVE ASSESSMENT ACTIVITIES

Since alternative assessment activities are designed to provide students an opportunity to demonstrate their learning in ways that are not measurable on "paper and pencil" tests, your providing meaningful evaluative feedback is essential to their growth. Using rubrics facilitates more useful feedback. (You might recall, a rubric is a scoring device that lists the criteria on which an activity is to be evaluated.) An effective rubric provides for gradations of quality from "outstanding" to "poor," or "excellent" to "not satisfactory." Evaluative criteria should be specific to the activity and inclusive of all aspects of the activity that you deem appropriate.

For example, suppose you have your students prepare and deliver an oral presentation on a proposed penny increase in the local sales tax. Criteria you may use for evaluating the effectiveness of the presentation would include not only the content shared with the other students regarding the pro's and con's of the tax proposal, but might also address the delivery skills—voice projection, eye contact with the audience, use of visual aids, and others. In other words, you establish what you believe are the appropriate criteria for both content and delivery and create a continuum of "degree of success." Thus, your evaluation will be consistent from one presentation to the next and you will also provide the students with the key factors required for success in the real world. Rubrics work best when they are appropriate for the particular class, easy to understand, and focus on the most important aspects of the project.

Rubrics are useful because they clearly communicate to the students the expectation you have for their performance. By knowing expectations up front, students are better able to strive for acceptable quality, rather than guess. Rubrics also help students evaluate their own work as they prepare. As they consider their performance in light of the rubric, students can make appropriate adjustments ahead of time and avoid embarrassing catastrophes in their final presentation. From a defensive perspective, the analytical and objective nature of rubrics also minimize chances that students will question their project grades. This frequently happens with today's consumer-oriented students when a holistic letter grade is assigned or when points are taken off for various things that students are likely to perceive as trivial. In addition, rubrics make your assessment duties more focused and thus less time-consuming, and reduce the self-doubt you might experience by using a less objective method. While it might take time to develop the rubric itself, the simplified assessment it provides expedites decision making and minimizes explanations of your grading. On those rare occasions when a student asks for an explanation, it will be easier for you to reconstruct your thinking as you review the "scoring" directed by the rubric. Appendix 9.2, a model rubric for students making an in-class, instructional presentation in a public speaking or other course, can be easily adapted to a wide range of related situations.

DEALING WITH PLAGIARISM

As you evaluate student papers and related work, there will no doubt be times when you suspect plagiarism. Some clues include individual student work that far exceeds the quality of their previous work and the use of language which is inconsistent with their previously displayed style. If your course requires extensive student research, be sure to include your clear definition of plagiarism in your syllabus and embellish it with examples and further explanations, both at the time of its review and when you actually make an assignment. Spell out the penalties, taking into account institutional or departmental policies where they exist. Your class policy will also want to deal with the knotty challenge of students submitting work they had done for a previous course or one they are taking concurrently.

In a day when students can easily download reams of material on countless topics from the Internet and obtain papers from peers or through commercial services and other creative ways, discovering the source of plagiarized material is growing increasingly difficult. Resist the temptation to do nothing—your honorable students deserve better. At the same time, be extremely careful about making statements that would be perceived as an accusation even when you feel the evidence is substantial.

When you suspect student plagiarism, your best tactic is usually to hold a timely conference with the student. Point out, through specific examples, the inconsistencies with previously written work that caught your attention and wait for the student to react. You are likely to receive three responses: anger over what is perceived as an accusation, denial that what has been done constitutes plagiarism, or a tacit admission of guilt. Be careful to say nothing you might later regret. Close your conference by saying you will consult appropriate resources before a final decision is made.

THROUGH THE ADJUNCTS' EYES

Margaret:

The success of our first exam encouraged me to expand my parameters of evaluating student performance. I really believe in the value of having students analyze case problems, with an eye toward their applying the concepts to their present workplace or to an emerging management style that they will someday employ. The one weakness of my exam was that I initially graded the essay too subjectively. My scores would have been challenging to defend! Before returning the exams to the students, I developed a point system for each aspect of the writing—content, mechanics, conclusion—and re-scored the tests. As I employ additional case problem analysis, it will be important to develop a consistent evaluation system which I can review with students prior to developing their responses. I talked with another business professor who called this a "rubric."

Karen:

Really disappointed with the first exam I gave my students, I developed an alternative scoring plan that could help them salvage a good grade for the course. There are 4 or 5 really good students, however, who remain really anxious over their test results. Although I have always been a good test-taker, I realize there are many otherwise bright people who simply do not perform well on exams. As I was contemplating a corrective action I might take, I noticed an announcement on the bulletin board inside the faculty lounge about a free workshop the college is sponsoring on "alternative assessment." I'm going to attend it to get some additional ideas on how I might address the grade situation that now exists in my class.

Juan:

One of the pleasant outcomes of teaching in a different environment has been the chance to gather ideas on effective teaching from a wider range of professors. One person whom I spoke to about evaluating students told me about portfolios, which are apparently increasing in importance in some of the career preparation programs. He showed me several that were not only impressive in appearance and content, but that clearly demonstrated the students' mastery of essential course concepts. Several of my community college students would really respond to a more authentic method of assessment than exams, so I'm going to work up a way to give them a trial in my class.

TIPS FOR THRIVING

Effective instructors are continually looking for ways to improve their delivery of a particular course. As you teach a course for the first time and students submit their projects, ask yourself which of those submitted might provide students in subsequent terms with a clearer understanding of the assignment. Students who submit work of this quality will likely be flattered if you ask to borrow their project at the end of the course to use as a model for future students. Explain, of course, that the student retains "ownership" of the project and can have it back whenever he or she desires. (If they want to maintain the original, few would mind your making a photocopy.) When displaying the project for subsequent classes, take special precautions that it not get out of your sight—for it is truly priceless to the creator.

REVIEW OF KEY POINTS

- Alternative assessment supports and reinforces student-directed learning.
- Alternative assessment encourages students to integrate concepts learned into their everyday lives.
- Genuine learning is enhanced by giving students choices in the nature of assignments and the evaluative criteria.
- Consider portfolios as a potential alternative assessment tool.
- Develop rubrics to guide evaluation of student projects.
- Fit alternative assessment activities to the destinations of students.
- Deal proactively and deliberately with suspected plagiarism.

SUGGESTED READINGS

Annis, L. & Jones, C. (1995). Student portfolios: Their objectives, development, and use. In P. Seldin (Ed.), *Improving college teaching* (pp. 181–190). Bolton, MA: Anker.

Baron, J. B., & Wolf, D. P. (Eds.). (1996). *Performance-based student assessment: Challenges and possibilities.* Ninety-Fifth Yearbook of the National Society for the Study of Education. Chicago: University of Chicago.

Knowles, M. S. (1975). *Self-directed learning.* New York: Association Press.

Knowles, M. S. (1986). *The adult learner: A neglected species.* Houston: Gulf.

Pintrich, P. R., & Johnson, G. R. (1990). Assessing and improving students' learning strategies. In M. D. Svinicki (Ed.), *The changing face of college teaching* (New directions for teaching and learning No. 42) (pp. 83–92). San Francisco: Jossey-Bass.

12

BRINGING THE COURSE TO AN EFFECTIVE CONCLUSION

Focus Questions

- How do you energize a class that seems to be losing some of its momentum?
- How do you manage the critical questions related to final student grades?
- What end-of-term procedures can you expect?

Even though you have been careful to effectively manage the key mileposts in your class—the first meeting, the first examination, and the mid-term— you will most likely experience some loss of momentum as you approach the last few weeks of the term. This is due to such common factors in your and your students' lives as the juggling of multiple responsibilities and the mental fatigue it engenders. It is critical that you remain on common ground with students and offer regular encouragement. Resist the temptation to blame students for "slacking off"—it tends to become a self-fulfilling prophecy. This chapter will help you deal with the issues that frequently arise as you seek to lead the class to the finish line.

DEALING PROACTIVELY WITH A LOSS OF MOMENTUM

As you enter the last few weeks of the term, it is common for some students to demonstrate tell-tale signs of fatigue and loss of momentum:

- Arriving late to or excessively missing class
- Assignments that are late or below acceptable standards

- A decline in mental engagement and/or participation in class discussions
- A decline in spontaneity and sense of humor

As in personal or work relationships, the key to solving the situation is proactive, positive communications. Assuming you have done most of the things previously recommended, you are probably well positioned to achieve success if you will simply talk with students. If the problem is widespread and students have developed a team spirit, you might want to talk to the entire class at the beginning of a class session. Otherwise, you would probably achieve better results in addressing students individually. Be careful to use a constructive approach and a nonjudgmental tone of voice or you might create more harm than improvement.

Gently share your concern, identify some of the behaviors you have observed, and give students the opportunity to react a bit. Expect to hear how much they enjoy the course and your instruction followed by the challenges they are experiencing. Demonstrate clearly again that you believe in win–win relationships and remind them of the goals you set as you began the course together. Gain their commitment to the importance of those goals and reinforce your determination. At the same time, let them know you are enthusiastic and supportive and will exceed their expectations in energizing the class if they will agree to finish the course strongly.

It is common after the midpoint of the term to have a student stop coming to class altogether. While your initial reaction might be that the student has lost commitment, more often than not it is because the student became overwhelmed by the multiple demands on his or her time. Since your goal has been to build win–win relationships with students, we suggest you telephone such students at home to rekindle a dialogue that encourages them to return and finish the course. Be prepared to hear a wide variety of excuses and comments—some which you will probably easily accept, others which might seem trivial. Listen genuinely and try to understand the perspective of those who may have had quitting modeled often in their lives. Be willing to offer some specific type of relief to the student, such as an extra tutoring session or an extension in the due date of an assignment. Be sure to communicate a high level of performance you would in turn expect from the student. Offering such an "olive branch" to students demonstrates an unexpected level of concern to which many will respond in a very positive way.

In your approach to class sessions, clearly demonstrate your concern and willingness to be part of the solution by using responsive teaching techniques to energize the course:

- Shorten the length of lecture sessions.
- Employ more cooperative learning activities, engaging students in the application of concepts covered earlier in the course.

- Use more audiovisual materials and action-based activities, which engage the minds of students.
- Schedule an upbeat guest speaker who will tie together several key concepts of the course, emphasizing the analysis, synthesis, and evaluation steps of Bloom's Taxonomy.
- Provide feedback which is positive, timely, and specific, to students collectively and individually, as frequently as possible.

The energy you invest will be far less than the emotional letdown you would feel at the end of the course if you did nothing to address the situation.

THE CHALLENGE OF DETERMINING GRADES

One of the thorniest challenges facing contemporary college and university instructors is the awarding of final course grades. On one hand, most instructors seek to establish and maintain a standard of true excellence for their courses, to motivate students toward producing their best work and to demonstrate traditional values to their colleagues. On the other hand, instructors realize that students will, other things being equal, enroll first in the classes taught by professors who award higher grades, contributing to the "recruit, retain, and satisfy" mindset so often tacitly promoted by instructional leaders concerned about maintaining enrollments. Factor in employer and family expectations affecting students, and the situation becomes even more challenging.

In recent years, "grade inflation" has permeated the culture of American higher education in spite of the efforts of many academics to stifle it. While most who study the situation agree that grade inflation is most prevalent at highly selective private colleges, grades at public universities and less selective institutions have risen also. Against this contemporary context, adjunct professors typically bring to their teaching the grading standards they experienced as students—sometimes decades earlier. In the higher education environment which has changed so dramatically in recent years, holding on to what many consider artificially high standards can be an Achilles heel for adjunct professors.

The task of determining final course grades is typically filled with a great deal of ambiguity at most institutions. While the formalized precept of academic freedom dictates that each professor may, within reasonable parameters, deliver instruction and assign grades according to personal standards, some institutions employ methods of monitoring final course grades. One common method employs a "grade justification" or similarly-titled form, which instructors who assign a disproportionate number low and/or high grades are required to use to clarify their grading decisions. It is critical for new instructors to fully understand and adhere to the formal grading protocols of the institution.

In addition, each institution, and often departments within the institution, follow an informal posture toward determining final grades. Many factors feed the development of the informal posture toward grading, including historical precedent, philosophy of instructional leaders, nature of the student body, and the philosophy of competing institutions and those to which students might transfer. The expectations of parents and other stakeholder groups can also be significant. The new adjunct professor should solicit input on this issue from a variety of sources before assigning grades for the first course taught. Clearly there is an ethical problem inherent in this dilemma which might require significant dialogue and personal reflection.

Given a clear understanding of the full context of the issue of assigning grades, the professor must deal with the dynamics of the students in each particular course. Many younger students have been conditioned through their secondary educations to expect higher grades than many instructors believe they may deserve. Thus, while many students are highly dissatisfied by grades lower than they expect, they often are not highly motivated to pursue higher grades. Nontraditional students, grounded in a different grading paradigm, are often highly motivated to achieve higher grades and will often exert much additional effort to achieve one more point on a grade.

Some highly successful contemporary instructors assign relatively low grades to students who fail to achieve at a satisfactory level. Ultimately, you are the standard setter for each course you teach, and personal discretion has been historically supported. The key to managing final course grades lies in consistently communicating, reinforcing, awarding, and defending your standards, while remaining focused on the best interests of your students.

CONDUCTING EFFECTIVE CLOSING CLASS MEETINGS

Nearly as much as the first class meeting, the final session or two are critical to the success of each instructor. Through the administration of the final course examination and often the students' evaluations of the course and instructor, the closing class meetings establish within the mind of each student a paradigm of holistic evaluation. The perception that is reinforced in those final sessions will largely influence the students' sense of personal achievement, as well as their attitude toward the instructor and their total learning experience.

With so much riding on the outcome, it is critical to manage effectively each aspect of the closing class meetings. Be sure to:

- Prepare an agenda of items you should address prior to giving the final examination or distributing student evaluation forms.
- Create a professional visual image to students entering the classroom—clean boards, appropriately arranged desks, and lack of clutter.
- Manage the predictable tension of exam-taking by greeting students by name as they enter the classroom—in a relaxed, reassuring manner, being careful not to discount the importance of the exam.
- If a student evaluation is to be completed, clearly outline the procedures and leave the classroom with your briefcase of examinations.
- Thank students for their effort in the class and reassure them that the energy they invested in the course will pay off in some specifically mentioned way.
- Using your agenda as a guide, review key items such as the status of projects or papers which students may have submitted, and when and how examination scores will be available.
- Encourage progress toward students' educational goals by identifying the next logical course(s) within the curriculum which each should take, including specific information such as course number, dates, time, and instructor.
- If known, identify the next course you expect to be teaching for the institution and encourage students to enroll.
- Immediately before distributing the final exam, ask if there are any last-minute questions specific to the exam.
- While preparing to distribute the final examination, specify the procedures for submitting it and answer sheets if used, along with directions for students' picking up graded assignments you have ready for distribution.
- Avoid saying much more—students are inherently anxious about the final exam and want to "get on with it."
- As students leave following the exam, quietly say a warm "good bye" to each at the door, sharing some bit of personalized, positive feedback (perhaps about a well-done assignment) and wish them well as they pursue their goals.

Students vividly remember those few teachers who "go the extra mile" to ensure they learned not only the subject matter, but the context into which that subject matter fits. By managing the last moments of the course effectively, you increase the likelihood that your students will retain the same vivid perception of you and will be encouraged to pursue their educational goals even more passionately than before they enrolled in your course.

In the days following the conclusion of the course, don't be surprised if your more engaged students seek you out, via telephone or in person, to bring to closure their feelings about their experience with you. In a time punctuated with colorful accusations of all sorts, you would probably do well to be a bit cautious, but be assured that most efforts of students are genuine and pleasant. Such encounters are among the most gratifying within the overall teaching experience.

SUBMITTING END OF TERM REPORTS

By the end of the term, you will have been provided a final grade roll and most likely some standard report forms required by the institution or department. Remember that timeliness is crucial in the submission of these materials, so plan accordingly. If details related to the materials or procedures are unclear, consult the adjunct faculty handbook, the secretary of your instructional leader, or other resource well in advance of the deadline.

A word about confidentiality. Many of us attended college when professors commonly posted the names and final course grades on their office doors, and most of us probably did not care for the practice. The federal Buckley Amendment requires professors to maintain the privacy of information related to students, including grades. Such information should not be shared with anyone other than the student, including parents who could conceivably telephone you and build their request for information on the fact that they are paying the tuition bill. Be understanding, but be firm and professional in dealing with such requests.

THROUGH THE ADJUNCTS' EYES

Karen:

As the semester has progressed, I have become even busier at the law firm. I am embarrassed that my preparation for the last two class meetings probably totals three hours—twenty minutes here, fifteen minutes there, etc. I didn't get the chance to flesh out some of the ideas for alternative assessment or to spend much time re-working the final exam Mr. Jackson used before. The students didn't perform much better on the final than the mid-term. Averaging the final course grades yielded nearly two-thirds C's and no A's in the entire class.

While I still see the rain-making possibilities of teaching, I wonder if I'm cheating the students by not having more time to prepare for class.

Margaret:

The informal evaluation was a real "wake-up call" for me. Since then, I used no videos and only one guest speaker. She was well received, largely because of a four-week lapse between her and the previous speaker. The classroom has become much livelier as I've developed activities based on actual personal experiences during my last few years in management. On the final exam, I used an exercise, worth 20% of the exam score, which students worked on in a group after completing and submitting the individual portion of the exam. That activity clearly reinforced to students the movement in industry today toward team-based management, and every one of the students, although surprised, performed very well.

As one of the students, Jan, was leaving after completing her final exam, she made a point to thank me for a "terrific" course, then went on to say that she had decided to pursue a career as a human resource manager. That one heartfelt comment made all the challenges of the semester worth it!

Juan:

After I used the role-playing exercise, the remainder of the semester went very smoothly. I felt connected to the students—like I was a partner in the achievement of their educational goals.

The final exam was designed to be practical and realistic—representative of the kinds of issues that students would need to handle at work. Several students far exceeded their previous exam scores, which indicated that they had not only mastered the material but developed a lot more self-confidence. Comparing grades from this class with my undergraduate course at the university, I realize that, while the community college students didn't score as high on exams, they seemed to have developed a much deeper understanding of the course material.

TIPS FOR THRIVING

As students leave the final class meeting, think about providing each with some very inexpensive memento of the course. It might be something funny, such as a photocopy of a cartoon that related to a particularly memorable classroom discussion. It might be something highly useful, such as a government pamphlet that relates to some health or safety issue. It might be something very thought-provoking, such as a memorable quote from a revered figure studied during your course. Whatever it is, let it be uplifting and speak to who you are and to your philosophy of teaching. Give it with a smile, shared eye contact, thanks, and a warm handshake.

As your initial teaching experience concludes, remember to say "thanks" to those who helped your efforts:

- A card to your instructional leader(s) and their administrative assistant(s), as well as campus resources, such as librarians, who were especially useful
- Personally expressed thanks to custodians, security guards, and others without whom your duties would have been much more difficult to perform
- Appropriate tokens of appreciation to family members and work colleagues whose willingness to carry a share of your load made things go more smoothly and upon whom you will continue to depend as you teach

REVIEW OF KEY POINTS

- Look for tell-tale signs of the loss of student momentum.
- Expect to invest class time in energizing students' progress toward the conclusion of your course.
- Remind students of the learning objectives you established together early in the course.
- Pursue, via telephone, students who stop coming to class.
- Calculate and monitor students' overall grades throughout the course.
- Become familiar with department and institutional formal and informal policies regarding grade distribution.
- Carefully plan and orchestrate the closing two meetings of the class.
- Submit end-of-term reports in a prudent and timely fashion.
- Consistently maintain the confidentiality of students' grades and related information.

SUGGESTED READINGS

Duffy, D. K., & Jones, J. W. (1995). *Teaching within the rhythms of the semester.* San Francisco: Jossey-Bass.

Gose, B. (1997, July 25). "Efforts to curb grade inflation get an F from many critics." *The Chronicle of Higher Education, 43*(46).

13

EVALUATING YOUR TEACHING

Focus Questions

- Why should you informally evaluate your performance throughout the course?
- How can you effectively solicit meaningful feedback from students and colleagues?
- What are the common procedures for end-of-term evaluation?

Legislators, taxpayers, parents, students, and other stakeholders in the American system of higher education—increasingly focused on a global society and marketplace—have become increasingly concerned about life-long, effective learning. As the business community has embraced a "quality movement," institutions of higher education have been mandated by various governmental entities and their regional accrediting associations to embrace more intensive measurements of their output. Increasingly accountable to their stakeholders, colleges and universities must (sometimes over the objections of academic traditionalists) be prepared to convincingly document the learning of their graduates. That emphasis has filtered down to the classroom level, impacting every professor—new or veteran, full-time or adjunct. "Teaching without learning is just talking." (Angelo & Cross, 1993).

A key characteristic of those dedicated to long-term success is their commitment to continuous self-improvement. Because of the nature of their environment, adjunct professors especially must "own" the process—data gathering, evaluation, and implementation of corrective measures—from the very outset of their teaching. Their teaching improves by continually focusing on which concepts or skills are most essential for students, regularly assessing student progress, and identifying ways to more effectively facilitate student learning. Virtually all institutions employ formal instructor evaluation procedures. But an adjunct professor's waiting passively for the first round of student evaluations, or the less-common classroom observation by instructional leader, is quite risky. Increasingly market-oriented, discipline leaders are hesitant to continue to employ a new adjunct professor who garners student complaints about their teaching or receives even a smattering of seriously unsatisfactory feedback in the formal student evaluation process. Nearly always, ineffective teaching methods and negative student perceptions could have been uncovered and corrected had more proactive measures been employed early in the term.

CONDUCTING INFORMAL STUDENT EVALUATIONS

Human beings typically have some very paradoxical views of evaluation. While we want feedback to affirm our self-efficacy, we are often reluctant to ask for it out of fear of rejection. Resistance to initiating evaluation of one's performance is often greatest among the least experienced in any particular endeavor. Thus, new adjunct professors, who often perceive the greatest risk in asking for help, are harmed the most from not receiving it while benefitting the most when it is provided. Stated more succinctly, adjunct professors who fail to improve dramatically in their early teaching assignments are often not asked to return. A similar paradox exists for evaluators, who may be reluctant to provide meaningful evaluative data for fear of having their identity attached to the evaluative comments. Therefore, in seeking feedback from those capable of providing it, be sensitive to their perspective so you can access it most liberally.

Clearly the key to effective evaluation in your classroom is to make it a natural, informal, on-going component of your regular practices. Most students who have not previously had their opinions so actively solicited typically respond very positively. Actively involving students in ongoing evaluation is a strategy that has been employed successfully for decades by instructors committed to continuous self-improvement. The key mileposts during a course when evaluation is especially useful for instructors, as well as natural to gather, include the following:

- At the end of the first class meeting
- Immediately after the first examination, or following the submission of first project
- At mid-term
- At the end of the term, when a formal process is typically employed

Using the first three mileposts to gather data effectively enables you to discover problems before they become difficult to overcome. Furthermore, it encourages students to provide you additional individualized feedback on a regular basis and reduces the chances a student will harbor a complaint that shows up for the first time on the formal, end-of-the-term evaluation. We will look at each a bit more closely.

If you followed the suggestions for conducting an effective first class meeting in Chapter 6, you should have begun to create an environment where students feel very comfortable providing useful feedback. At the end of that first class meeting, take full advantage of this dynamic. Provide each student a 3 × 5 index card or other uniform piece of paper, encouraging anonymity and a sense of personal security in providing honest feedback. After placing a container near the exit door, write the items listed in Chapter 6 or several items from the following list on the board:

- What was your biggest surprise during this class today/tonight?
- Who was the most interesting student you met today/tonight? Why?
- What one thing are you most looking forward to in this class?
- What is the biggest challenge you see for yourself in this class?
- What aspect(s) of the class, syllabus, etc. do you have a question about?

Tell students how genuinely committed you are to getting the course off to a successful beginning. Ask them to invest a few minutes in the success of their course by responding. Direct them to drop their cards, unsigned, into the receptacle as they leave the room to go home, and thank them for their input. Do not look at the cards until you get home, to your office, or wherever you prepare for class.

As you review these comments, you probably will be pleasantly surprised at how much students enjoyed the first class meeting and the frankness some expressed in their responses. You would be well advised to review the cards carefully, identify any patterns that might be evident, and make notes from which you might make a few positive comments to open the following class period. Most importantly, you should strongly consider making a small adjustment in classroom procedures or some other significant aspect of the course to signal that you are fully invested in the informal evaluation process.

A second natural milepost for seeking evaluation from students is following the first examination or submission of their first major assignment—prior to those items being graded. Employing the same procedure used at the end of the first class meeting, write several items on the board, such as those on the following list:

- What was your biggest challenge in completing this assignment (or preparing for this exam)?
- What would you do differently on this assignment/test if you could?

- Which resource (library, fellow student, other teacher) did you most rely on for help?
- Without making the assignment (or test) shorter (or easier), what suggestion, if any, would you make so that the assignment would be even more worthwhile?

As in the first evaluation, you probably will be surprised by the quality and quantity of feedback which this activity elicits. Having asked for their feedback, you are obligated to do something with it, most likely by reacting to their comments when opening the following class meeting. You may get some creative excuses for what turned out to be less than exemplary work. While you probably want to resist the frequent request to lower your standards, you might want to consider implementing some of the comments when you assign the next project or as you clarify expectations for the following examination.

Your third natural milepost for eliciting informal student evaluative comments is at mid-term. By that point, students likely will have completed several assignments and one or more tests or quizzes. Having conducted the first two evaluations, you are likely to have created an environment where students are fairly comfortable sharing their deeper feelings. Employ the same procedure as before while asking students to respond to several of the following:

- What have you most benefitted from in the course to this point?
- What would you like to have left out, added, or modified?
- How would you assess your own efforts to this point?
- What would you like to add during the remainder of the term?
- On a scale of 1 (poor) to 10 (outstanding), what score would you give the course at this point?

The questions should elicit your most detailed responses to date, providing you with significant data for contemplating changes which you might want to consider for the remainder of the term, or for employing the next time you teach the course. Again, you should react somewhat to responses at the following class meeting to demonstrate your commitment to the concept of continuous improvement. You might also expect some pointed critical comments by this point. Resist the urge to strike back at the class over such comments, or to single out the person who might have made them. Protect the integrity of the process and be constructive.

In addition to these periodic surveys, we have found it useful to solicit conversational feedback from key students throughout the term. The results of your first exam and volunteered student feedback will help you identify the several students, typically found in most classes, who are most invested in its outcome and most able to provide you effective feedback on your teaching performance. Several times during the middle of the term, ask this group to stay at the end of class and help you assess progress in the class.

Gathering this data informally throughout the term will enable you to produce an ever-richer learning experience for the overwhelming majority of your students and make teaching much more rewarding. In addition, it should reduce the amount of negative feedback you would have otherwise received on the formal, end-of-the-term student evaluation so critical to the future decisions of your instructional leader.

ARRANGING INFORMAL OBSERVATIONS BY COLLEAGUES

Another extremely valuable activity you might employ early in your teaching career is to invite your mentor, peer adjunct, or other experienced instructor with whom you have developed rapport to attend your class, observe your teaching, and provide feedback. You might ask them to use the form found in Appendix 13.2 or the official form of the institution, but be aware that some colleagues will resist such a degree of formality and the degree of criticism it inherently engenders. Having someone especially familiar with the course might optimize the quality of the feedback, but feedback of a general nature from someone totally unfamiliar with the course is probably better than no feedback at all.

Realize there is significant risk in this process unless you are absolutely comfortable with the person observing your teaching and they are comfortable playing this role. Many will decline, for perfectly understandable reasons, so resist applying pressure of any kind. The simple fact that you invited them to participate in the process might plant a seed that will bear the fruit of useful feedback later. In addition, realize there probably is less need to initiate this action when the institution does not employ a formal observation process. One of your primary motivations is to learn from others' experiences when there is a formal process in place that you must satisfy.

FORMAL STUDENT RATINGS

At nearly every American college and university it is common practice to employ a system of student evaluation of instructor effectiveness and courses at the conclusion of each term. Many professors dread this experience, for some perfectly understandable reasons. They frequently make their opinions on the issue known to their peers, and sometimes even to students. Although admittedly imperfect, the practice of conducting student evaluations and of instructional leaders relying on their results is a given. To openly criticize the process invites the creation of some unhealthy psychological dynamics in the classroom or between the professor and administrator. As stated earlier, the process especially affects the continued employment of new adjunct professors. Therefore, you are encouraged to view student evaluation in its most positive light—as an opportunity to gain feedback that will enable you to improve the quality of your instruction in succeeding courses and enable instructional leaders to make more valid decisions about future course assignments.

Most formal student evaluation processes employ a form, standard to a particular instructional unit or to the institution as a whole. The form typically contains a series of closed-end statements, such as:

- The instructor was knowledgeable in the subject area.
- The instructor was well prepared for each class meeting.
- The instructor presented the material in a clearly understandable manner.
- The course examinations and other evaluative measures, e.g., projects, fairly and accurately measured students' mastery of the course material.
- The methods of instruction were effective and appropriate for this course.
- The instructor used class time wisely, including starting and ending on time.

A Likert scale is typically employed, with categories from *strongly agree* through *strongly disagree,* (or some similar system), to which numerical values can be assigned. Such a system enables the calculation of an overall score and allows instructional leaders to make a variety of comparisons. Most forms also include several open-ended questions that enable students to comment on a wide range of issues. Since the results on the student evaluation are so critical, you would be very wise to obtain a copy of the form used in your teaching situation well in advance of its administration date.

To protect the anonymity of students and validity of results, most colleges and universities have developed precise procedures for administering student evaluations. While these vary somewhat among institutions, these procedures typically include:

- Scheduling of the activity at the close of the term
- Administration of the evaluation, and transport of forms, by someone other than the instructor—e.g., an administrator, peer teacher or student
- The instructor leaving the classroom during the administration of the evaluation
- The availability of the completed forms for the professor to review only after the submission of student grades and end-of-term reports, or after a specific date

Taking liberties with these procedures, even unintentionally, is viewed by many instructional leaders as a breach of ethical standards. Therefore, be very careful to clarify explicitly the procedures employed in your situation before administering your first student evaluation.

To achieve their goal of improving teaching effectiveness, the student ratings process must be effectively managed by each professor. First, students must be provided sufficient reflective time to complete the form. Scheduling the activity as the last item of a given class meeting, or immediately before a timed final exam, is likely to lead to insufficient and ineffective input by students. The activity should be introduced effectively by the instructor; a statement of the value and seriousness of the process must be emphasized. Lastly, the evaluation forms must be carefully reviewed shortly after the completion of the term while the issues that might arise from their contents are still fresh in your mind.

Be aware that the new adjunct professor is often surprised the first few times student evaluations are reviewed. Students who are shy, unassertive, or "mean-spirited" will sometimes rate your performance below what you believe it should be, or they may write comments that are a total surprise and perhaps blatantly unfair. No one likes to be judged, especially by those whose judgement is frequently not well intended. However, the formalization of a student voice in the instructional process creates a positive dynamic. When fully understood and appropriately managed, it provides you the most effective and consistent source of data upon which to improve your instruction. Your efforts to informally gather evaluative data throughout the term will likely prevent the type of significant negative feedback that sometimes overwhelms the new adjunct professor.

FORMAL OBSERVATION/EVALUATION
BY INSTRUCTIONAL LEADER

Many colleges and universities conduct formal observations of adjunct professors' teaching, though less frequently than the administration of student evaluations. The timing and other factors influencing formal observations make them a less-than-perfect but useful tool for faculty development. As with student evaluations, you can maximize the rewards of observations through a constructive perspective on their potential, and sound management practices.

First, you must thoroughly understand the process employed in your teaching situation. Gather answers to as many of the following questions as possible:

- Who conducts the observation? Does the observer prefer to be briefly introduced to the students or treated as "a fly on the wall"?

- Are the observations announced in advance or are they spontaneous?
- Are you permitted input into the selection of the particular class meeting that will be observed—such as by providing a list of classes when examinations or other activities would create an inappropriate atmosphere?
- Is a form used to guide the observation? If so, is a copy available for you to review in advance? (A copy of a typical observation form is found in Appendix 13.2.)
- What unwritten factors contribute to the unique perspective of the person most likely to observe your teaching?
- How do the observation results factor into later decisions that affect you?
- Is a follow-up meeting with an instructional leader standard? How is it scheduled?

Besides helping you develop a grounded strategy for achieving success in the observation, knowing the answers to these and related questions will markedly reduce the anxiety you experience during this situation. In addition, your chances of success will have been markedly improved by employing the informal methods of evaluation suggested earlier in this chapter.

Regardless of the combination of methods employed by your institution to evaluate teaching performance, it is critical to demonstrate to instructional leaders that you are actively involved in the process of continuously improving your classroom performance. Even if not required in the institution's stated procedures, seek a brief appointment to discuss the results of formal procedures. If you are able to speak with your instructional leader, listen carefully to his or her counsel. Carefully share your reactions to the formal evaluation procedures and to feedback gathered through the informal methods you used. Highlight some of the changes you propose to incorporate into future courses you might be assigned. Keep the session brief and focused, with the goal of simply reinforcing your commitment to excellence.

SELF-EVALUATION OF YOUR TEACHING

The instructor who regularly engages in systematic self-evaluation will unquestionably derive greater reward (and less potential damage) from the formal methods of evaluation commonly employed by colleges and universities. Regular self-evaluation is especially important early in your part-time career as you seek to develop insights and skills that will form habits you can incorporate into your continually evolving teaching style.

One method for providing structure to an ongoing system of self-evaluation is to keep a journal of reflections on your teaching experiences. Regularly invest 15 or 20 introspective minutes following each class meeting to reflect and note the techniques that attained a positive reaction from students. Word processors are especially convenient and effective in helping you get the words "just right." Focus especially on the strategies and events in class that you feel could be improved. Focus also on the key mileposts, such as the first class meeting, administration of the first examination, and the review of the results of your examinations. Committing your thoughts to paper and editing them to reflect your precise thoughts and emotions enables you to develop more effective habits, build confidence in your teaching performance, and make more effective comparisons later.

We would suggest that you invest additional self-evaluation time at the midpoint of your course, much the same way a business conducts an audit or a college or a university conducts a self-study as a component of the accreditation process. Appendix 13.1 is an instrument for guiding a self-assessment. Depending on your course, institution, or other circumstances, you might want to modify the instrument to more effectively achieve your goals. The key is to begin your own self-assessment early in the course and to synthesize your findings with informal inputs from students and peers to develop a valid assessment of your strengths and needs at any particular point in time.

THROUGH THE ADJUNCTS' EYES

Juan:

Yesterday, I reviewed the evaluations of my course in the dean's office and am very pleased! While undergraduates at the university provided little feedback other than an occasional complaint about a trivial item, the community college students were quite free in their comments— mostly positive and a very few negative. They cited my "openness," "willingness to change," and "ability to treat each student as an individual." In addition, there were several expressions of thanks for making the course rewarding and memorable.

Karen:

In evaluating my own performance in the course, I realize that while Mr. Jackson's materials made the transition to teaching easier, they also prevented me from receiving the emotional reward that I was seeking. When, not "if," I teach again—be it next term or later—I will agree to do so only when it appears there will be more time to prepare to the level that students truly deserve.

My student evaluations were surprisingly good. Several noted I was "well prepared" (even though at times I didn't feel I was), "fair," and "used class time wisely." I realize that students had been provided only a small view of my capabilities as a college instructor.

Margaret:

When I phoned after the end of the term, my department chair called my student evaluations "glowing." Although I was a little nervous going in to review them, I found out he was right! Comments like "the best course I've ever taken," "extremely relevant to the real world," and "thanks for giving me a new, inside view of the corporate world" made the investment of time and emotional energy well worth it. Several also reminded me not to overuse videos and guest speakers and to emphasize the interactive case problems. While I've heard a couple of my fellow adjunct professors criticize the student evaluation process—"Who are they to evaluate me?"—I find it extremely useful in providing information on which I can rely to improve my teaching next semester.

TIPS FOR THRIVING

In recent years, a wide range of professionals from attorneys to business executives have markedly improved their job performance by employing video recorders in their preparation efforts. High-achieving adjunct professors would do well to follow their example.

While you might employ this strategy totally alone, a more effective method might be to do it in concert with another instructor—perhaps your mentor or other veteran instructor, or even a new adjunct professor colleague. Taping a 10 to 15 minute mini-lesson, then debriefing it using the observation evaluation form in the chapter appendix, would prove to be an especially valuable experience. Critiquing a videotaped session, rather than trying to recall the exact dynamics of a particular class, provides objectivity and is therefore more likely to effect change. Involving another instructor as an informal coach will enable you to gain from their experience and perspective and will reduce the chances of your engaging in self-deprecation.

Finally, reflect on your experiences from the nonacademic world, in which motivated and competent young professionals saw their careers stall in their tracks or even come to a crashing end. Often, it was due to a single off-hand remark at a company function, or to an inappropriate tone of voice with a client who was unknowingly connected in some mysterious way to an executive of the company. Early in your adjunct teaching career you enter a new "fish bowl," not unlike that of a prominent corporation. Unfortunately, we are often judged by a remark or action taken out of context by an observer who communicates it through his or her "personal filters" to a key decision-maker. As you seek to continue this most rewarding part-time experience, become especially careful about making comments in, or even outside, class that serve no useful purpose.

We once knew a promising adjunct professor whose part-time career at one institution was quietly terminated due to a derogatory comment about the local public school system. Unknown to the instructor at the time of the remark, the class included the spouse of a prominent school principal. The course had nothing at all to do with the system of public education or any other link that would have made the comment appropriate. While adjunct professors enjoy the protection of "academic freedom," privileges under it are not absolute. Most of us were provided with two ears and one mouth for a good reason!

REVIEW OF KEY POINTS

- Conduct informal student evaluations at the end of the first class meeting, following the first examination, and at mid-term.
- Informal student evaluations provide you significant data on which to build your teaching style.
- Informal evaluations reduce potential problems that would otherwise show up in the formal end-of-the semester evaluation.
- Ask open-ended questions likely to solicit grounded responses.
- Involve peer instructors or your mentor in observing and giving coaching tips on your teaching.
- Early in the term, obtain copies of the student evaluation form and observation criteria form from your instructional leader.
- Follow guidelines precisely when administering formal student evaluations.
- Maintain a journal to self-evaluate your early teaching experiences.

SUGGESTED READINGS

Centra, J. (1993). *Reflective faculty evaluation*. San Francisco: Jossey-Bass.

Fink, L. D. (1995). Evaluating your own teaching. In P. Seldin (Ed.), *Improving college teaching* (pp. 191–204). Bolton, MA: Anker.

Weimer, M., Parrett, J., & Kerns, M. (1988). *How am I teaching?* Madison, WI: Magna.

Weimer, M. (1990). What to do when somebody criticizes your teaching. In M. Weimer & R. A. Neff (Eds.), *Teaching college: Collected readings for the new instructor* (pp. 143–144). Madison, WI: Magna.

APPENDIX 13.1   SELF-ASSESSING MY TEACHING

1. How do I typically begin the class?
   Briefly review key points of previous class? Use "advance organizers"? Share current news events? Share "real-life" examples to which students are likely to relate?

2. Where/how do I position myself in class?
   Stand behind a podium or table? Regularly move throughout classroom? Sit on a table edge to speak less formally and create collegiality?

3. How do I move in the classroom?
   Back and forth across the front, looking down in a contemplative manner, or toward students and back to the front creating a sense of active interchange?

4. Where are my eyes usually focused?
   On lecture notes? On rear wall of classroom? Scanning eyes of students?

5. Do I facilitate students' visual processing of course material?
   Is a chalkboard or overhead projector used to reinforce key points? Do I overwhelm students' ability to process by displaying too many words at once, or do I write (or display) points in rhythm with their processing speed?

6. Do I change the speed, volume, energy, and tone of my voice?
   Are students likely to perceive which points are more critical?

7. How do I ask questions of students?
   Call student by name before posing question? Rhetorically, then provide an answer myself? Of the entire class, expecting a volunteered response?

8. How often, and when, do I smile or laugh in class?
   Do students smile or laugh with me?

9. How do I react when students are inattentive?
   Ignore it and "plow through the material?" Nonjudgmentally, state what I see and encourage students to explain?

10. How do I react when students disagree or challenge what I say?
    React as if threatened? Acknowledge the viewpoint then objectively explain its weaknesses?

11. How do I typically end a class?
    With planned material unaddressed? Smoothly, predictably?

APPENDIX 13.2 TEACHING OBSERVATION WORKSHEET

Professor: *Date:*   *Room:*

Course Title: *Time:*

Course ID#:   *Number of students present:*

1. Appropriate visual impact created?
2. Effective introduction to lesson?
3. Student participation elicited?
4. Expertise in subject matter demonstrated?
5. Variety of teaching methods used?
6. Energy and enthusiasm demonstrated?
7. Verbal communications effective?
8. Effective nonverbal communications?
9. Classroom management effective?
10. Appropriate support materials used?

Additional Comments:

14

BUILDING YOUR PART-TIME TEACHING CAREER

Focus Questions

- How do you develop a following among students?
- What opportunities are available for continually improving your teaching performance?
- How do you increase the long-term benefits of your part-time teaching career?

As you read or re-read this chapter, most or all of your first term of teaching is probably behind you. This book has alerted you to some of the joys and challenges you would experience, but there undoubtedly have been others you did not expect. There have been totally unforgettable students, and perhaps a few you would like to forget immediately. You probably can cite several examples of "seeing the light go on" in students' eyes, experiencing the reward for which all good teachers strive. Chapter 13 guided you through the process of thoroughly evaluating your teaching performance in objective, analytical ways. As you end the term, you have a great deal of data to process, much of which your mind wants to evaluate in holistic, subjective terms.

On an academic level, you most likely can discuss insights you have developed about concepts within your course which are now much more clear because of the experience of having had to examine them from one or more new perspectives. Unquestionably, you have learned more about teaching from being directly involved in it than you have learned from reading this or any other book. But, would you do it again? Although your discipline leader is likely to be asking you that question soon, avoid giving a hasty answer. You owe it to him or her, to yourself, but most of all, to students, to provide as grounded an answer as possible. To achieve that degree of insight requires significantly more evaluation and analysis.

REVISITING YOUR GOALS

Chapter 1 identified some of the major objectives that may have attracted you to adjunct teaching. They included:

- The opportunity to share wisdom you have gathered over the years with those who might benefit and to engage in stimulating intellectual and emotional activity
- Enhancing your potential for success in your full-time career by building credibility and making contacts
- The opportunity to make new social contacts among students and employees of the college or university
- The chance to repay a psychological "debt" to a teacher or other important person who influenced your success
- The opportunity to explore a potential full-time career in education
- The chance to earn additional income

Whether these or other statements accurately reflect the reasons that attracted you to pursuing part-time teaching, it is critical at this milepost in your development that you invest some quiet time in revisiting the reason(s) you decided to pursue adjunct teaching. Because of your background and present circumstances, as well as conditions within the institution, some of these goals may prove unachievable. Now is the time to identify and process those issues rather than to continue pursuing objectives that have little chance of attainment. Invest the time, through journal entries and talking with your mentor, that will enable you to resolve your expectations with reality. The result will be that whichever path you pursue will be best for you, for the institution, and for the students who will increasingly depend on you for the grounded wisdom they so badly need.

DEVELOPING YOURSELF AS A TEACHER

In recent years, many successful business leaders have promoted the concept of "total quality management" (TQM), sometimes referred to as "continuous quality improvement" (CQI). Increasingly, institutions of higher education have embraced these principles as well. One of the major precepts of this approach is that successful workers must "own" their continuous development within the chosen career. Assuming you have decided to continue the pursuit of your adjunct career, it is a philosophy you need to embrace. Within higher education, the principle of continuous self-improvement has long been acknowledged within the research requirements of professors. Only in recent years has it been integrated into the increasingly more critical teaching aspects of the profession.

One approach to self-development within the educational arena encourages "critical reflection"—a continuous process of self examination through four distinct lenses:

- Autobiographical reflection
- Students' eyes
- Colleagues' perceptions and experiences
- Literature of the profession (Brookfield, 1995)

The preceding chapters have identified some sources of data for each of these—journal entries, informal and formal student evaluations, informal peer evaluations, and formal observation by instructional leaders, to name a few. Each chapter has also suggested additional readings that would help you expand your knowledge base and gain new perspectives. Remembering that we tend to read a great deal in areas in which our knowledge base is already significant, and less in areas in which we are most deficient, seek out new, diverse topics. The key to achieving real growth is to do something now with this information, thoroughly processing and applying it to your individual situation.

Assuming student evaluations were performed for your course, you have perhaps the most valuable source of data available for helping you formulate a grounded understanding of your teaching efforts. Typically, most colleges and universities will make student evaluations available to adjunct professors shortly after the completion of the term. Plan to make an appointment to review them at a leisurely pace, then if possible, discuss your perceptions with the discipline leader. Expect there to be some predictable feedback, but also anticipate some surprises. Expect to feel somewhat attacked, even if critical responses represent only a small portion of the total evaluative data. Expect to find yourself trying to guess "Who in the world wrote that?" Most of the feedback will be true, at least in the perception of the student who wrote it—as imperfect as those students often are. Embrace their comments, for it is probably the best information you have upon which to build any improvement. Since you will likely read the especially critical responses several times, invest the time to read the positive comments a second or third time as well.

Allow yourself a bit of time to reflect before discussing your reactions with the discipline leader. He or she probably values this process of student input a great deal, and most likely recalls how hurtful such comments were the first time his or her classroom performance was reviewed. Teaching is one of life's most challenging activities—especially the first time it is attempted. Your discipline leader probably has coached new adjunct professors before, and respects vulnerability, insightful reflection, and genuine dialogue much more than defensive posturing. Therefore, when you talk, be yourself, but your *best* self—analytical, constructive, and professional.

Before meeting with the discipline leader, review his or her "bigger picture" and seek to assess how your delivery of the course helped the department achieve its overall academic goals. Be prepared to share the specific strengths of your teaching experience, based on the input of students, evaluators of other types, and especially on your own ongoing self-assessment. Identify several items you clearly need to improve. The better the match between others' assessments and your self-assessment, the more confidence and trust the discipline leader will have in your judgement and the more likely he or she will be to extend the opportunity for you to teach again. Review the program curriculum and course descriptions found in the college catalog, as well as the schedule of courses for the upcoming term, and be prepared to make a valid assessment of the other courses you believe you could successfully teach.

Lastly, find out where the successful adjunct professors "hang out" before or after class and position yourself there. Buy some coffee or cold drinks for others and uncover those who, like you, are committed to self-improvement in the classroom. As in any activity, there will be naysayers who seem to thrive on negativity; keep your distance. Strive to make one or two new friends rather than be known to everybody. Seek out campus resources for improving your teaching—faculty development centers or workshops and seminars that increasing numbers of colleges and universities are making available to their part-time faculty members. Update your knowledge about the institution's course reimbursement policy and enroll in a public speaking or computer class. Adjunct professors who report a sense of isolation seldom take advantage of the many everyday and inexpensive resources that are so commonly available on college campuses to those who seek them out.

BUILDING YOUR FOLLOWING AMONG STUDENTS

As stated before, higher education is increasingly a market-driven endeavor. Besides your delivery of high-quality, well-received instruction, probably the single biggest factor that impacts your continued employment as an adjunct professor is the ability to attract, retain, and satisfy students. Stated another way, that means developing a following among students who not only will enroll in subsequent courses you will teach, but who will recommend you to their friends and work colleagues. If the instructional leader perceives that your being identified as the instructor for the course was the determining factor in its attaining satisfactory enrollment, you have satisfied a critical criterion for continued employment. But how do you attain such a student following?

You probably can cite several students with whom you developed very rewarding relationships during the term. You no doubt can clearly identify also several blunders you made. Developing a strong following among students involves the time- and energy-intensive process of maximizing the number and quality of positive student relationships, while minimizing the negative encounters.

Whether or not you have conceptualized it, you develop a relationship with every single student in your class. Ultimately, the student defines the nature of that relationship. Some want on-call, personalized attention frequently throughout the course, while others would prefer not much more than for you to recognize them by name. Chapter 6 encouraged you to have students complete a "student profile" form that provides you some baseline information on which to build your knowledge of the student. You were also encouraged to keep those forms in a notebook where you keep other critical information, which you brought to each class meeting. Use the back of the profile form throughout the course to note developments with each student, record meetings or phone calls you held, and other useful information. Following the conclusion of the course, add the final grade and perhaps a reflective, evaluative comment. Such record keeping helps you learn more about each student, so that you can better tailor your instruction to their needs. It also provides information upon which you can build an on-going dialogue, at the beginning and end of class meetings and during breaks, throughout the course. It also provides you a file to which you can refer when recruiting students for subsequent courses.

Information gathered through "student profile" forms and your ongoing dialogue with students also enables you to help them build relationships with other students. We are not talking about sharing privileged information or "fixing students up" for dating, but, with their prior approval, increasing the common bonds between students. For example, a student who identified him- or herself as having served militarily in the Middle East might be identified as a potential resource for another student's research paper on some cultural practice indigenous to that area. Students' perceiving that you are looking out for their better interests and playing an active part in their synthesis of information is a win–win situation for all. Such perceptions contribute to the development of a student following so critical to your long-term success.

Finally, demonstrate to students your humanness. When possible, stop at the student union before class for a snack or refreshment and strike up a conversation with students you meet. Attend campus cultural or sporting events, greeting your students by name when you encounter them. When their body language indicates, share a few words and introduce yourself to their friends. You might be surprised at how such simple actions will not only enrich your classroom environment, but create a following among students who often are more isolated than you might expect.

DEVELOPING YOUR RELATIONSHIP WITH THE INSTRUCTIONAL LEADER

Much as you have grown to know each of your students, it is imperative as well that you actively seek to better understand the background, approach, and style of your instructional leader. A reminder of a caution stated earlier is ensure that you "Fit in before you seek to stick out." That is, demonstrate your understanding and acceptance of the culture of the instructional unit before making recommendations that you believe will make things better. Assume that the policies and procedures the instructional leader employs are predicated on sound information and experience, even though their intent might not be fully understandable based on your experience. Although there will probably be an appropriate time for you to share your suggestions, be careful to develop those carefully and share them only when a signal is sent that they are desired.

Once you have established your ability to recruit, retain, and satisfy students, your credibility with the instructional leader will grow rather significantly. Remember that one of the major reasons you have been invited to join the instructional team is your ability to link the course you teach to the "real world" into which the institution sends its students. Continually assess your ability to help the discipline leader achieve his or her noninstructional goals, such as your ability to attract new markets of students or extend the reach of the department by offering courses in additional settings (for example, at your full-time place of employment). After you formulate several suggestions, complete with contextual information and the names and telephone numbers of contact persons, make an appointment to share your perspective with your instructional leader. Your ability to help the instructional leader expand the program will markedly increase your perceived value to the department's overall mission.

Lastly, remember to say "thank you" on a regular basis to those who help you—not only the instructional leaders, but the support staff as well. Your card or small gift can go a long way toward achieving results that many adjunct instructors can only dream about.

CROSS-FERTILIZATION WITH YOUR FULL-TIME CAREER

Just as your full-time career certainly can stimulate your growth within the institution's instructional programs, your teaching offers significant benefits for the other arenas of your life, including your full-time employment. Such synergistic dynamics, in turn, hold the potential for enlarging the sphere of your influence and your total rewards.

Many businesses have come to realize the importance of continually developing their employees to utilize the technological tools and better understand the rapidly changing dynamics of today's marketplace—mirroring the "learning organization" concept espoused by Peter Senge in his blockbuster book *The Fifth Discipline*. Your ability to access educational and training resources for the benefit of your full-time employer, or even the civic and social organizations to which you belong, have great potential for expanding your influence on and off campus.

As your emerging abilities and contacts become increasingly important in the business world, be careful not to over-sell them to your full-time employer. While learning organizations are unquestionably growing in number and quality, a fair amount of managers in the private sector distrust those in academe. Nurture your core of supporters carefully, encouraging each to build links with others to slowly increase momentum. Your getting "out front" too boldly can be risky to the growth of your influence.

THE FUTURE OF THE ADJUNCT PROFESSORSHIP

The growth in employment of adjunct professors over the past twenty years shows strong signs of continuation well into the future. Institutions of higher education are changing dramatically in the way they deliver their mission. Many full-time faculty initially employed during the rapid growth of the late 1960s and early 1970s have recently retired or are rapidly approaching retirement. Mature students are returning to school, many for the first time in decades, and in the process are demanding more relevant and specialized instruction. Pressures increase on colleges and universities from taxpayers and donors to become more accountable and reduce budgets, commonly believed to be bloated by inefficiency fed by tenure and other traditional practices of higher education.

You have begun your journey into college teaching at a most opportune time. Colleges and universities increasingly are awakening to the value you provide and are committing themselves to providing the resources required for you to teach more effectively and efficiently. At the same time, expectations of your classroom performance by instructional leaders will rise. Having assumed ownership of your own development, as evidenced by your reading of this book and other activities, will position you well among other adjunct professors. Become a mentor to others and your personal rewards will not only increase, but the additional resources you attract in return will enhance your further development.

MAXIMIZING YOUR LONG-TERM OPTIONS

In recent years, the nature of work in America has undergone fundamental change. Few people will any more be employed by the same organization for a majority of their working lives. Many will work as independent contractors, concurrently performing closely related tasks for several different organizations. As full-time professors reach retirement age, their employing institutions will likely seek to supplant their teaching with more adjunct professors and with instruction delivered through a variety of distance learning methods, including television and the Internet. The full-time professors remaining will become as much invested in the program-building aspects of their departments as they are in the teaching aspects.

Your ability and willingness to employ the strategies suggested in this book will serve you well for the new paradigm in higher education. The flexibility and creativity required to operate effectively in several different arenas will pay huge competitive dividends for your career. Your ability to link resources to facilitate the achievement of complex goals will be rewarded richly. Your work life will become increasingly satisfying as you grow in your ability to identify potential connections between higher education, business, government, and service organizations. The fact that you have learned a fuller range of rewards from education will enable you to take advantage of changing situations while others are scrambling to react. You have started down an exciting road—enjoy its special potential to change people forever.

THROUGH THE ADJUNCTS' EYES

Margaret:

As I look back on my initial teaching experience, I, like any good businessperson, must revisit my goal in pursuing this position initially. Although I had some challenges along the way, it's clear from the student evaluations, as well as my own instincts, that my goal of being successful in order to open additional opportunities was achieved. The challenges I experienced probably made the end product sweeter than it would have been had the road been completely smooth. The skills in "reading" people and accessing their feelings, which I developed in my management career, are among the most critical for an instructor to possess. Knowing instinctively how effectively I was communicating and how I was challenging students to do their best work was very satisfying.

The biggest difference between my management career and teaching was in the excitement demonstrated by students when they grasped a concept or achieved a personal goal. Launching a new career—whether you're entering business or the teaching profession—is a very exciting enterprise!

Karen:

As I reflect on my first teaching assignment, I realize the importance of developing my own teaching style. Relying too much on someone else's approach—especially given their differences in age, gender, and philosophy of education—stifles the need for personal achievement that has clearly driven the other aspects of my life. If asked by the department chair if I would teach again, I must accept only if time is available to design the course "my way." When I recall my goal for entering teaching, I must admit that teaching enabled me to connect with people in the community who could help grow my legal career.

Juan:

As I pause to contemplate my future in teaching, I first realize the fundamental difference in mission between the university and community college. Serving as a professor at the university requires research and publishing, with a lower emphasis on teaching performance, while building a faculty career in the community college is exclusively focused on teaching success. Although I really prefer teaching, there were difficulties in connecting with the growing percentage of nontraditional students who challenge many things in the classroom. While I realize that a career in either type of institution is highly competitive and requires careful planning and networking, I would prefer to investigate the possibilities within each for a bit longer before making a firm commitment to pursue one over the other.

TIPS FOR THRIVING

Besides the normal reading you will do within your discipline area, your professional development would be greatly enriched by periodically reading materials geared to the broader higher education community. *The Chronicle of Higher Education,* available at nearly all college and university libraries and many public ones, as well as through individual subscription, is a weekly publication dedicated to providing a rich variety of information. Its regular sections include: The Faculty, Research, Information Technology, Government and Politics, Money and Management, Students, Athletics, Opinion and Arts, and a Gazette that lists promotions, retirements, and deaths within the higher education community. Each edition of the *Chronicle* also includes a Bulletin Board—the most widely accepted source of job openings in higher education. While its annual subscription cost might be outside the budget of someone who teaches part-time, it is a valuable resource to review periodically at the college library. Besides, hanging out there enriches the texture of your adjunct teaching experience, providing you a view of students and other faculty that you might not otherwise get.

Academic conferences, highly varied in scope, size, and length, are another resource you might want to access periodically. Some are international in scope and attract tens of thousands of attendees and hundreds of presenters, while others are more localized and attract fewer than one hundred attendees and but a few presenters. The National Adjunct Faculty Guild sponsors an annual conference dedicated to the unique interests and needs of adjunct faculty. You can access conference information and other organizational services through their web site—<http://www.sai.com/adjunct>. Besides major presentations and plenary sessions of specialized topics, conferences often also include an exposition of textbooks, software, and other teaching materials of interest to faculty and administrators. *The Chronicle of Higher Education* publishes a special edition twice yearly featuring upcoming conferences, as well as announcements in regular editions. Smaller scale conferences might be promoted directly to instructional leaders, so ask if this might be a possibility. A few colleges and universities provide funds for adjunct professors to attend conferences which offer the potential of reward to the institution.

In addition, there are other opportunities that might be appropriate self-development activities, depending on the discipline area, nature of the educational culture, and so forth. For example, colleges and universities sometimes sponsor, perhaps in conjunction with other institutions, activities of interest to teachers at all levels of education. Workshops on highly specialized topics, which may be free or require only a nominal fee, are especially popular. Like the full-fledged academic conferences, these activities provide rich opportunities for talking with potential colleagues and for sharing teaching ideas and experiences. In the process, you might build mutually beneficial relationships that will last throughout your teaching career.

REVIEW OF KEY POINTS

- Building your career as an adjunct professor begins with revisiting the goals that attracted you to the field initially.
- Continuous self-development of your teaching skills is consistent with contemporary practices of the business world.
- "Critical reflection" encourages you to examine your teaching through the eyes of your own autobiography, your students, your colleagues, and through professional literature.
- Initiate debriefing of your student evaluations with your instructional leader.
- Embrace your role in recruiting, retaining, and satisfying students.
- Begin to proactively build your relationship with your instructional leader by fully understanding his or her background, approach, and style.
- Finds ways to synergize your relationship with your instructional leader and other arenas of your life.
- Maximize your long-term options by understanding the changing nature of work and dovetailing your career-building efforts.

SUGGESTED READINGS

Brookfield, S. (1995). *Becoming a critically reflective teacher.* San Francisco: Jossey-Bass.
Marchese, T. (1991, November). TQM reaches the academy. *American Association for Higher Education Bulletin.*
Senge, P. (1990). *The fifth discipline.* New York: Currency Doubleday.

REFERENCES

Ailes, R. (1996). *You are the message: Getting what you want by being who you are.* New York: Doubleday.

Angelo, T., & Cross, K. P. (1993). *Classroom assessment techniques: A handbook for college teachers* (2nd ed.). San Francisco: Jossey-Bass.

Annis, L., & Jones, C. (1995). Student portfolios: Their objectives, development, and use. In P. Seldin (Ed.), *Improving college teaching* (pp. 181–190). Bolton, MA: Anker.

Armstrong, T. (1994). *Multiple intelligences in the classroom.* Alexandria, VA: Association for Supervision and Curriculum Development.

Arden, E. (1995, July 21). Ending the loneliness and isolation of adjunct professors. *The Chronicle of Higher Education, 46*(45), A44.

Avakian, A. N. (1995, June/July). Conflicting demands for adjunct faculty. *Community College Journal, 65*(6), 34–36.

Bank, J. (1994). *Outdoor development for managers* (2nd ed.). Aldershot, UK: Gower.

Banta, T. W. (1996). Using assessment to improve instruction. In R. J. Menges & M. Weimer (Eds.), *Teaching on solid ground: Using scholarship to improve practice* (pp. 363–384). San Francisco: Jossey-Bass.

Baron, J. B., & Wolf, D. (Eds.). (1996). *Performance-based student assessment: Challenges and possibilities.* Ninety-fifth Yearbook of the National Society for the Study of Education. Chicago, IL: University of Chicago Press.

Berne, E. (1964). *The games people play.* New York: Ballantine.

Bianco-Matthis, V., & Chalofsky, N. (Eds.). (1996). *The adjunct faculty handbook.* Thousand Oaks, CA: Sage.

Biles, G. E., & Tuckman, H. P. (1986). *Part-time faculty personnel management policies.* New York: American Council on Education/Macmillan.

Blanchard, K., & Johnson, S. (1982). *The one minute manager.* New York: Berkley Books.

Bloom, A. (1987). *The closing of the American mind.* New York: Simon & Schuster.

Bloom, B. S. & others (1956). *Taxonomy of learning objectives:* Volume One: *The cognitive domain.* New York: McKay.

Boice, R. (1992). *The new faculty member: Supporting and fostering professional development.* San Francisco: Jossey-Bass.

Bridges, J. (Writer & Director). (1973). *The paper chase [Film].* Beverly Hills, CA: Twentieth Century Fox.

Bridges, W. (1994, September 19). The end of the job. *Fortune, 130*(6). 61–74.

Brookfield, S. (1990). *The skillful teacher.* San Francisco: Jossey-Bass.

Brookfield, S. (1995). *Becoming a critically reflective teacher.* San Francisco: Jossey-Bass.

Caine, R. N., & Caine, G. (1991). *Making connections: Teaching and the human brain.* Alexandria, VA: Association for Supervision and Curriculum Development.

Candy, P. (1991). *Self direction for lifelong learning.* San Francisco: Jossey-Bass.

Carnegie, D. (1962). *The quick and easy way to effective speaking.* New York: Pocket Books.

Centra, J. (1993). *Reflective faculty evaluation.* San Francisco: Jossey-Bass.

Cohen, M. (1992). *Benefits on a budget: Addressing adjunct needs.* Paper presented at the annual meeting of the Speech Communication Association, Chicago, IL (ERIC Document Reproduction Services No. ED 355 578)

Cordes, C. (1998, January 16). As educators rush to embrace technology, a coterie of skeptics seeks to be heard. *The Chronicle of Higher Education, 44*(19), A25–A26.

Coulter, M. M. (1993). Modern teachers and postmodern students. *Community College Journal of Research and Practice, 17*(1), 51–58.

Covey, S. (1989). *The seven habits of highly effective people.* New York: Simon & Schuster.

Cross, K. P. (1994). Involving faculty in TQM through classroom assessment. In T. O'Banion (Ed.), *Teaching and learning in the community college* (pp. 143–159). Washington, DC: The Community College Press.

Danielson, C., & Abrutyn, L. (1997). *An introduction to using portfolios in the classroom.* Alexandria, VA: Association for Supervision and Curriculum Development.

Davis, J. (1993). *Better teaching, more learning.* Phoenix, AZ: The Oryx Press.

Davis, S. (1995). *The effect of a pedagogically-based staff development program for adjunct community college faculty.* Unpublished doctoral dissertation, George Mason University, Fairfax, Virginia.

Dewey, J. (1916). *Democracy and education.* New York: Macmillan.

Diamond, R. M. (1998). *Designing and assessing course and curricula: A practical guide.* San Francisco: Jossey-Bass.

Digest of Education Statistics, 1996. National Center for Education Statistics. U.S. Department of Education, Office of Educational Research and Improvement. NCES 96–133.

Doucette, D. (1994). Transforming teaching and learning using information technology. *Community College Journal, 65*(2), 18–24.

Duffy, D. K., & Jones, J. W. (1995). *Teaching within the rhythms of the semester.* San Francisco: Jossey-Bass.

Dunham, S. M. (1996). What college teachers need to know. In R. J. Menges & M. Weimer (Eds.), *Teaching on solid ground: Using scholarship to improve practice* (pp. 297–313). San Francisco: Jossey-Bass.

Eble, K. (1994). *The craft of teaching.* San Francisco: Jossey-Bass. *Educational Leadership* (Teaching for Authentic Student Performance) Vol. 54, No. 4. December 1996/January 1997. Association for Supervision and Curriculum Development.

Ericson, E. E. (1998, January/February). Gen X is OK, Part 1. *The American Enterprise, 9*(1), 38–41.

Erwin, J., & Andrews, H. (1993, November/December). State of part-time faculty services at community colleges in a nineteen-state region. *Community College Journal of Research and Practice, 17*(6), 555–562.

Erwin, T. D. (1991). *Assessing student learning and development.* San Francisco: Jossey-Bass.

Fink, L. D. (1995). Evaluating your own teaching. In P. Seldin (Ed.), *Improving college teaching* (pp. 191–204). Bolton, MA: Anker.

Flood, B. J., & Moll J. K. (1990). *The professor business: A teaching primer for faculty.* Medford, NJ: Learned Information.

Gappa, J., & Leslie, D. (1993). *The invisible faculty: Improving the status of part-timers in higher education.* San Francisco: Jossey-Bass.

Gappa, J. (1984). *Part-time faculty: Higher education at the crossroads.* [Association for the Study of Higher Education Research Report Number 3]. Washington, DC: Clearinghouse on Higher Education.

Gardner, H. (1983). *Frames of mind: The theory of multiple intelligences.* New York: Basic Books.

Gold, J. (1997, September 12). Student evaluations deconstructed. *The Chronicle of Higher Education, 44*(3), B8.

Gose, B. (1997, July 25). Efforts to curb grade inflation get an F from many critics. *The Chronicle of Higher Education, 43*(46).

Grieve, D. (1995). *A handbook for adjunct/part-time faculty and teachers of adults* (3rd ed.). Elyria, OH: Info-Tec.

Gross, R. (1995, October/November). Defining the future: The new mandate for distance learning in the 21st century. *Community College Journal, 66*(2), 28–33.

Grunert, Judith (1997). *The course syllabus: A learning-centered approach.* Bolton, MA: Anker.

Gup, T. (1997, November 21). The end of serendipity. *The Chronicle of Higher Education, 44*(13), A52.

Hakim, C. (1994). *We are all self-employed.* San Francisco: Berrett-Koehler.

Hall, R. M., & Sandler, B. R. (1983). Academic mentoring for women students and faculty: A new look at an old way to get ahead. *Project on the Status and Education of Women.* Washington, DC: Association of American Colleges.

Hammonds, K. H., & Jackson, S., with DeGeorge, G., & Morris, K. (1997, December 22). The new university. *Business Week,* 96–102.

Harnish, D., & Wild, L. (1993, May/June). Peer mentoring in higher education: A professional development strategy for faculty. *Community College Journal of Research and Practice, 17*(3), 272–282.

Harris, T. (1967). *I'm O. K., you're O. K.* New York: Avon.

Heller, S. (1996, March 1). Bowling alone. *The Chronicle of Higher Education, 42*(24).

Hersey, P., & Blanchard, K. (1982). *Management of organizational behavior.* Englewood Cliffs, NJ: Prentice-Hall.

Hill, S., Bahnik, M., & Dobos, J. (1989, January). The impact of mentoring and collegial support on faculty success: An analysis of support behavior, information adequacy, and communication apprehension. *Communication Education, 38,* 15–33.

Himmelfarb, G. (1996, November 1). A neo-Luddite reflects on the internet. *The Chronicle of Higher Education, 43*(10), A56.

Howe, N., & Strauss, B. (1993). *13th gen: Abort, retry, ignore, fail?* New York: Vintage Press.

Jacobs, L., & Chase, C. (1992). *Developing and using tests effectively.* San Francisco: Jossey-Bass.

Janzow, F., & Eison, J. (1990). Grades: Their influence on students and faculty. In M. D. Svinicki (Ed.), *The changing face of college teaching* (New Directions for Teaching and Learning No. 42) (pp. 93–102). San Francisco: Jossey-Bass.

Joyce, M., Weil, M., with Showers, B. (1992). *Models of teaching, 4th edition.* Boston: Allyn & Bacon.

Keil, K. L. (1998, January/February). An intimate portrait of generation X. *The American Enterprise, 9*(1), 49–51, 59.

Kent, N. (1996, May 7). Community colleges confront alternative futures. *Community College Times, 8*(9), 2–3.

Kindsvater, R., Wilen, W., & Ishler, M. (1996). *Dynamics of effective teaching* (3rd ed.). White Plains, NY: Longman.

Knowles, M. (1975). *Self-directed learning.* New York: Cambridge.

Knowles, M. (1980). *The modern practice of adult education: From pedagogy to andragogy.* San Francisco: Jossey-Bass.

Knowles, M. (1984). *The adult learner: A neglected species.* Houston: Gulf.

Kram, K., & Isabella, L. (1985, March). Mentoring alternatives: The role of peer relationships in career development. *Academy of Management Journal, 28*(1), 110–132.

Kram, K. (1983, December). Phases of the mentor relationship. *Academy of Management Journal, 26,* 608–625.

Kubiszyn, T., & Borich, G. (1996). *Educational testing and measurement: Classroom application and practice* (5th ed.). New York: HarperCollins.

Lankard, B. (1993). Part-time instructors in adult and vocational education. *ERIC Digest.* (ERIC Document Reproduction Services No. ED 363 797)

Lauridsen, K. (1994). A contemporary view of teaching and learning centers for faculty. In T. O'Banion (Ed.), *Teaching and learning in the community college* (pp. 229–244). Washington, DC: The Community College Press.

Leatherman, C. (1997, November 7). Do accreditors look the other way when colleges rely on part-timers? *The Chronicle of Higher Education, 44*(11).

Leatherman, C. (1997, October 10). Growing use of part-time professors prompts debate and call for action. *The Chronicle of Higher Education, 44*(7).

Lee, J., & Maitland, C. (1995, June 5). Faculty profile reveals surprises. *Community College Week, 7*(21), 4–5.

Lesko, P. D. (1995, December 15). What scholarly groups should do to stop adjuncts' exploitation. *The Chronicle of Higher Education, 42*(15).

Levinson, D., Darrow, C., Klein, E., Levinson, M., & McKee, B. (1978). *The seasons of a man's life.* New York: Knopf.

Lofland, J., & Lofland, L. (1984). *Analyzing social settings.* Belmont, CA: Wadsworth.

Lowther, M. A., Stark, J. S., & Martens, G. G. (1989). Preparing course syllabi for improved communications. *Research Program on Curriculum Design: Influences and Impacts.* Ann Arbor, MI: The National Center for Research to Improve Postsecondary Teaching and Learning.

Lyons, R. (1996). *A study of the effects of a mentoring initiative on the performance of new adjunct community college faculty.* Unpublished doctoral dissertation, University of Central Florida, Orlando.

Lyons, R. E., & Kysilka, M. L. (1997, April 18). *A comprehensive development program for new adjunct community college faculty.* Paper presented at the eighth annual national conference on college teaching and learning, Jacksonville, Florida.

MacGregor, J. (1990). Collaborative learning: Shared inquiry as a process of reform. In M. D. Svinicki (Ed.), *The changing face of college teaching* (New Directions for Teaching and Learning No. 42) (19–30). San Francisco: Jossey-Bass.

Magnan, R. (Ed.) (1990). *147 practical tips for teaching professors.* Madison, WI: Magna Publications.

Maitland, C. (1995, September). Part-time faculty in community colleges. *Community College Week, 8*(4), 4.

Marchese, T. (1991, November). TQM reaches the academy. *American Association for Higher Education Bulletin.*

Margolis, F. M., & Bell, C. R. (1986). *Instructing for results.* San Diego: Pfeiffer and Associates.

McGaughey, J. (1985). Parttime faculty: Integrity and integration. In D. Puyear (Ed.), *Maintaining institutional integrity: New direction for community colleges, No. 52.* San Francisco: Jossey-Bass.

McGrath, D., & Spear, M. (1988, January/February). A professorate is in trouble and hardly anyone recognizes it. *Change, 20*(1), 26, 53.

McGuire, J. (1993, June). Part-time faculty: Partners in excellence. *Leadership Abstracts, 6*(6).

McKeachie, W. (1994). *Teaching tips* (9th ed.). Lexington, MA: D.C. Heath.

Merriam, S. (1983, Spring). Mentors and proteges: A critical review of the literature. *Adult Education Quarterly, 33*(3), 161–173.

Merriam, S. (1988). *Case study research in education: A qualitative approach.* San Francisco: Jossey-Bass.

Merriam, S., & Brockett, R. (1997). *The profession and practice of adult education.* San Francisco: Jossey-Bass.

Milton, O. (1978). *On college teaching: A guide to contemporary practice.* San Francisco: Jossey-Bass.

O'Banion, T. (1995, December/January). A learning college for the 21st century. *Community College Journal, 66*(3), 18–23.

Notar, E. (1994). *Solving the puzzle: Teaching and learning with adults.* New York: Rivercross.

Palmer, P. K. (1997, November/December). The heart of a teacher. *Change, 29*(6), 14–21.

Phillips-Jones, L. (1982). *Mentors and proteges.* New York: Arbor House.

Pintrich, P. R., & Johnson, G. R. (1990). Assessing and improving students' learning strategies. In M. D. Svinicki (Ed.), *The changing face of college teaching* (New Directions for Teaching and Learning No. 42) (pp. 83–92). San Francisco: Jossey-Bass.

Quinn, B. J. (1980). *The influence of same-sex and cross-sex mentors on the professional development and personality characteristics of women in human services.* Unpublished doctoral dissertation, Western Michigan University, Kalamazoo.

Rawles, B. A. (1980). *The influence of a mentor on the level of self-actualization of American scientists.* Unpublished doctoral dissertation, Ohio State University, Columbus.

Richardson, R. C. (1992, Summer). The associate program: Teaching improvement for adjunct faculty. *Community College Review, 20*(1), 29–34.

Richardson, R., & Elliott, D. (1994). Improving opportunities for underprepared students. In T. O'Banion (Ed.), *Teaching and learning in the community college* (pp. 97–114).Washington, DC: The Community College Press.

Roche, G. (1979). Much ado about mentors. *Harvard Business Review, 20*(24), 26–28.

Rothenberg, D. (1997, August 15). How the web destroys the quality of students' research papers. *The Chronicle of Higher Education, 43*(49).

Roueche, J., Roueche, S., & Milliron, M. (1995). *Strangers in their own land: Part-time faculty in American community colleges.* Washington, DC: Community College Press.

Roueche, J., & Roueche, S. (1994). Creating the climate for teaching and learning. In T. O'Banion (Ed.), *Teaching and learning in the community college* (pp. 21–40). Washington, DC: The Community College Press.

Rudenstine, N. (1997, February 21). The internet and education: A close fit. *The Chronicle of Higher Education, 43*(24), A48.

Sacks, P. (1996). *Generation X goes to college.* Peru, IL: Open Court.

Schaub, D. J. (1998). Gen X is OK, Part II. *The American Enterprise, 9*(1), 42–45.

Schneider, A. (1998, March 13). More professors are working part time, and more teach at 2-year colleges. *The Chronicle of Higher Education, 44*(27), A14–A16.

Senge, P. (1990). *The fifth discipline.* New York: Currency-Doubleday.

Shapiro, E., Haseltine, F., & Rowe, M. (1978, Spring). Moving up: Role models, mentors and the patron system. *Sloan Management Review, 19,* 51–58.

Sheehy, G. (1995). *New passages.* New York: Random House.

Sinetar, M. (1987). *Do what you love, the money will follow.* New York: Dell.

Solomon, R., & Solomon, J. (1993). *Up the university: Re-creating higher education in America.* Reading, MA: Addison-Wesley.

Stark, J., & Lattuca, L. (1997). *Shaping the college curriculum.* Boston: Allyn & Bacon.

Svinicki, M. D. (1990). Changing the face of your teaching. In M. D. Svinicki (Ed.), *The changing face of college teaching* (New Directions for Teaching and Learning No. 42) (pp. 5–15). San Francisco: Jossey-Bass.

Treichler, D. G. (1967). Are you missing the boat in training aids? *Audio-visual communications.* New York: United Business Publications.

Trigwell, K. (1995). Increasing faculty understanding of teaching. In W. A. Wright (Ed.), *Teaching improving practices: Successful strategies for higher education* (pp. 76–100). Bolton, MA: Anker.

Tuckman, H. P. (1978, December). Who is part-time in academe? *AAUP Bulletin,* 305–315.

Upcraft, M. L. (1996). Teaching and today's college students. In R. J. Menges & M. Weimer (Eds.), *Teaching on solid ground: Using scholarship to improve practice* (pp. 21–41). San Francisco: Jossey-Bass.

Vaillant, G. (1997). *Adaptation to life.* Boston: Little, Brown.

Valent, R. (1992). *Community college part-time faculty: Factors which influence their expressed staff development needs.* Unpublished doctoral dissertation, Widener University, Chester, PA.

Vella, J. (1994). *Learning to listen, learning to teach.* San Francisco: Jossey-Bass.

Wagner, R. J., & Roland, C. C. (1993). *Facilitators: One key factor in implementing successful experience-based training and development programs.* Unpublished monograph.

Walton, P. (1998, February 10). X-ers as employees. *BankersNews, 6*(3), 1, 3.

Weimer, M., & Neff, R. A. (Eds.). (1990). *Teaching college: Collected readings for the new instructor.* Madison, WI: Magna Publications.

Weimer, M., Parrett, J., & Kerns, M. (1988). *How am I teaching: Forms and activities for acquiring instructional input.* Madison, WI: Magna Publications.

Wilson, R. (1998, January 16). New research casts doubt on value of student evaluations of professors. *The Chronicle of Higher Education, 44*(19), A12–A14.

Wislock, R. (1993). What are the perceptual modalities and how do they contribute to learning? In D. Flannery (Ed.), *Applying cognitive learning theory to adult learning* (pp. 5–13). San Francisco: Jossey-Bass.

Witt, A., Wattenbarger, J., Gollattscheck, J., & Suppiger, J. (1994). *America's community colleges: The first century.* Washington, DC: The Community College Press.

Yantz, P., & Bechtold, C. (1994, February). *Part-time faculty: Here today, not gone tomorrow, or professional development of part-time faculty and the changing role of division chairpersons.* Paper presented at the International Conference for Community College Chairs, Deans and other Instructional Leaders, Phoenix, AZ. (ERIC Document Reproduction Services No. ED 369 428)

INDEX